Made|Simple™

MEXICAN

Easy and delicious dishes for every meal

Publications International, Ltd.

Copyright © 2025 Publications International, Ltd.

All rights reserved. This publication may not be reproduced or quoted in whole or in part by any means whatsoever without written permission from:

Louis Weber, CEO
Publications International, Ltd.
8140 Lehigh Ave
Morton Grove, IL 60053

Permission is never granted for commercial purposes.

Made Simple is a trademark of Publications International, Ltd.

Photographs on front cover and pages 29 and 187 copyright © Shutterstock.com.

Pictured on the front cover: Beef and Cheese Nachos *(page 28)*.

Pictured on the back cover: Weeknight Chicken Tacos *(page 83)* and Guacamole *(page 50)*.

ISBN: 978-1-63938-831-8

Manufactured in China.

8 7 6 5 4 3 2 1

Microwave Cooking: Microwave ovens vary in wattage. Use the cooking times as guidelines and check for doneness before adding more time.

WARNING: Food preparation, baking and cooking involve inherent dangers: misuse of electric products, sharp electric tools, boiling water, hot stoves, allergic reactions, foodborne illnesses and the like, pose numerous potential risks. Publications International, Ltd. (PIL) assumes no responsibility or liability for any damages you may experience as a result of following recipes, instructions, tips or advice in this publication.

While we hope this publication helps you find new ways to eat delicious foods, you may not always achieve the results desired due to variations in ingredients, cooking temperatures, typos, errors, omissions or individual cooking abilities.

Let's get social!

@Publications_International

@PublicationsInternational

www.pilbooks.com

CONTENTS

- 4   **BREAKFAST**
- 26   **APPETIZERS & SNACKS**
- 52   **SOUPS & STEWS**
- 82   **TACOS, BURRITOS & QUESADILLAS**
- 118   **MAIN DISHES**
- 154   **SIDE DISHES & SALADS**
- 178   **DESSERTS & DRINKS**
- 188   **INDEX**

BREAKFAST

CHORIZO HASH

- 2 unpeeled russet potatoes, cut into ½-inch pieces
- 3 teaspoons salt, divided
- 8 ounces Mexican chorizo sausage, casings removed
- 1 yellow onion, chopped
- ½ red bell pepper, chopped (about ½ cup)
- Fried, poached or scrambled eggs (optional)
- Sliced avocado and chopped fresh cilantro (optional)

1. Fill medium saucepan half full with water. Add potatoes and 2 teaspoons salt; bring to a boil over high heat. Reduce heat to medium-low; cook 8 minutes. (Potatoes will be firm.) Drain.

2. Meanwhile, crumble chorizo into large cast iron skillet; cook and stir over medium-high heat 5 minutes or until lightly browned. Add onion and bell pepper; cook and stir 4 minutes or until vegetables are softened.

3. Stir in potatoes and remaining 1 teaspoon salt; cook 10 to 15 minutes or until vegetables are tender and potatoes are lightly browned, stirring occasionally. Serve with eggs, if desired; garnish with avocado and cilantro.

MAKES 4 SERVINGS

BREAKFAST

MEXICAN OMELET ROLL-UPS WITH AVOCADO SAUCE

- 8 eggs *or* 2 cups liquid egg substitute
- 2 tablespoons milk
- ¾ teaspoon salt, divided
- 1 tablespoon vegetable oil
- 1½ cups (6 ounces) shredded Monterey Jack cheese
- 1 large tomato, seeded and chopped
- ¼ cup chopped fresh cilantro
- 8 corn tortillas
- 1½ cups salsa (optional)
- 2 medium avocados, chopped
- ¼ cup sour cream
- 2 tablespoons finely chopped onion
- 1 jalapeño or serrano pepper, chopped (optional)
- 2 teaspoons lime juice
- ¼ teaspoon minced garlic

1. Preheat oven to 350°F. Spray 13×9-inch baking dish with cooking spray.

2. Whisk eggs, milk and ½ teaspoon salt in medium bowl until blended. Heat oil in large nonstick skillet over medium heat. Add egg mixture; cook 5 minutes or until eggs are set but still soft, stirring occasionally to form large curds. Remove from heat. Stir in cheese, tomato and cilantro.

3. Spoon about ⅓ cup egg mixture evenly down center of each tortilla. Roll up tortillas and place seam side down in prepared dish. Pour salsa evenly over tortillas, if desired.

4. Cover tightly with foil and bake 20 minutes or until heated through.

5. Meanwhile, process avocados, sour cream, onion, jalapeño pepper, lime juice, remaining ¼ teaspoon salt and garlic in food processor or blender until smooth. Serve roll-ups with avocado sauce.

MAKES 8 SERVINGS

BREAKFAST

SPICY MEXICAN FRITTATA

- 1 jalapeño pepper, stemmed and seeded
- 1 clove garlic
- 1 medium tomato, peeled, quartered and seeded
- ½ teaspoon ground coriander
- ½ teaspoon chili powder
- 1 tablespoon vegetable oil
- ½ cup chopped onion
- 1 cup thawed frozen corn
- 8 eggs
- ¼ cup milk
- ½ teaspoon salt
- ¼ teaspoon black pepper
- ¼ cup (1 ounce) shredded farmer or mozzarella cheese

1. Place jalapeño pepper and garlic in food processor or blender; process until finely chopped. Add tomato, coriander and chili powder; process until tomato is almost smooth.

2. Heat oil in large nonstick skillet over medium heat. Add onion; cook and stir 5 minutes or until tender. Stir in tomato mixture and corn; cook 3 to 4 minutes or until liquid is almost evaporated, stirring occasionally.

3. Whisk eggs, milk, salt and black pepper in medium bowl. Add egg mixture to skillet. Cook without stirring 2 minutes or until eggs begin to set. Run large spoon around edge of skillet, lifting eggs to allow uncooked portion to flow underneath. Remove skillet from heat when eggs are almost set but surface is still moist.

4. Sprinkle with cheese. Cover; let stand 3 to 4 minutes or until surface is set and cheese is melted. Cut into wedges to serve.

MAKES 4 SERVINGS

BREAKFAST

CHORIZO AND CHEDDAR BREAKFAST CASSEROLE

- 8 ounces Mexican chorizo sausage, casings removed
- 1 cup diced onion
- 1 green bell pepper, chopped
- 1 jalapeño pepper, chopped
- 6 eggs
- 1 cup biscuit baking mix
- ¾ cup buttermilk
- ½ teaspoon salt
- ½ teaspoon black pepper
- 1 cup (4 ounces) shredded Cheddar cheese
- ¼ cup chopped fresh cilantro
- Sour cream and chopped tomato (optional)

1. Preheat oven to 350°F. Spray 8- or 9-inch square baking dish with nonstick cooking spray.
2. Heat large nonstick skillet over medium heat. Add chorizo; cook 4 minutes or until browned, stirring to break up meat. Drain fat.
3. Add onion, bell pepper and jalapeño to skillet; cook and stir 6 minutes or until vegetables are crisp-tender. Spread mixture evenly in prepared baking dish.
4. Whisk eggs, baking mix, buttermilk, salt and black pepper in medium bowl until well blended. Pour evenly over chorizo mixture.
5. Bake 45 to 50 minutes or until knife inserted into center comes out clean. Sprinkle evenly with cheese and cilantro. Let stand 10 minutes or until cheese is melted. Serve with sour cream and tomato, if desired.

MAKES 6 TO 8 SERVINGS

BREAKFAST

BLACK BEAN AND MUSHROOM CHILAQUILES

- 2 tablespoons olive oil
- 1 medium onion, chopped
- 1 green bell pepper, chopped
- 1 jalapeño or serrano pepper, seeded and minced
- 2 cans (about 15 ounces each) black beans, rinsed and drained
- 1 can (about 14 ounces) diced tomatoes
- 1 package (8 ounces) whole white mushrooms, cut into quarters
- 1½ teaspoons ground cumin
- 1½ teaspoons dried oregano
- ½ teaspoon salt
- 1 cup (4 ounces) shredded sharp Cheddar cheese
- 6 cups tortilla chips, crushed

1. Heat oil in medium skillet over medium heat. Add onion, bell pepper and jalapeño pepper; cook 5 minutes until onion softens, stirring occasionally. Stir in beans, tomatoes, mushrooms, cumin, oregano and salt; cook 10 minutes or until mushrooms are tender, stirring occasionally.

2. Remove from heat. Sprinkle cheese over bean mixture; cover and let stand until cheese is melted. Place tortilla chips in bowls; top with bean mixture.

MAKES 6 SERVINGS

SCRAMBLED EGGS AND TORTILLAS

¼ cup vegetable oil

2 small (6-inch) corn tortillas, cut in half and cut into ½-inch slices

¾ teaspoon salt, divided

4 eggs

1 Heat oil in medium skillet over medium-high heat until hot (tortilla strip dropped in oil will sizzle). Add tortilla strips; cook 1 minute or until light golden and almost crisp. Remove with tongs to paper towel-lined plate; sprinkle with ¼ teaspoon. Drain all but 1 tablespoon oil from skillet.

2 Whisk eggs and remaining ½ teaspoon salt in medium bowl until well blended. Heat same skillet over medium heat. Add eggs; cook and stir about 1 minute or until almost set, stirring and lifting edge of egg to allow uncooked portion to flow underneath. Add tortilla strips; cook and stir 1 to 2 minutes or until eggs are firm. Serve immediately.

MAKES 2 SERVINGS

BREAKFAST

CHORIZO AND EGGS

- 1 teaspoon vegetable oil
- 1 pound Mexican chorizo sausage, casings removed
- 6 eggs
- Salt and black pepper

1. Heat oil in large skillet over medium-high heat. Add chorizo; cook 5 minutes, stirring to break up meat.

2. Beat eggs in medium bowl. Add to skillet with chorizo; cook 2 to 3 minutes, stirring and lifting edge of egg to allow uncooked portion to flow underneath until eggs are softly scrambled.

MAKES 4 SERVINGS

BREAKFAST

- ¼ teaspoon salt, divided
- 1 plum tomato, diced
- 2 eggs
- ⅛ teaspoon black pepper
- 2 teaspoons vegetable oil or butter, divided
- 4 (6-inch) flour tortillas
- ½ cup (2 ounces) shredded Monterey Jack cheese
- 1 cup baby spinach
- 1 green onion, finely chopped
- ¼ cup crumbled feta or goat cheese
- Sour cream, salsa and/or hot pepper sauce (optional)

SPINACH AND EGG QUESADILLAS

1. Sprinkle ⅛ teaspoon salt over tomato in small bowl; set aside. Whisk eggs, remaining ⅛ teaspoon salt and pepper in medium bowl until well blended.

2. Heat 1 teaspoon oil in small nonstick skillet over medium heat. Add egg mixture; cook without stirring 1 minute. Cook 2 to 3 minutes or just until eggs are softly set but not dry, stirring frequently. Remove to plate. Wipe out skillet with paper towel.

3. Place two tortillas on work surface. Sprinkle each with 2 tablespoons Monterey Jack cheese; top with ½ cup spinach and half of scrambled eggs. Sprinkle with half of tomato, half of green onion, remaining Monterey Jack and feta cheeses. Top with remaining tortillas.

4. Heat ½ teaspoon oil in same skillet over medium heat. Add one quesadilla; cook 2 to 3 minutes per side or until lightly browned. Repeat with remaining ½ teaspoon oil and quesadilla. Cut into quarters; serve with sour cream, if desired.

MAKES 2 SERVINGS

BREAKFAST

MEXICAN BREAKFAST BURRITO

- 8 eggs *or* 2 cups liquid egg substitute
- ½ teaspoon salt
- ⅛ teaspoon black pepper
- 1 tablespoon vegetable oil
- ⅓ cup canned black beans, rinsed and drained
- 2 tablespoons sliced green onions
- 2 (10-inch) flour tortillas
- ¼ cup (1 ounce) shredded Cheddar cheese
- 3 tablespoons salsa

1. Whisk eggs, salt and pepper in medium bowl until well blended. Heat oil in large nonstick skillet over medium heat. Pour egg mixture into skillet; cook about 5 minutes or until eggs begin to set, stirring occasionally. Stir in beans and green onions; cook 3 minutes or just until cooked through, stirring frequently.

2. Spoon mixture evenly down center third of tortillas; top with cheese. Roll up to enclose filling. Cut in half; serve with salsa.

MAKES 4 SERVINGS

BREAKFAST

BREAKFAST BEANS AND RICE

- 1 package (10 ounces) frozen brown rice
- 2 tablespoons vegetable oil
- 1 cup diced onions
- 1 medium poblano chile pepper, seeded and diced
- ½ (15-ounce) can black beans, rinsed and drained
- 1 cup seeded diced tomatoes
- ¼ cup chopped fresh cilantro
- 2 teaspoons paprika
- ¾ teaspoon salt
- 1 lime, quartered

1. Cook rice according to package directions.
2. Meanwhile, heat oil in large nonstick skillet over medium-high heat. Add onions and poblano pepper; cook and stir 4 to 5 minutes or until lightly browned.
3. Add beans, tomatoes, cilantro, paprika and salt; cook and stir 1 minute. Remove from heat. Stir in rice; squeeze lime wedges over each serving.

MAKES 4 SERVINGS

BREAKFAST

HUEVOS RANCHEROS CASSEROLE

- 6 corn tortillas
- 1 cup refried black beans
- 1 cup salsa, plus additional for serving
- 10 eggs
- ¾ cup milk
- ½ teaspoon salt
- 1 cup (4 ounces) shredded Mexican cheese blend

1. Preheat oven to 400°F. Spray 13×9-inch baking dish with nonstick cooking spray.

2. Line prepared baking dish with tortillas, overlapping as necessary. Spread beans evenly over tortillas; top with 1 cup salsa.

3. Whisk eggs, milk and salt in large bowl until blended. Pour over tortillas and beans; sprinkle with cheese. Cover with foil.

4. Bake 30 minutes. Remove foil; bake 5 minutes or until center is set and edges are lightly browned and pulling away from sides of dish. Cut into squares. Serve warm with additional salsa.

MAKES 6 SERVINGS

BREAKFAST

SPICY SCRAMBLED EGGS AND TOMATOES

- 8 eggs
- ½ teaspoon salt
- 2 tablespoons butter
- 2 tablespoons vegetable oil
- ⅓ cup finely chopped onion
- 2 to 4 fresh serrano peppers, finely chopped
- 2 medium tomatoes, seeded, chopped and drained

1. Whisk eggs and salt in medium bowl.
2. Heat butter and oil in large nonstick skillet over medium heat until butter melts. Add onion and peppers; cook and stir 1 minute or until hot but not soft.
3. Stir in tomatoes. Increase heat to medium-high; cook and stir 1 minute or until tomatoes are hot.
4. Add egg mixture to skillet. Cook without stirring 1 minute. Cook 2 minutes, stirring gently until eggs are softly set.

MAKES 4 SERVINGS

BREAKFAST BURRITOS

- 1 tablespoon butter
- ½ cup red or green bell pepper, chopped
- 2 green onions, sliced
- 6 eggs
- 2 tablespoons milk
- ¼ teaspoon salt
- 4 (7-inch) flour tortillas, warmed
- ½ cup (2 ounces) shredded Colby Jack or Mexican cheese blend
- ½ cup salsa

1. Melt butter in medium nonstick skillet over medium heat. Add bell pepper and green onions; cook and stir about 3 minutes or until vegetables are softened.

2. Beat eggs, milk and salt in medium bowl until blended. Pour mixture into skillet. Reduce heat to low; cook until eggs are softly set with no liquid remaining, stirring gently.

3. Spoon one fourth of egg mixture down center of each tortilla; top with 2 tablespoons cheese. Fold in sides of tortillas to enclose filling. Serve with salsa.

MAKES 4 SERVINGS

APPETIZERS & SNACKS

WHITE SPINACH QUESO

- 1 tablespoon olive oil
- 1 clove garlic, minced
- 1 tablespoon all-purpose flour
- 1 can (12 ounces) evaporated milk
- ½ teaspoon salt
- 2 cups (8 ounces) shredded Monterey Jack cheese, divided
- 1 package (10 ounces) frozen chopped spinach, thawed and squeezed dry
- Optional toppings: pico de gallo, guacamole, chopped fresh cilantro and queso fresco
- Tortilla chips

1 Preheat broiler.

2 Heat oil in medium saucepan over medium-low heat. Add garlic; cook and stir 1 minute without browning. Add flour; whisk until smooth. Slowly whisk in evaporated milk in thin, steady stream. Stir in salt. Cook about 4 minutes or until slightly thickened, whisking frequently. Add 1½ cups Monterey Jack; whisk until smooth. Stir in spinach. Pour into medium cast iron skillet; sprinkle with remaining ½ cup Monterey Jack.

3 Broil 1 minute or until cheese is melted and browned in spots. Top with pico de gallo, guacamole, cilantro and queso fresco. Serve immediately with tortilla chips.

MAKES 4 TO 6 SERVINGS

APPETIZERS & SNACKS

BEEF AND CHEESE NACHOS

- 8 ounces ground beef
- ½ cup chopped onion
- 2 cloves garlic, minced
- 2 teaspoons chili powder
- 1 teaspoon ground cumin
- ½ teaspoon salt
- ½ teaspoon dried oregano
- ½ bag tortilla chips
- 1 cup (4 ounces) shredded Chihuahua or Monterey Jack cheese
- ½ cup halved grape tomatoes
- ¼ cup guacamole
- Optional toppings: pico de gallo, sour cream and/or sliced jalapeños

1. Cook beef, onion and garlic in large skillet over medium-high heat 6 to 8 minutes or until beef is no longer pink, stirring to break up meat. Drain fat. Add chili powder, cumin, salt and oregano; cook and stir 1 minute.

2. Preheat broiler. Spread chips in 11×7-inch baking dish or pan; sprinkle with cheese.

3. Broil 2 to 4 minutes or until cheese is melted. Top with beef, tomatoes, guacamole and desired toppings.

MAKES 4 TO 6 SERVINGS

APPETIZERS & SNACKS

CHIPOTLE CHICKEN QUESADILLAS

- 1 package (8 ounces) cream cheese, softened
- 1 cup (4 ounces) shredded Mexican cheese blend
- 1 tablespoon minced canned chipotle pepper in adobo sauce
- 5 (10-inch) flour tortillas
- 5 cups shredded cooked chicken (about 1¼ pounds)
- Optional toppings: guacamole, sour cream, salsa and chopped fresh cilantro

1. Combine cream cheese, Mexican cheese blend and chipotle pepper in large bowl; mix well.

2. Spread ⅓ cup cheese mixture over half of one tortilla. Top with about 1 cup chicken. Fold tortilla over filling and press gently. Repeat with remaining tortillas, cheese mixture and chicken.

3. Heat large nonstick skillet over medium-high heat. Cook quesadillas in batches 2 to 3 minutes per side or until lightly browned.

4. Cut each quesadilla into four wedges. Serve with desired toppings.

MAKES 20 WEDGES

APPETIZERS & SNACKS

CHICKEN WINGS IN CERVEZA

- 1½ pounds chicken wings or drummettes
- 1 teaspoon salt
- 1 teaspoon dried thyme
- ⅛ teaspoon black pepper
- 1 bottle (12 ounces) Mexican beer

1. Cut off and discard wing tips. Cut each wing in half at joint. Place wings in large bowl; sprinkle with salt, thyme and pepper. Pour beer over wings; toss to coat. Cover and refrigerate 2 to 6 hours.

2. Preheat oven to 375°F. Line baking sheet with foil; spray with nonstick cooking spray.

3. Drain wings, reserving marinade. Arrange wings in single layer on prepared baking sheet.

4. Bake 40 minutes or until wings are cooked through and well browned on all sides, turning and basting with reserved marinade occasionally. *Do not brush with marinade during last 5 minutes of baking.* Discard remaining marinade.

MAKES 6 SERVINGS

Note

When using drummettes, simply place them in the marinade without cutting.

APPETIZERS & SNACKS

CHICKEN FAJITA NACHOS

- 2 tablespoons vegetable oil, divided
- 2 red bell peppers, cut into thin strips
- 1 onion, cut in half and thinly sliced
- 2 tablespoons fajita seasoning mix (from 1¼-ounce package), divided
- 2 tablespoons water, divided
- 12 ounces boneless skinless chicken breasts, cut into 2×1-inch strips
- 4 cups tortilla chips (about 30 chips)
- ½ cup (2 ounces) shredded Cheddar cheese
- ½ cup (2 ounces) shredded Monterey Jack cheese
- 1 jalapeño pepper, seeded and thinly sliced
- 1 cup shredded lettuce
- ½ cup salsa
- Sour cream and guacamole (optional)

1. Heat 1 tablespoon oil in large skillet over medium-high heat. Add bell peppers and onion; cook 5 minutes or until vegetables are tender and browned in spots, stirring frequently. Transfer to large bowl; stir in 1 tablespoon fajita seasoning mix and 1 tablespoon water.

2. Heat remaining 1 tablespoon oil in same skillet over medium-high heat. Add chicken; cook 7 to 10 minutes or until cooked through, stirring occasionally. Add remaining 1 tablespoon fajita seasoning mix and 1 tablespoon water; cook and stir 3 to 5 minutes or until chicken is coated.

3. Preheat broiler. Spread chips in 11×7-inch baking dish or pan; top with vegetables, chicken, Cheddar, Monterey Jack and jalapeño pepper.

4. Broil 2 to 4 minutes or until cheeses are melted. Top with lettuce and salsa; serve with sour cream and guacamole, if desired.

MAKES 4 SERVINGS

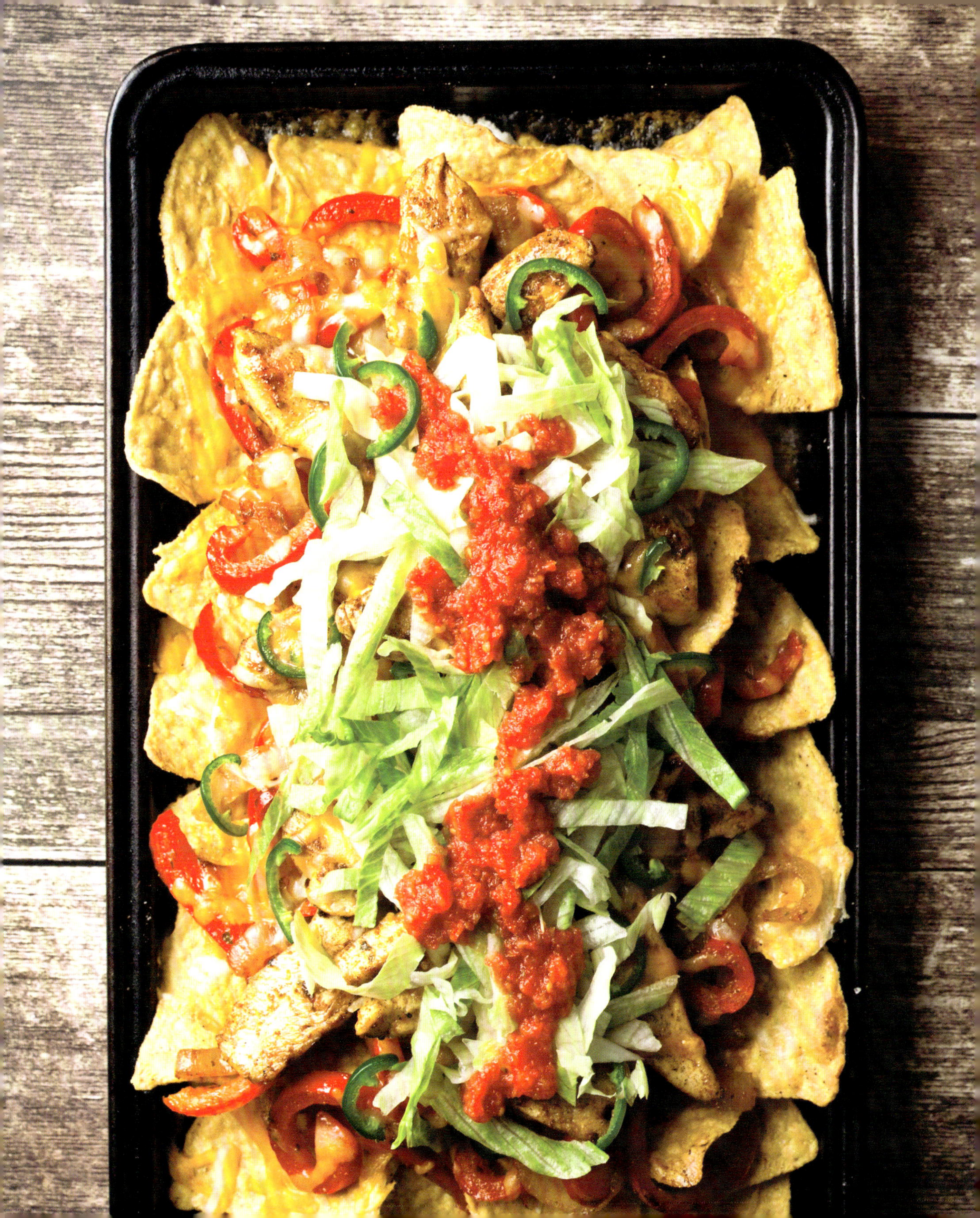

APPETIZERS & SNACKS

TORTILLA PIZZA WEDGES

- 2 teaspoons vegetable oil
- 1 cup thawed frozen corn
- 1 cup thinly sliced mushrooms
- 4 (6-inch) corn tortillas
- ¼ cup pasta sauce
- 1 to 2 teaspoons chopped jalapeño pepper
- ¼ teaspoon dried oregano
- ¼ teaspoon dried marjoram
- ½ cup (2 ounces) shredded Chihuahua or mozzarella cheese

1. Preheat oven to 450°F. Heat oil in large skillet over medium heat. Add corn and mushrooms; cook and stir 4 to 5 minutes or until tender.

2. Place tortillas on baking sheet. Bake 4 minutes or until edges begin to brown.

3. Combine pasta sauce, jalapeño, oregano and marjoram in small bowl. Spread evenly over tortillas. Top evenly with corn and mushrooms. Sprinkle with cheese.

4. Bake 4 to 5 minutes or until cheese is melted and pizzas are heated through. Cut each pizza into four wedges.

MAKES 4 SERVINGS

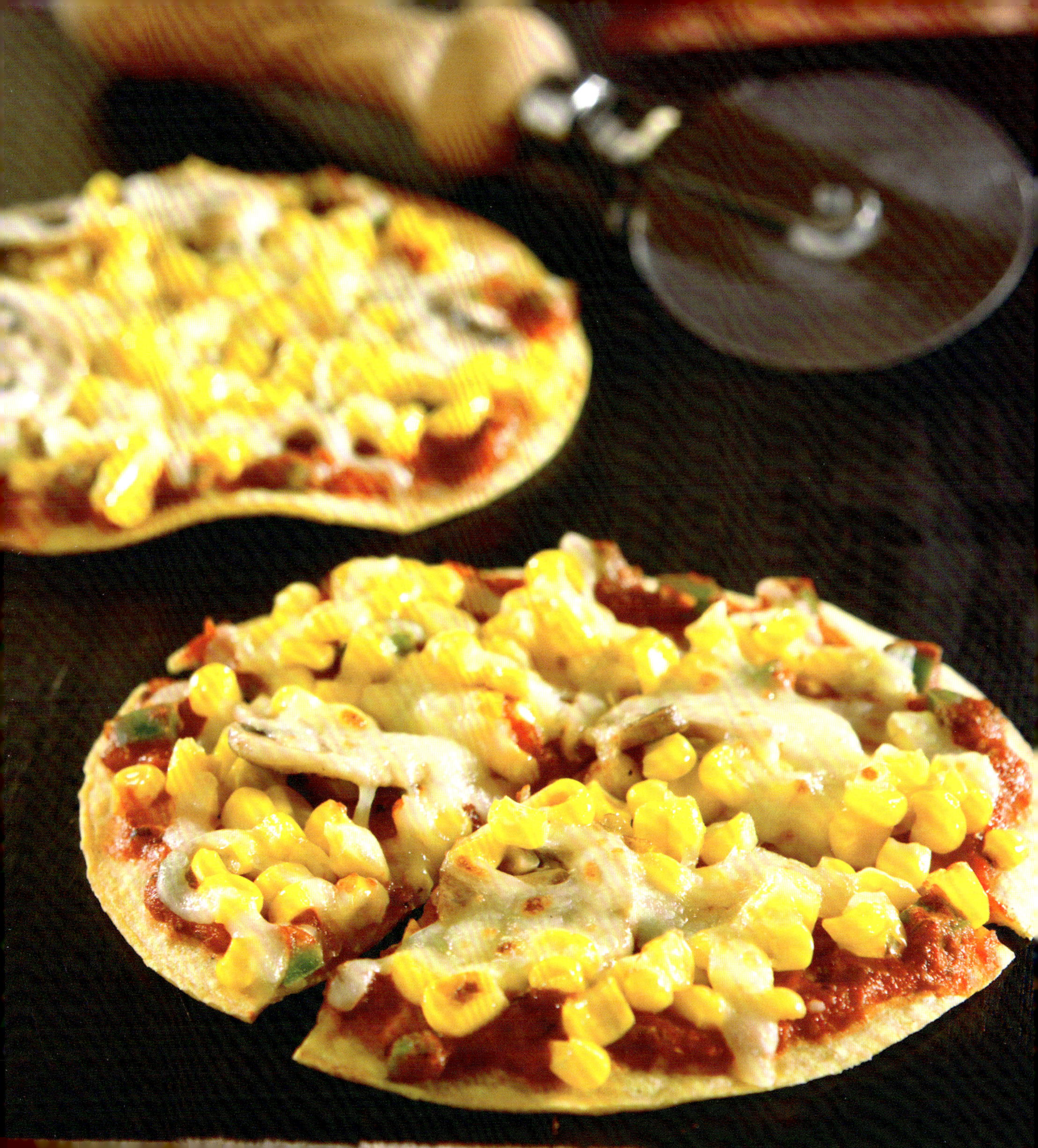

APPETIZERS & SNACKS

CORN TORTILLA CHIPS

12 (6-inch) corn tortillas, preferably day-old
Vegetable oil
½ to 1 teaspoon salt

1. If tortillas are fresh, let stand, uncovered, in single layer on wire rack 1 to 2 hours to dry slightly.

2. Stack 6 tortillas; cut through stack into 6 or 8 wedges. Repeat with remaining tortillas.

3. Heat ½ inch oil in deep heavy skillet over medium-high heat to 375°F; adjust heat to maintain temperature during cooking.

4. Working in batches, cook tortilla wedges 1 minute or until crisp, turning occasionally. Remove with slotted spoon; drain on paper towels. Sprinkle with salt.

MAKES 6 TO 8 DOZEN CHIPS

Note

Tortilla chips are best eaten fresh, but can be stored, tightly covered, 2 or 3 days. Reheat in 350°F oven a few minutes before serving.

SALSA

- 1 can (28 ounces) whole tomatoes, undrained
- 2 fresh plum tomatoes, seeded and chopped
- 2 tablespoons canned diced mild green chiles
- 1 tablespoon canned diced jalapeño peppers (optional)
- 1 tablespoon white vinegar
- 1 clove garlic, minced
- 1 teaspoon onion powder
- 1 teaspoon sugar
- 1 teaspoon ground cumin
- ½ teaspoon garlic powder
- ¼ teaspoon salt
- Tortilla chips

Combine canned tomatoes with juice, fresh tomatoes, green chiles, jalapeños, if desired, vinegar, garlic, onion powder, sugar, cumin, garlic powder and salt in food processor; process until finely chopped. Serve with tortilla chips.

MAKES 4½ CUPS

APPETIZERS & SNACKS

BEAN AND CORN NACHOS

- 1 tablespoon vegetable oil
- 1 cup chopped onion
- 1 tablespoon chili powder
- 2 teaspoons dried oregano
- 1 can (about 15 ounces) pinto beans or black beans, rinsed and drained
- 2 tablespoons water
- 48 corn tortilla chips
- 1¼ cups (5 ounces) shredded Monterey Jack cheese
- ¾ cup thawed frozen corn, drained
- 1 jar (2 ounces) pimientos, drained
- 3 tablespoons sliced black olives
- 2 to 3 tablespoons pickled jalapeño pepper slices, drained

1. Preheat oven to 375°F. Heat oil in medium saucepan over medium-high heat. Add onion; cook and stir 5 minutes or until onion is tender. Add chili powder and oregano; cook and stir 1 minute. Remove from heat.

2. Add beans and water; mash with fork or potato masher until blended but still chunky. Cover; cook over medium heat 6 to 8 minutes or until bubbly, stirring occasionally. Stir in additional water if beans become dry.

3. Spread chips on large baking sheet. Spoon beans over chips. Top with cheese, corn and pimientos. Bake 8 minutes or until cheese is melted. Sprinkle with olives and jalapeños.

MAKES 8 SERVINGS

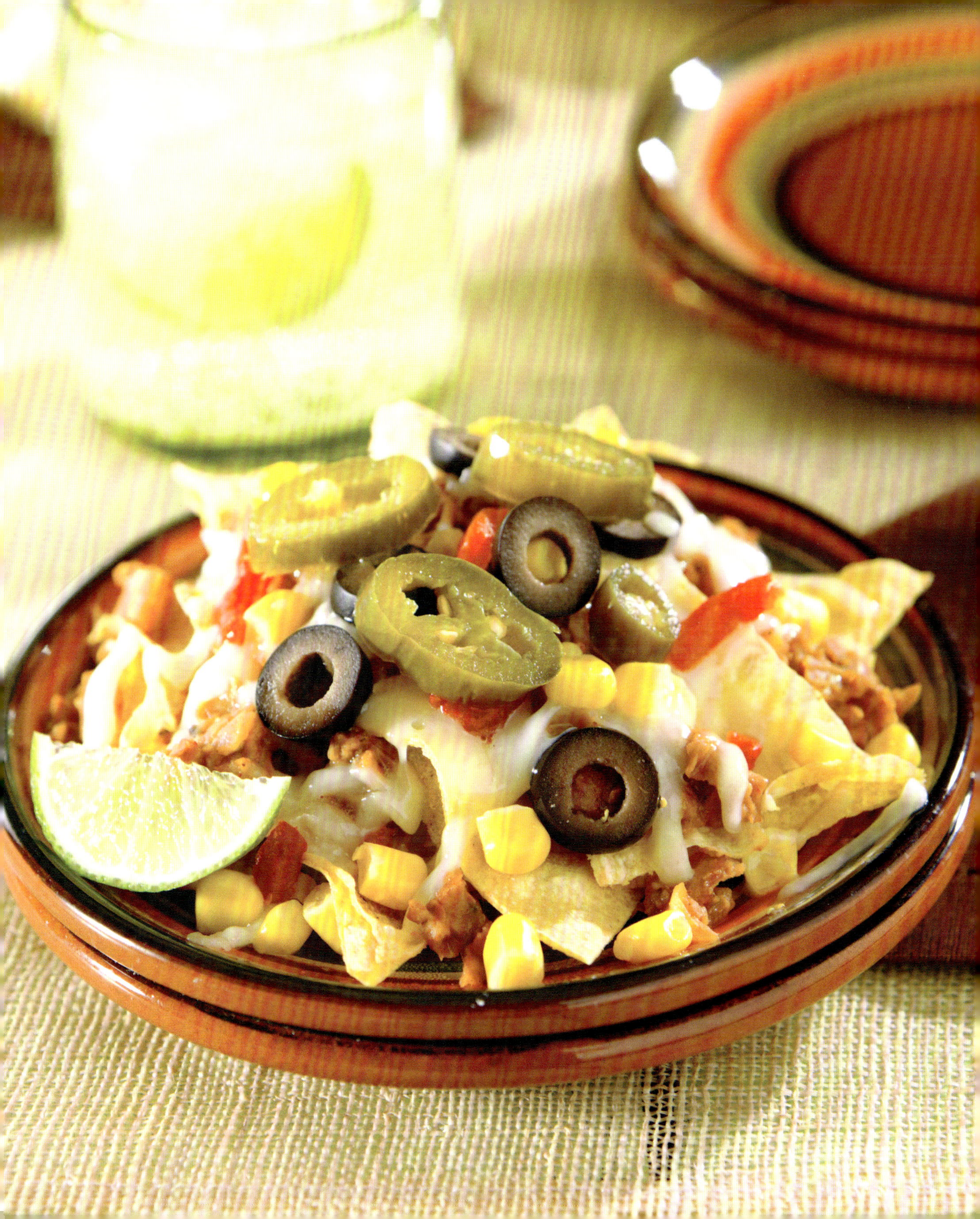

APPETIZERS & SNACKS

CORN SALSA

- 1 large poblano pepper
- 1 package (16 ounces) frozen white or yellow corn
- ¼ cup diced red onion
- ¼ cup chopped fresh cilantro
- 1 large jalapeño pepper, seeded and finely chopped
- 1 tablespoon lime juice
- 1 tablespoon lemon juice
- ½ teaspoon salt
- ⅛ teaspoon black pepper

1. Preheat oven to 400°F. Line small baking pan with foil.

2. Place poblano pepper on prepared pan; roast 40 minutes or until skin is charred and blistered, turning occasionally. Remove pepper to small bowl; cover with plastic wrap and let stand 10 minutes to loosen skin. Peel and dice poblano pepper, discarding stem and seeds.

3. Meanwhile, cook corn according to package directions; drain and cool completely (place in refrigerator or freezer to cool faster).

4. Place corn in large bowl. Add poblano, onion, cilantro, jalapeño, lime juice, lemon juice, salt and pepper; mix well. Let stand at least 30 minutes to blend flavors.

MAKES ABOUT 2½ CUPS

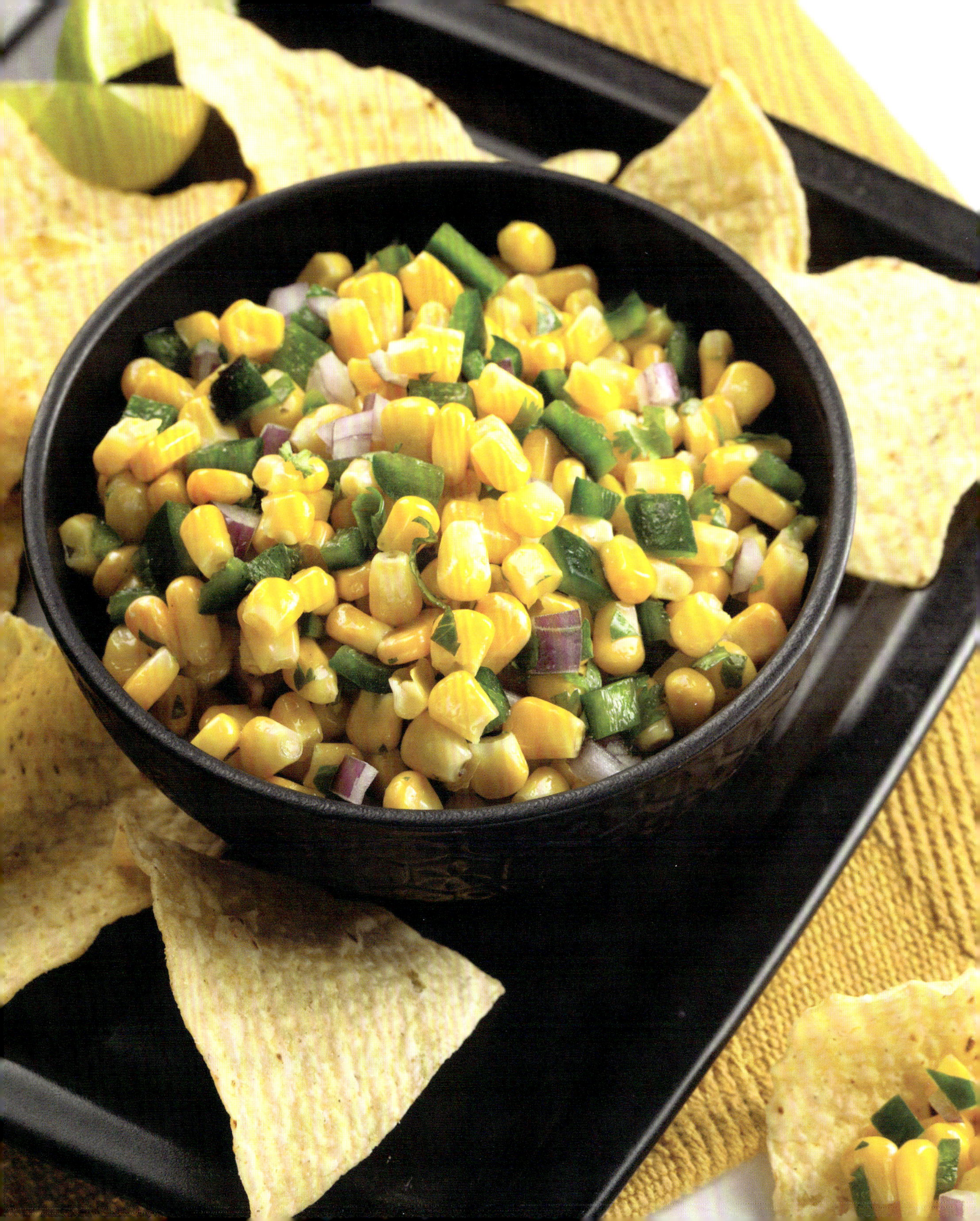

APPETIZERS & SNACKS

MINI CHEESE BURRITOS

- ½ cup refried beans
- 4 (8-inch) flour tortillas
- ½ cup chunky salsa
- 4 (¾-ounce) Cheddar cheese sticks or block Cheddar cut into sticks

1. Spread beans over tortillas, leaving ½ inch border around edges. Spoon salsa over beans.

2. Place cheese stick on one side of each tortilla. Fold edge of tortilla over cheese stick; roll up. Place burritos, seam side down, in microwavable dish.

3. Microwave on HIGH 1 to 2 minutes or until cheese is melted. Let stand 1 to 2 minutes before serving.

MAKES 4 SERVINGS

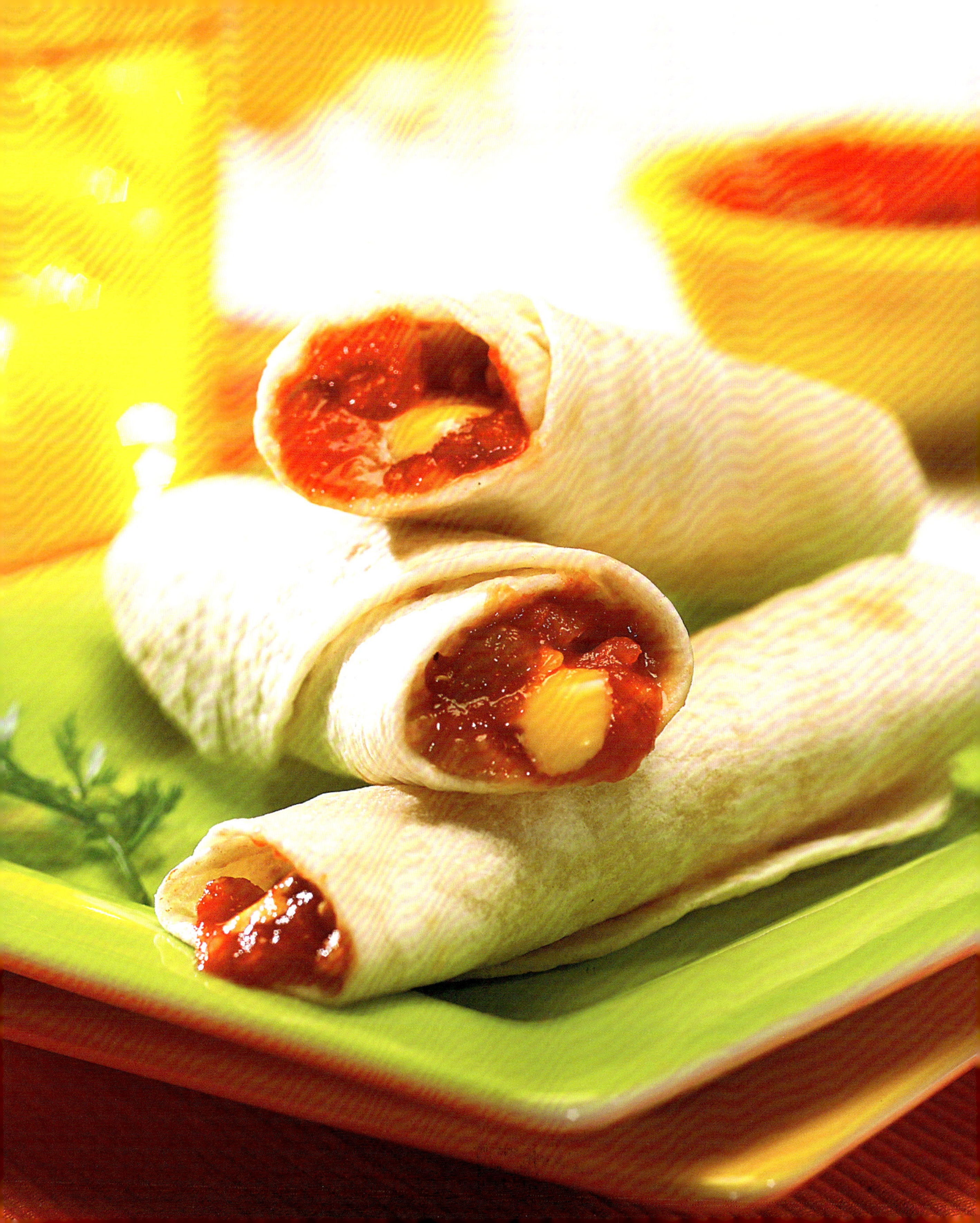

APPETIZERS & SNACKS

SALSA SHRIMP

- 1 cup chunky salsa
- 1 can (4 ounces) diced mild green chiles
- 2 teaspoons honey
- ¼ teaspoon hot pepper sauce
- 1 pound large cooked shrimp, peeled and deveined (with tails on)

Chopped fresh cilantro, lime wedges and sliced jalapeño pepper (optional)

1. Combine salsa, chiles, honey and hot pepper sauce in medium bowl; mix well.

2. Add shrimp; toss to coat. Cover and refrigerate 2 hours before serving. Serve with cilantro, lime wedges and jalapeños, if desired.

MAKES ABOUT 6 SERVINGS

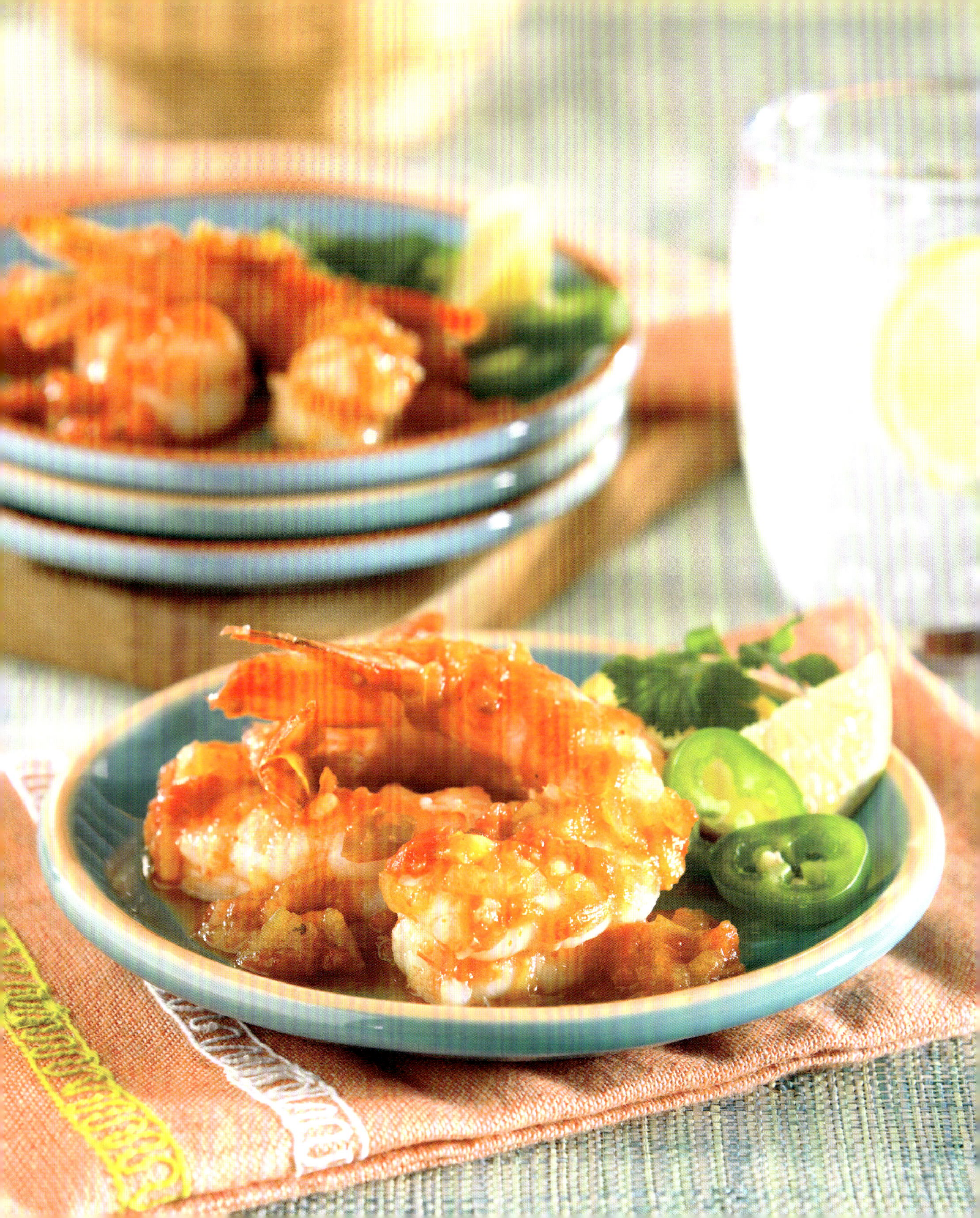

APPETIZERS & SNACKS

AVOCADO SALSA

- 1 medium avocado, diced
- 1 cup chopped onion
- 1 cup chopped peeled cucumber
- 1 Anaheim or jalapeño pepper, seeded and chopped
- ½ cup chopped fresh tomato
- 2 tablespoons chopped fresh cilantro
- ½ teaspoon salt
- ¼ teaspoon hot pepper sauce

1. Combine avocado, onion, cucumber, Anaheim pepper, tomato, cilantro, salt and hot pepper sauce in medium bowl; mix gently.
2. Cover and refrigerate at least 1 hour before serving.

MAKES ABOUT 4 CUPS

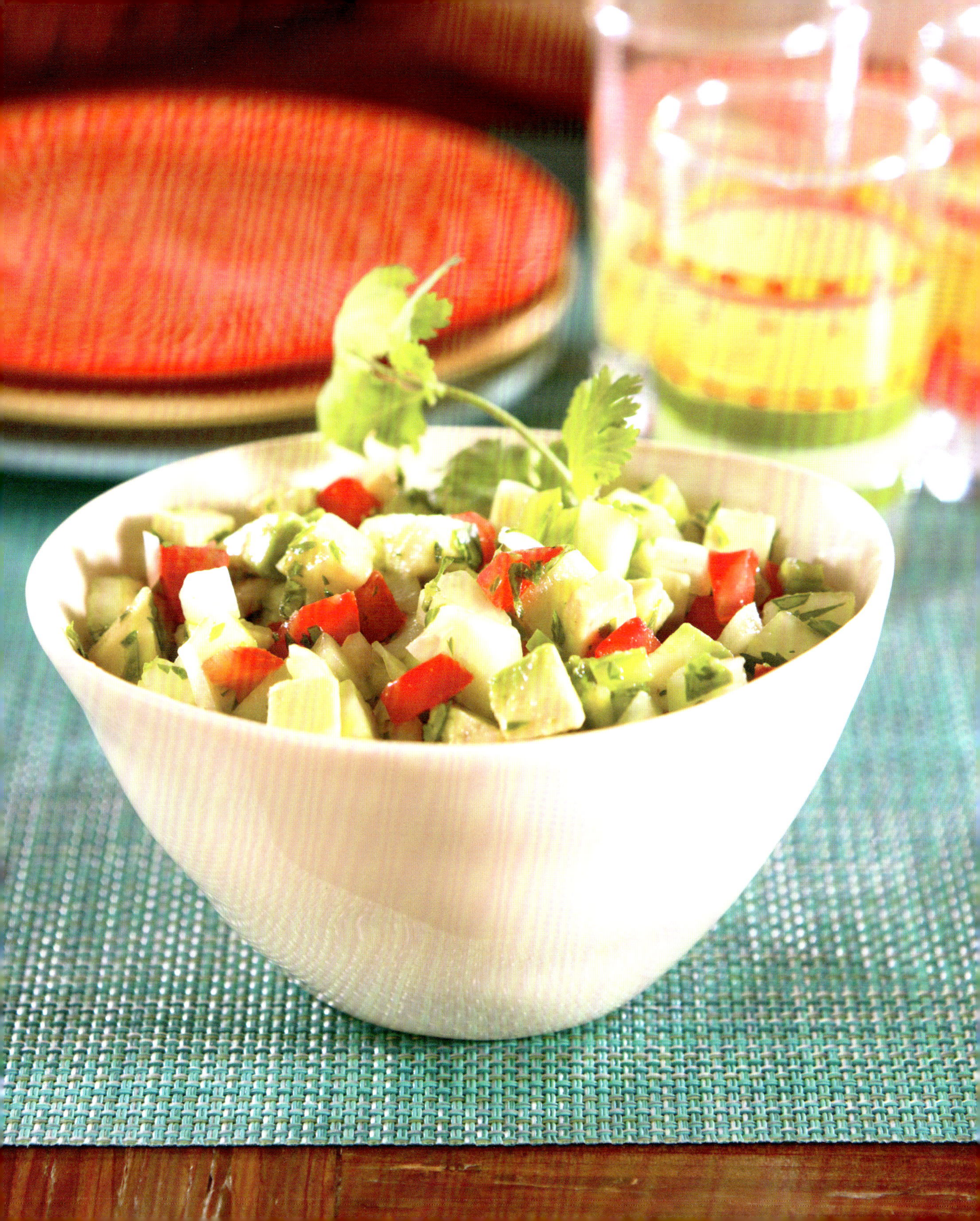

GUACAMOLE

- 2 large ripe avocados
- 2 teaspoons fresh lime juice
- ¼ cup finely chopped red onion
- 2 tablespoons chopped fresh cilantro
- ½ jalapeño pepper, finely chopped
- ½ teaspoon salt

1. Cut avocados in half lengthwise around pits; remove pits. Scoop avocados into large bowl; sprinkle with lime juice. Mash to desired consistency with fork or potato masher.

2. Add onion, cilantro, jalapeño and ½ teaspoon salt; stir gently until well blended. Taste and add additional salt, if desired.

MAKES 2 CUPS

SALSA FRESCA

- 1½ cups finely chopped tomatoes
- ¼ cup finely chopped red onion
- 1 to 2 serrano or jalapeño peppers, stemmed seeded and minced
- 2 tablespoons finely chopped fresh cilantro
- 1 teaspoon lime juice
- ½ teaspoon salt

Combine tomatoes, onion, 1 serrano pepper, cilantro, lime juice and salt in medium bowl. Taste and add additional serrano pepper for spicier salsa. Let stand 30 minutes to 1 hour to allow flavors to blend.

MAKES 2 CUPS

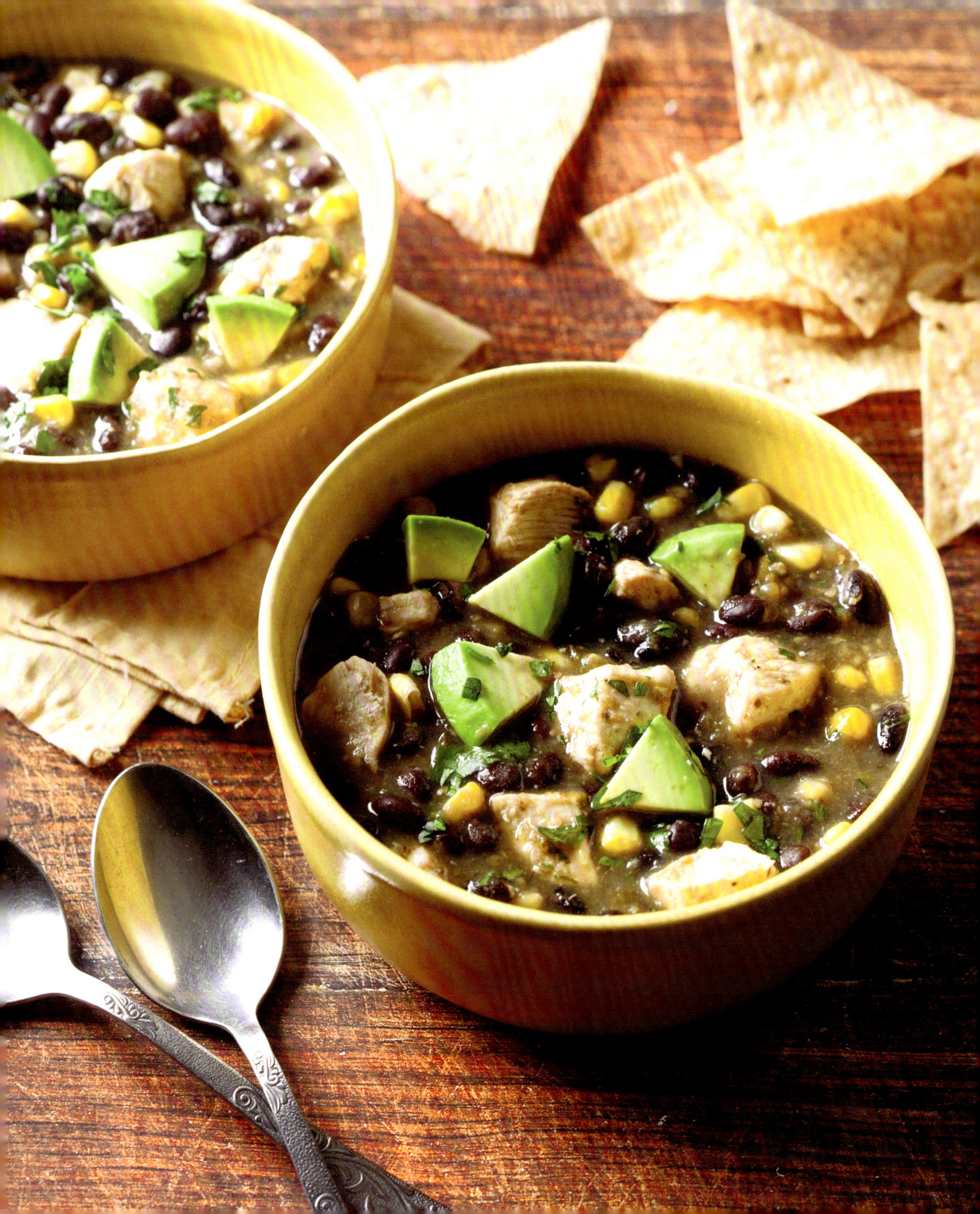

SOUPS & STEWS

SALSA VERDE CHICKEN STEW

- 1 tablespoon vegetable oil
- 1½ pounds boneless skinless chicken breasts, cut into ¾-inch pieces
- 2 cans (about 15 ounces each) black beans, rinsed and drained
- 1 jar (24 ounces) salsa verde
- 1½ cups thawed frozen corn
- ¾ cup chopped fresh cilantro
- Optional toppings: diced avocado, sour cream and/or tortilla chips

1. Heat oil in large saucepan over medium-high heat. Add chicken; cook and stir 5 minutes or until chicken begins to brown.

2. Stir in beans and salsa; bring to a simmer. Reduce heat to low; cover and cook 8 minutes.

3. Stir in corn; cook 3 minutes or until heated through. Remove from heat; stir in cilantro. Serve with desired toppings.

MAKES 4 TO 6 SERVINGS

SOUPS & STEWS

PORK CHILI VERDE

- 1½ pounds fresh tomatillos, peeled
- 5 serrano peppers, stemmed
- 2 cups water, divided
- 1 ounce jalapeño slices, undrained
- 2 cloves garlic
- 1 cup vegetable oil
- 2 pounds pork shoulder, trimmed and cut into 1-inch pieces
- 1 tablespoon salt
- 1 teaspoon garlic powder
- 1 teaspoon black pepper
- 1 teaspoon cornstarch

1. Place tomatillos and serrano peppers in medium saucepan; cover with 1 inch of water. Bring to a boil over medium-high heat. Reduce heat to medium; cook 15 minutes or until tomatillos are tender. Drain and place tomatillos and peppers in food processor or blender; add 1 cup water, jalapeño slices with liquid and garlic. Blend until smooth.

2. Heat oil in large skillet over medium-high heat. Cook pork in batches until browned on all sides. Remove to plate. Drain fat from skillet.

3. Return pork to skillet; add tomatillo mixture, salt, garlic powder and black pepper. Bring to a simmer over medium heat. Stir remaining 1 cup water into cornstarch in small bowl until smooth; stir into skillet. Cover and cook 30 minutes or until pork is tender, stirring occasionally.

MAKES 8 SERVINGS

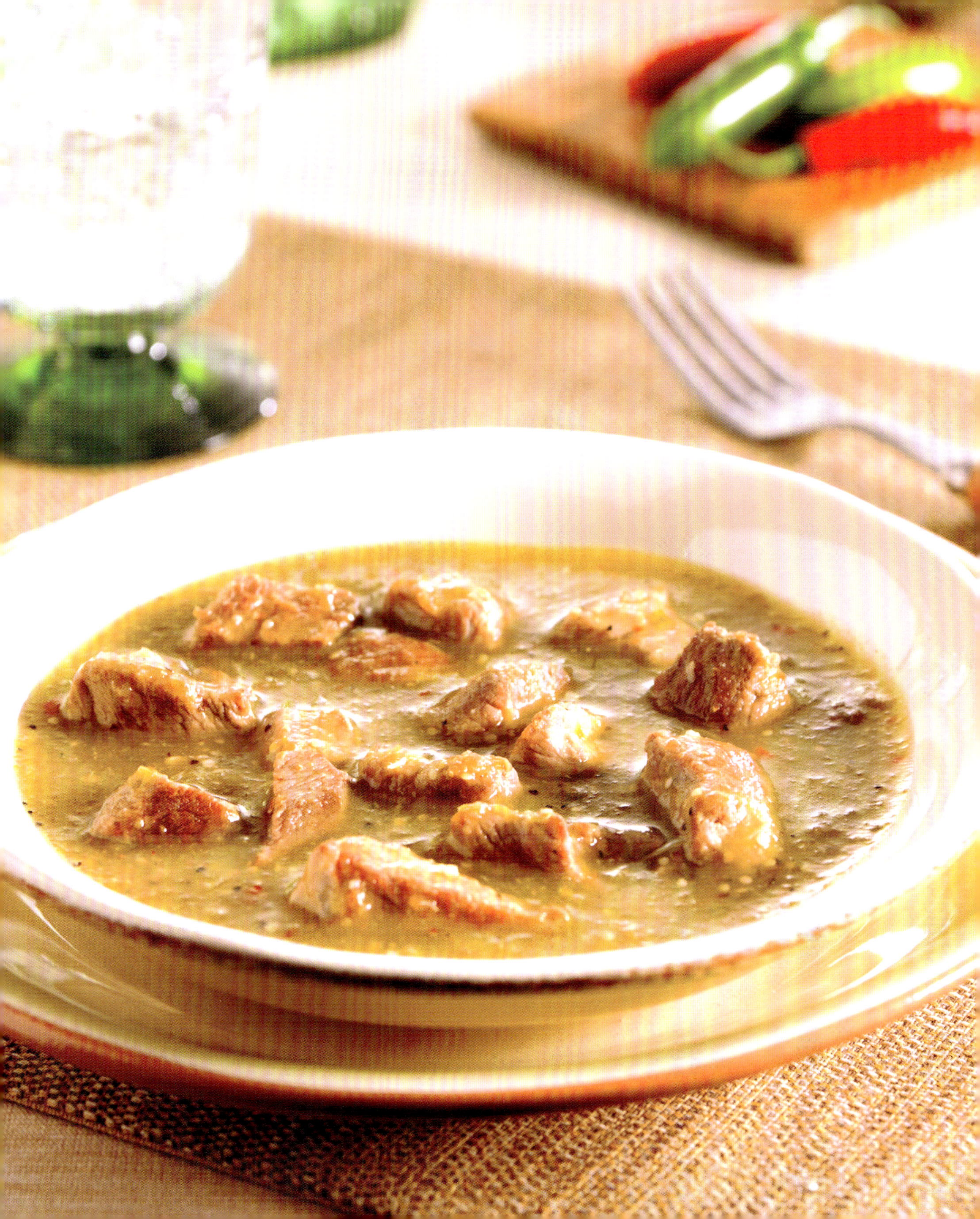

SOUPS & STEWS

BLACK BEAN SOUP

- 2 tablespoons vegetable oil
- 1 medium onion, diced
- 1 stalk celery, diced
- 2 carrots, diced
- ½ green bell pepper, diced
- 4 cloves garlic, minced
- 4 cans (about 15 ounces each) black beans, rinsed and drained, divided
- 4 cups (32 ounces) vegetable broth, divided
- 2 tablespoons cider vinegar
- 2 teaspoons chili powder
- ½ teaspoon salt
- ½ teaspoon ground red pepper
- ½ teaspoon ground cumin
- ¼ teaspoon liquid smoke
- Optional toppings: sour cream, chopped green onions and/or shredded Cheddar cheese

1. Heat oil in large saucepan or Dutch oven over medium-low heat. Add onion, celery, carrots, bell pepper and garlic; cook 10 minutes, stirring occasionally.

2. Combine half of beans and 1 cup broth in food processor or blender; process until smooth. Add to saucepan.

3. Stir in remaining beans, 3 cups broth, vinegar, chili powder, salt, red pepper, cumin and liquid smoke; bring to a boil over high heat. Reduce heat to medium-low; cook 1 hour or until vegetables are tender and soup is thickened, stirring occasionally. Serve with desired toppings.

MAKES 4 TO 6 SERVINGS

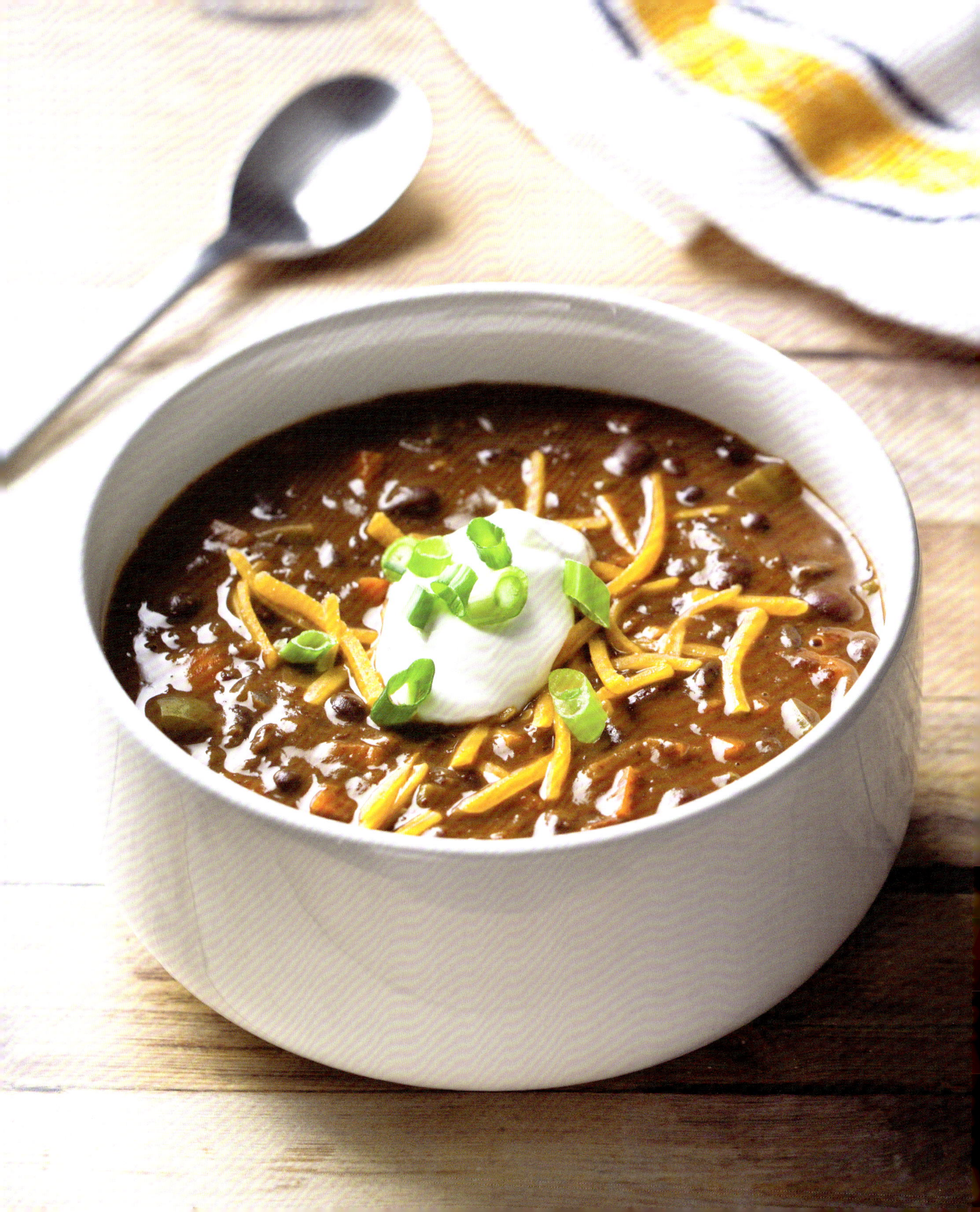

CHICKEN ENCHILADA SOUP

- 2 tablespoons vegetable oil, divided
- 1½ pounds boneless skinless chicken breasts, cut into ½-inch pieces
- ½ cup chopped onion
- 2 cloves garlic, minced
- 2 cans (about 14 ounces each) chicken broth
- 3 cups water, divided
- 1 cup masa harina
- 1 package (16 ounces) pasteurized process cheese product, cubed
- 1 can (10 ounces) mild red enchilada sauce
- 1 teaspoon chili powder
- ½ teaspoon salt
- ½ teaspoon ground cumin
- 1 large tomato, seeded and chopped
- Crispy tortilla strips*

*If tortilla strips are not available, crumble tortilla chips into bite-size pieces.

1. Heat 1 tablespoon oil in large saucepan or Dutch oven over medium-high heat. Add chicken; cook and stir 10 minutes or until no longer pink. Transfer to medium bowl with slotted spoon; drain any liquid from saucepan.

2. Heat remaining 1 tablespoon oil in same saucepan over medium-high heat. Add onion and garlic; cook and stir 3 minutes or until softened. Stir in broth.

3. Whisk 2 cups water into masa harina in large bowl until smooth. Whisk mixture into broth in saucepan. Stir in remaining 1 cup water, cheese product, enchilada sauce, chili powder, salt and cumin; bring to a boil over high heat. Stir in chicken. Reduce heat to medium-low; cook 30 minutes, stirring frequently. Ladle soup into bowls; top with tomato and tortilla strips.

MAKES 8 TO 10 SERVINGS

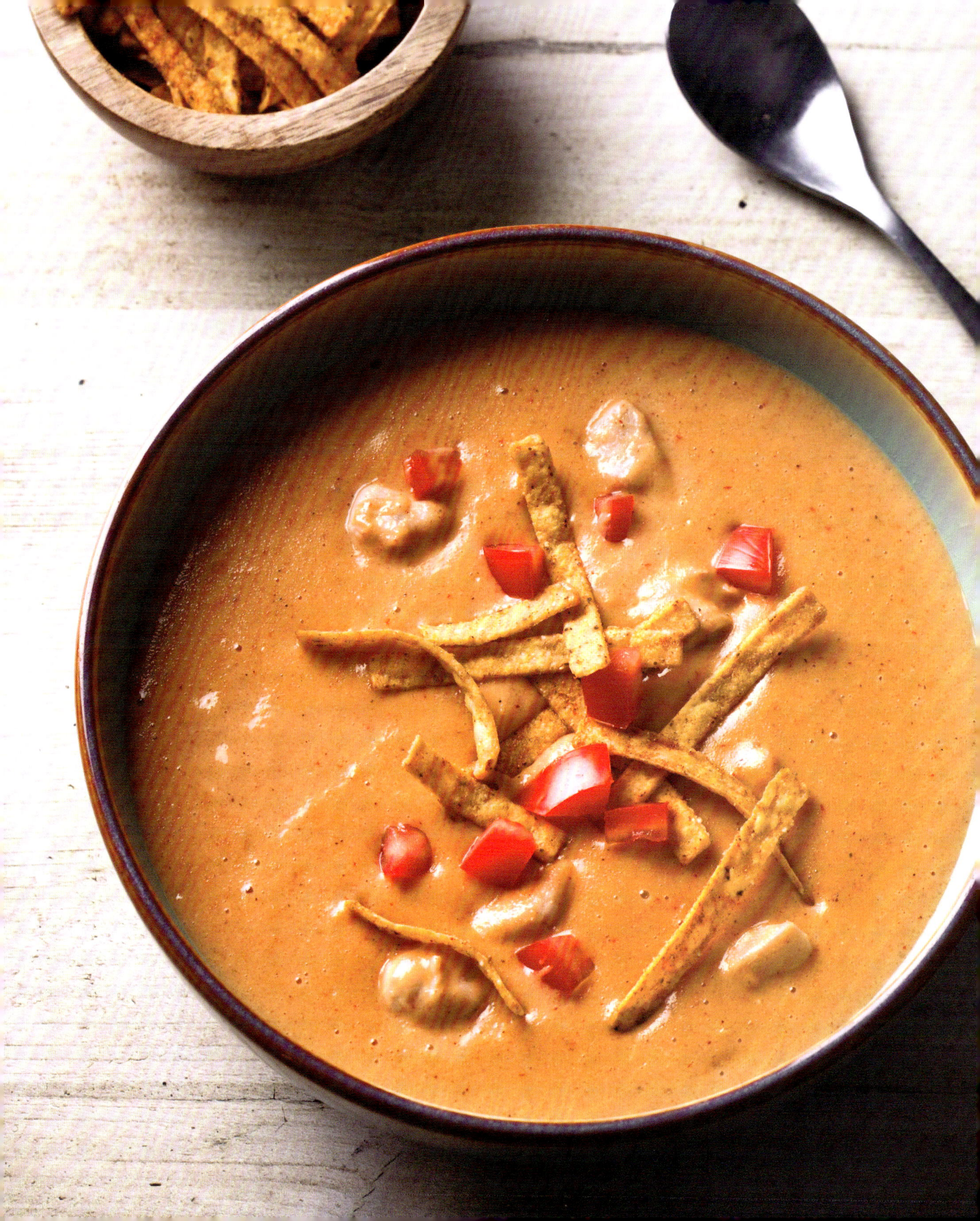

SOUPS & STEWS

POZOLE

- 1 tablespoon vegetable oil
- 1 large onion, chopped
- 1 tablespoon minced garlic
- 1 tablespoon dried oregano
- 1½ teaspoons ground cumin
- 2 cans (about 14 ounces each) chicken broth
- 1½ cups water
- 1 pound boneless skinless chicken breasts
- 2 cans (15 ounces each) yellow hominy, drained
- 1 red or green bell pepper, chopped
- 1 can (4 ounces) diced mild green chiles
- 1 can (2¼ ounces) sliced black olives, drained
- ½ cup lightly packed fresh cilantro, coarsely chopped
- Crispy tortilla strips

1 Heat oil in large saucepan over medium heat. Add onion, garlic, oregano and cumin; cover and cook about 6 minutes or until onion is golden brown, stirring occasionally. Add broth and water; cover and bring to a boil over high heat. Stir in chicken. Reduce heat to low; cover and cook 8 minutes or until chicken is no longer pink in center.

2 Remove chicken to plate; set aside until cool enough to handle. Cut into ½-inch pieces.

3 Meanwhile, add hominy, bell pepper, chiles and olives to broth; cover and bring to a boil over medium-high heat. Reduce heat to medium-low; simmer 4 minutes or until bell pepper is crisp-tender. Return chicken to saucepan; stir in cilantro. Top with tortilla strips.

MAKES 6 SERVINGS

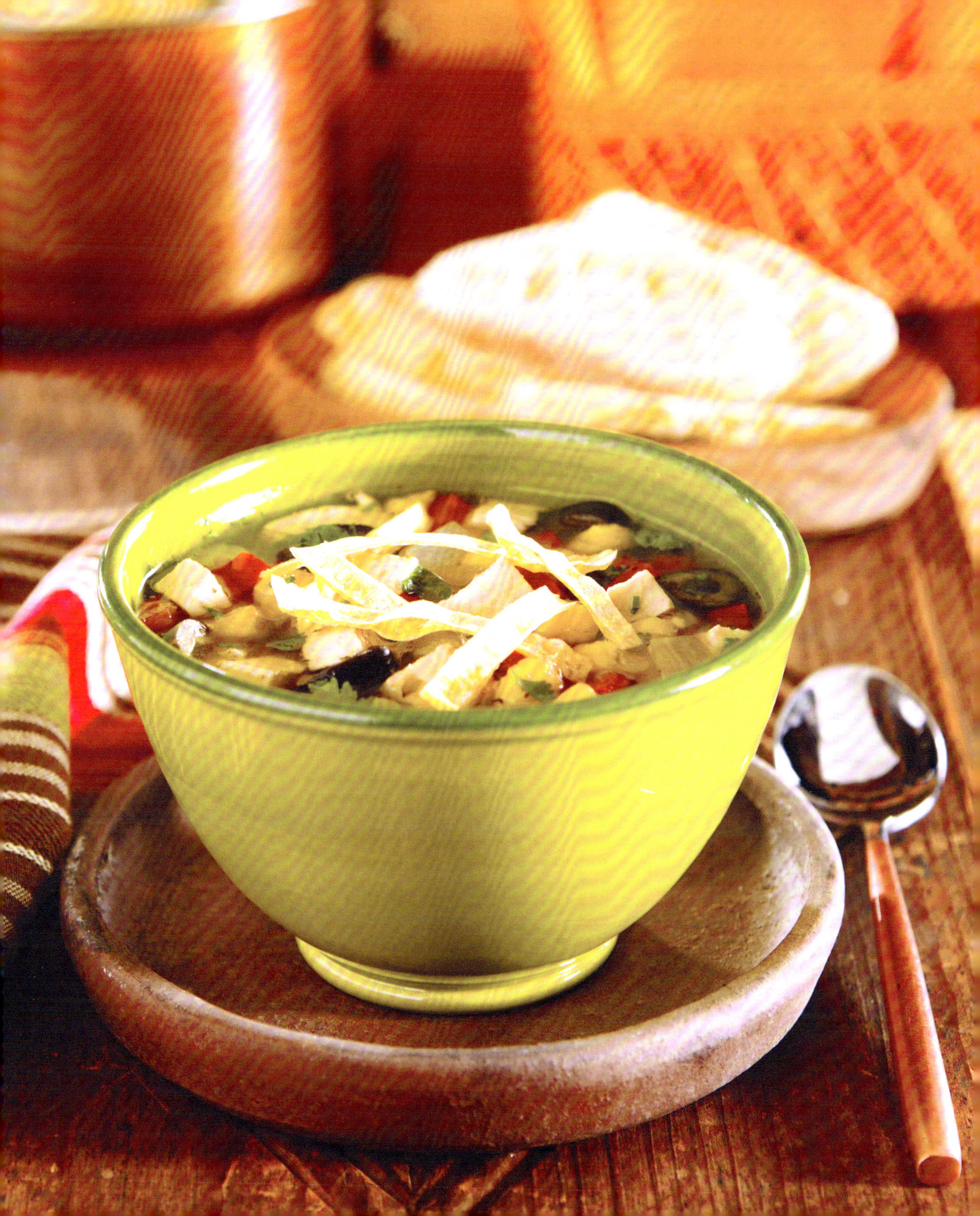

SOUPS & STEWS

CHUNKY ANCHO CHILI WITH BEANS

- 5 dried ancho chiles
- 2 cups water
- 2 tablespoons vegetable oil
- 1 onion, chopped
- 2 cloves garlic, minced
- 1 pound boneless beef top sirloin steak, cut into 1-inch cubes
- 1 pound boneless pork, cut into 1-inch cubes
- 1 to 2 fresh or canned jalapeño peppers, stemmed, seeded and minced
- 1 teaspoon salt
- 1 teaspoon dried oregano
- 1 teaspoon ground cumin
- ½ cup dry red wine
- 2 cans (about 15 ounces each) pinto or kidney beans, rinsed and drained

1. Rinse ancho chiles; remove stems, seeds and veins. Place in medium saucepan with water. Bring to a boil; turn off heat and let stand, covered, 30 minutes or until chiles are soft. Pour chiles with liquid into blender or food processor; process until smooth.

2. Heat oil in Dutch oven over medium heat. Add onion and garlic; cook and stir until onion is tender. Add beef and pork; cook until meat is lightly browned, stirring frequently. Add jalapeño peppers, salt, oregano, cumin, wine and ancho chile purée; bring to a boil.

3. Cover; reduce heat and simmer 1½ to 2 hours or until meat is very tender. Stir in beans. Simmer, uncovered, 30 minutes or until chili has thickened slightly.

MAKES 8 SERVINGS

Variation

To make chili with chili powder, use ⅓ cup chili powder and 1½ cups water in place of ancho chile purée. Reduce salt and cumin to ½ teaspoon each.

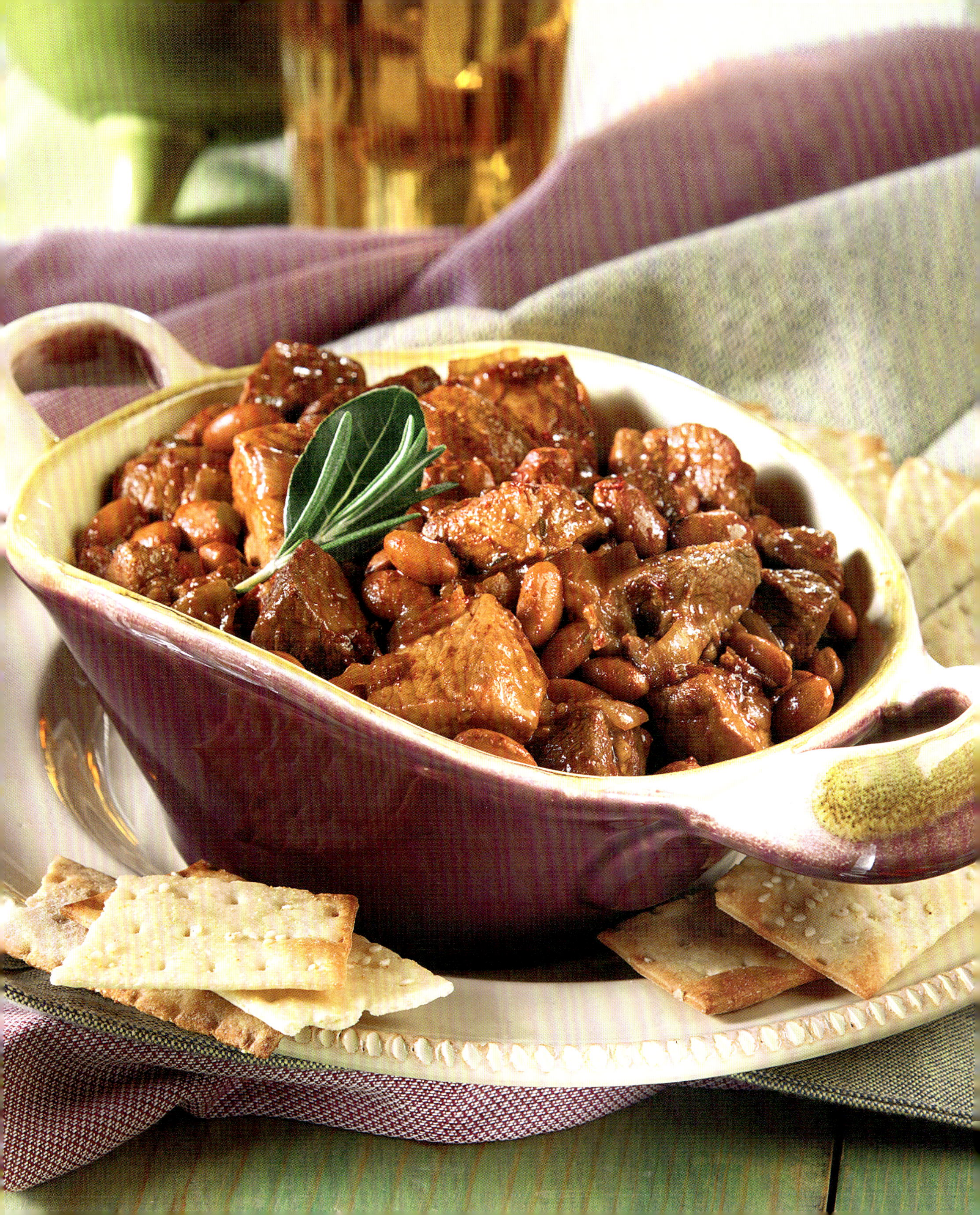

BEEF FAJITA SOUP

- 1 pound cubed beef stew meat
- 1 can (about 15 ounces) pinto beans, rinsed and drained
- 1 can (about 15 ounces) black beans, rinsed and drained
- 1 can (about 14 ounces) diced tomatoes with roasted garlic
- 1 can (about 14 ounces) beef broth
- 1½ cups water
- 1 green bell pepper, thinly sliced
- 1 red bell pepper, thinly sliced
- 1 onion, thinly sliced
- 2 teaspoons ground cumin
- 1 teaspoon seasoned salt
- 1 teaspoon black pepper
- Optional toppings: sour cream, shredded Monterey Jack or Cheddar cheese and/or chopped olives

Slow Cooker Directions

1. Combine beef, beans, tomatoes, broth, water, bell peppers, onion, cumin, seasoned salt and black pepper in slow cooker.
2. Cover and cook on LOW 8 hours. Serve with desired toppings.

MAKES 8 SERVINGS

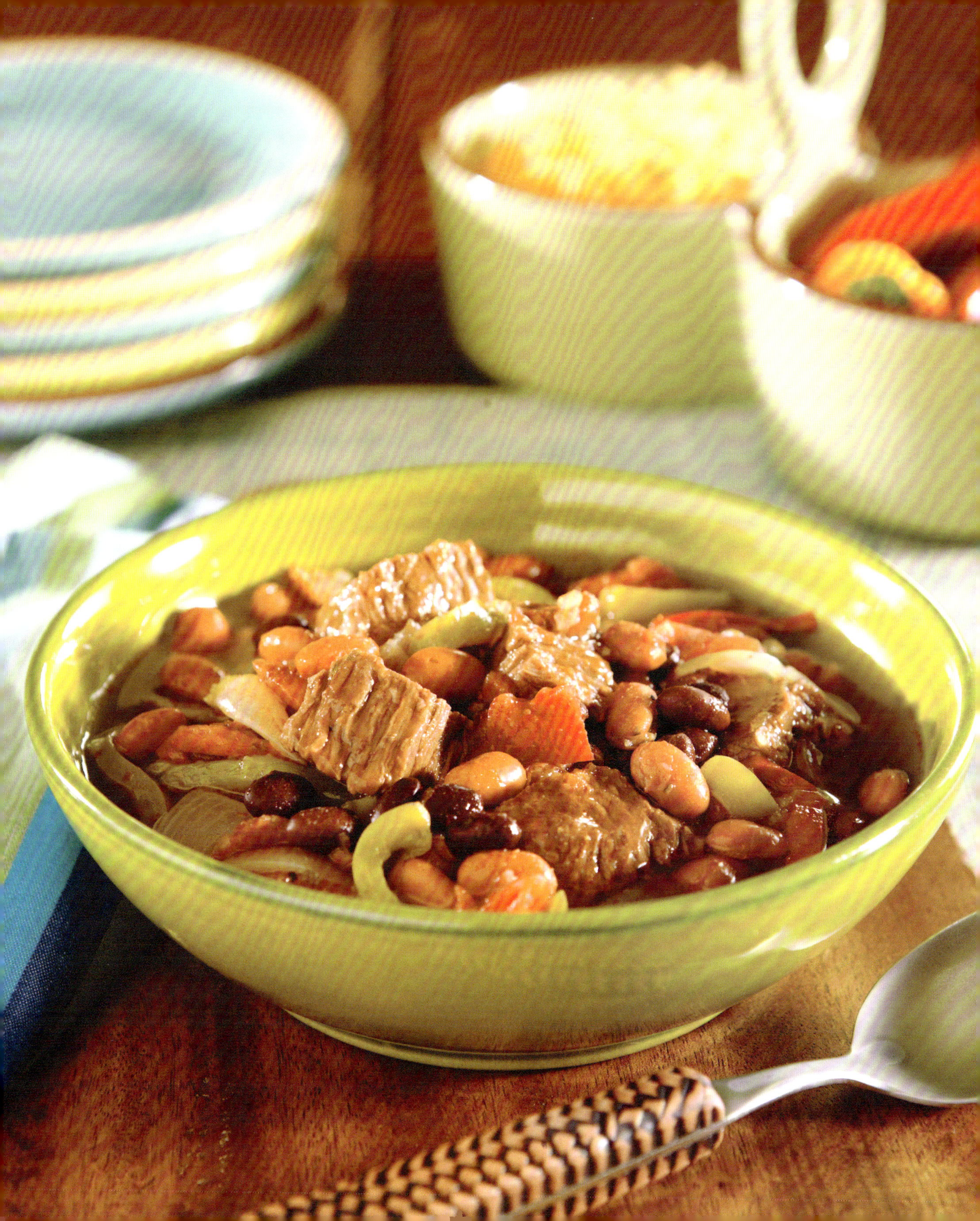

SOUPS & STEWS

MEXICAN TORTILLA SOUP

2 large very ripe tomatoes (about 1 pound), peeled, seeded and cut into chunks

⅔ cup coarsely chopped white onion

1 clove garlic

6 tablespoons vegetable oil, divided

7 cups vegetable broth

4 sprigs fresh cilantro

3 sprigs fresh mint (optional)

½ to 1 teaspoon salt

4 or 5 dried pasilla chiles

½ cup crispy tortilla strips

5 ounces Chihuahua or Monterey Jack cheese, cut into ½-inch cubes

¼ cup coarsely chopped fresh cilantro

1 Combine tomatoes, onion and garlic in blender or food processor; blend until smooth.

2 Heat 3 tablespoons oil in large saucepan over medium heat until hot. Add tomato mixture; cook 10 minutes, stirring frequently. Add broth and cilantro sprigs; bring to a boil over high heat. Reduce heat to low; simmer, uncovered, 20 minutes. Add mint, if desired, and salt; simmer 10 minutes. Remove and discard cilantro and mint sprigs.

3 Heat remaining 3 tablespoons oil in small skillet over medium-high heat. Add chiles; fry 30 seconds or until puffed and crisp, turning occasionally. *Do not burn chiles.* Drain on paper towel-lined plate. Cool slightly; crumble into coarse pieces.

4 Ladle soup into bowls; serve with chiles, tortilla strips, cheese and chopped cilantro.

MAKES 4 TO 6 SERVINGS

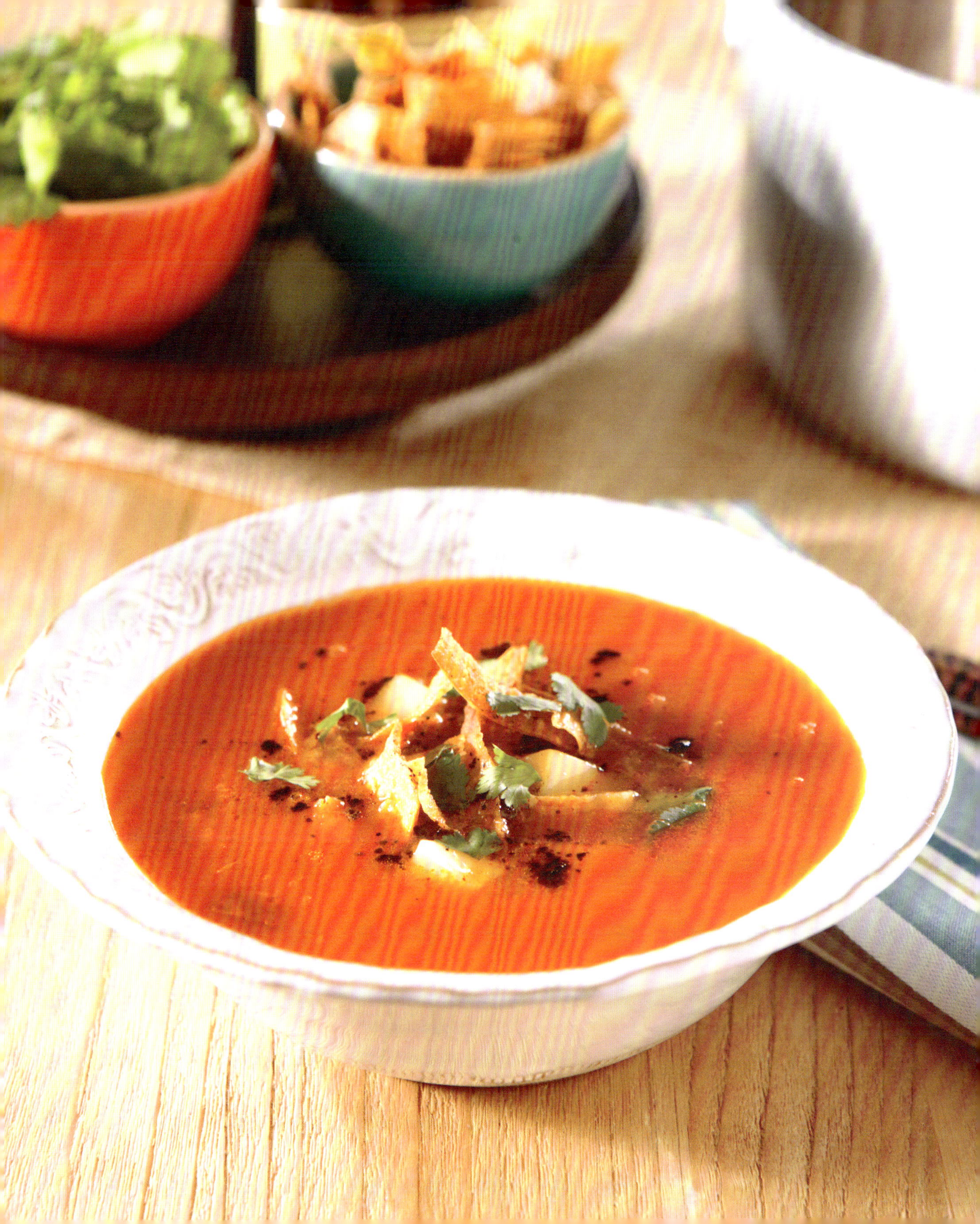

SOUPS & STEWS

CREAMY ROASTED POBLANO SOUP

6 large poblano peppers
1 tablespoon olive oil
¾ cup chopped onion
½ cup thinly sliced celery
½ cup thinly sliced carrots
1 clove garlic, minced
2 cans (about 14 ounces each) vegetable broth
1 package (8 ounces) cream cheese, cubed
Salt and black pepper

1. Preheat broiler. Line broiler pan or baking sheet with foil. Place poblano peppers on pan; broil 5 to 6 inches from heat source 15 minutes or until peppers are blistered and beginning to char, turning occasionally. Place peppers in medium bowl; cover with plastic wrap. Let stand 20 minutes.

2. Meanwhile, heat oil in large saucepan over medium-high heat. Add onion, celery, carrots and garlic; cook and stir 4 minutes or until onion is translucent. Stir in broth; bring to a boil. Reduce heat to medium-low; cover and simmer 12 minutes or until celery is tender.

3. Scrape skins from peppers with paring knife; remove stems and seeds. Add peppers to broth mixture.

4. Working in batches, process soup and cream cheese in food processor or blender until smooth. (Or use immersion blender.) Return soup to saucepan; cook and stir over medium heat 2 minutes or until heated through. Season to taste with salt and black pepper.

MAKES 4 SERVINGS

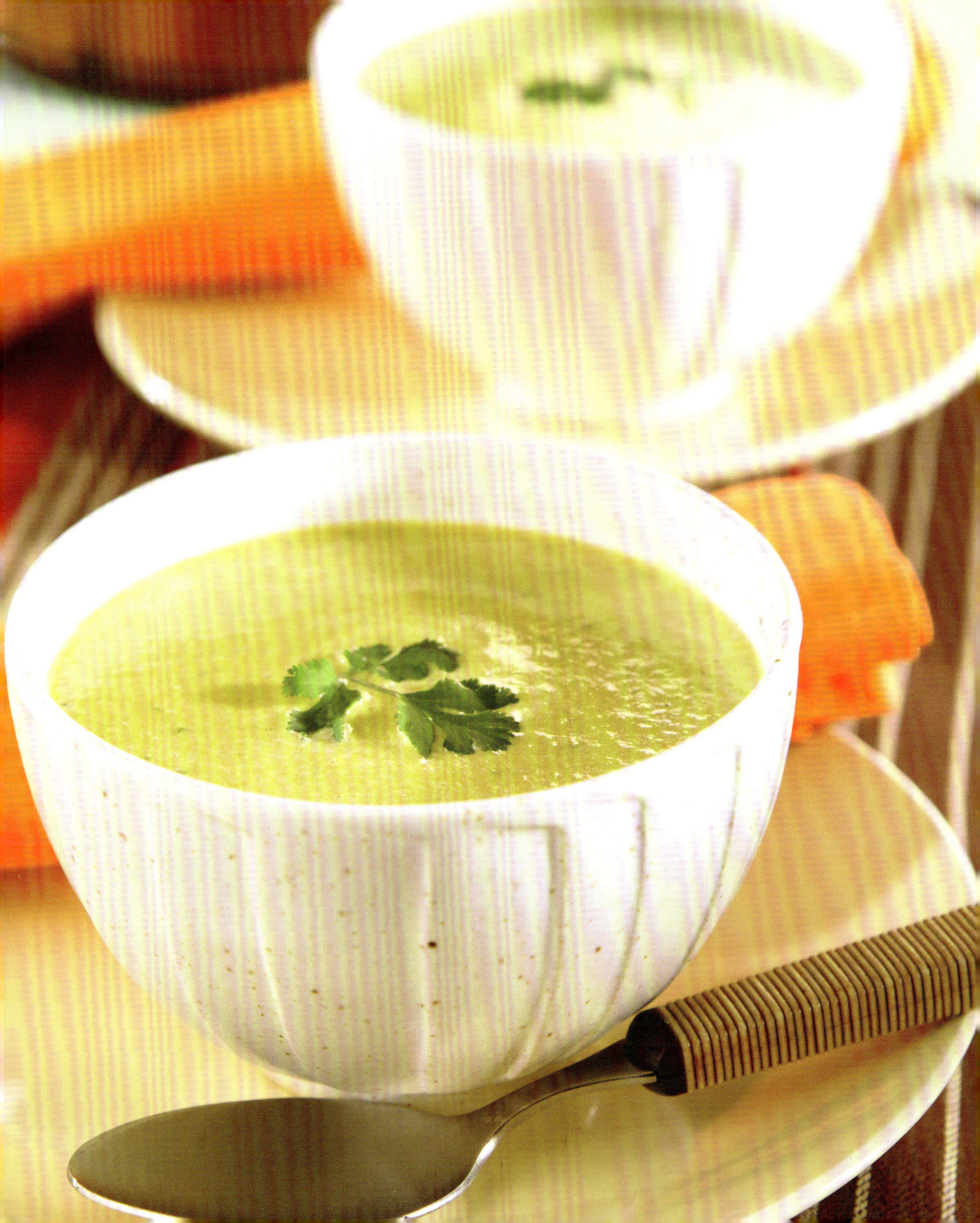

SOUPS & STEWS

CHILE VERDE CHICKEN STEW

- ⅓ cup all-purpose flour
- 1½ teaspoons salt, divided
- ¼ teaspoon black pepper
- 1½ pounds boneless skinless chicken thighs, cut into 1½-inch pieces
- 4 tablespoons vegetable oil, divided
- 1 pound tomatillos (about 9), husked and halved
- 2 onions, chopped
- 2 cans (4 ounces each) diced mild green chiles
- 1 tablespoon dried oregano
- 1 tablespoon ground cumin
- 2 cloves garlic, chopped
- 1 teaspoon sugar
- 2 cups chicken broth
- 8 ounces Mexican beer
- 5 unpeeled red potatoes, cut into 1-inch pieces

Optional toppings: chopped fresh cilantro, sour cream and/or shredded Monterey Jack cheese

1. Combine flour, 1 teaspoon salt and pepper in medium bowl. Add chicken; toss to coat. Heat 2 tablespoons oil in large saucepan or Dutch oven over medium heat. Add chicken in batches; cook 5 to 8 minutes or until lightly browned on all sides, stirring occasionally. Remove to bowl.

2. Heat remaining 2 tablespoons oil in same saucepan. Add tomatillos, onions, chiles, oregano, cumin, garlic, sugar and remaining ½ teaspoon salt; cook 20 minutes or until vegetables are softened, stirring occasionally and scraping up browned bits from bottom of saucepan. Stir in broth and beer until blended. Working in batches, process in food processor or blender until almost smooth. (Or use immersion blender.)

3. Return blended mixture to saucepan. Stir in potatoes and chicken; bring to a boil over medium-high heat. Reduce heat to low; cover and simmer 45 minutes or until potatoes are tender, stirring occasionally. Serve with desired toppings.

MAKES 6 SERVINGS

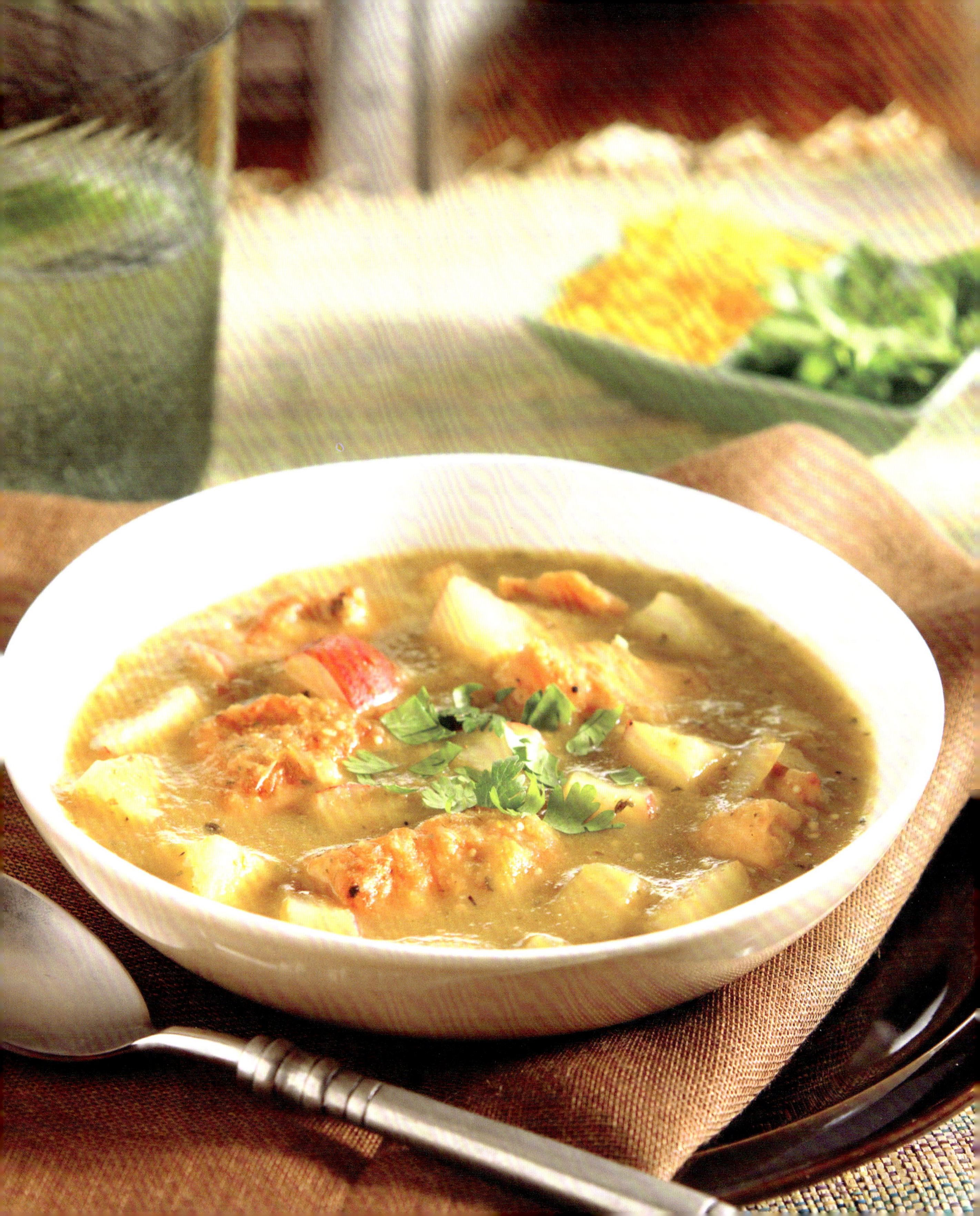

SOUPS & STEWS

TURKEY ALBONDIGAS SOUP

½ cup uncooked brown rice

Meatballs
- 1 pound ground turkey
- 2 tablespoons minced onion
- 2 teaspoons chopped fresh cilantro
- 2 teaspoons milk
- ½ teaspoon salt
- ½ teaspoon hot pepper sauce
- ¼ teaspoon dried oregano
- ¼ teaspoon black pepper

Broth
- 1 tablespoon olive oil
- ½ cup chopped onion
- 2 cloves garlic, minced
- 5 cups chicken broth
- 1 tablespoon tomato paste
- 2 teaspoons hot pepper sauce
- ½ teaspoon salt
- ¼ teaspoon black pepper
- 3 carrots, cut into rounds
- 1 zucchini, quartered lengthwise and cut crosswise into ½-inch slices
- 1 yellow squash, quartered lengthwise and cut crosswise into ½-inch slices
- Lime wedges and chopped fresh cilantro (optional)

1. Prepare rice according to package directions.

2. Meanwhile for meatballs, combine turkey, 2 tablespoons onion, 2 teaspoons chopped cilantro, milk, ½ teaspoon salt, ½ teaspoon hot pepper sauce, oregano and ¼ teaspoon black pepper in medium bowl; mix well. Shape mixture into 1-inch balls.

3. For broth, heat oil in large saucepan over medium heat. Add ½ cup onion and garlic; cook and stir until golden brown. Add broth, tomato paste, 2 teaspoons hot pepper sauce, ½ teaspoon salt and ¼ teaspoon black pepper; bring to a boil over high heat.

4. Reduce heat to low. Add meatballs and carrots to broth; simmer 15 minutes. Add zucchini, squash and cooked rice; simmer 5 to 10 minutes or just until vegetables are tender. Serve immediately with lime wedges and cilantro, if desired.

MAKES 4 SERVINGS

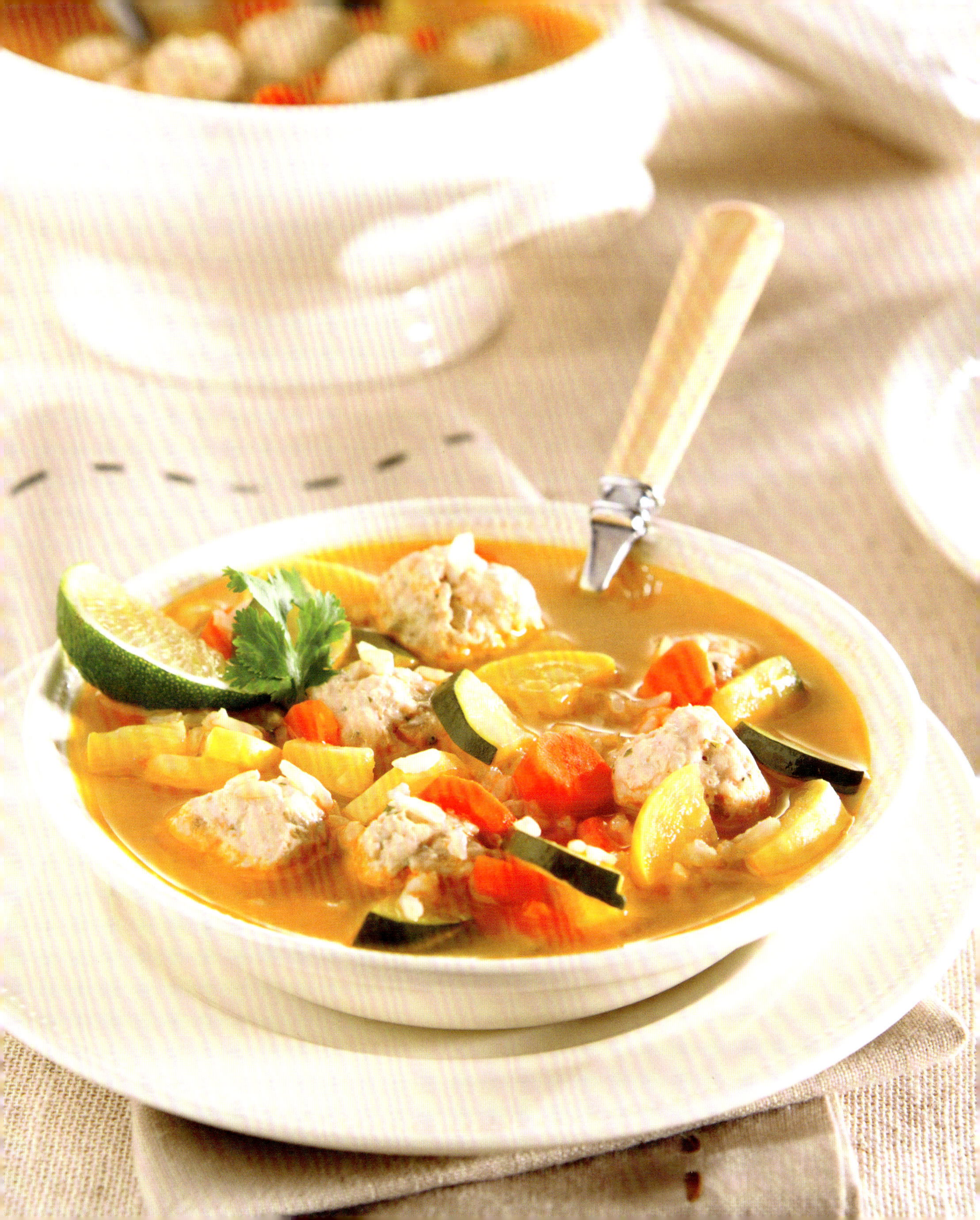

SOUPS & STEWS

TACO STEW

- 1 pound ground beef
- 1 cup chopped onion
- 1 can (16 ounces) pinto beans in Mexican-style sauce
- 1 can (about 14 ounces) stewed tomatoes, undrained
- 1 can (10 ounces) diced tomatoes with green chiles
- 1 tablespoon chili powder
- 1 teaspoon ground cumin
- ½ teaspoon salt
- 4 cups shredded iceberg lettuce
- ½ cup (2 ounces) shredded sharp Cheddar cheese
- ¼ cup chopped fresh cilantro (optional)
- Corn tortilla chips

1. Brown beef and onion in large saucepan over medium-high heat 6 to 8 minutes, stirring to break up meat. Add beans, stewed tomatoes with juice, diced tomatoes and green chiles, chili powder, cumin and salt; bring to a boil. Reduce heat to low; cover and simmer 10 minutes.

2. Divide lettuce among serving bowls; top with stew, cheese and cilantro, if desired. Serve with tortilla chips.

MAKES 4 SERVINGS

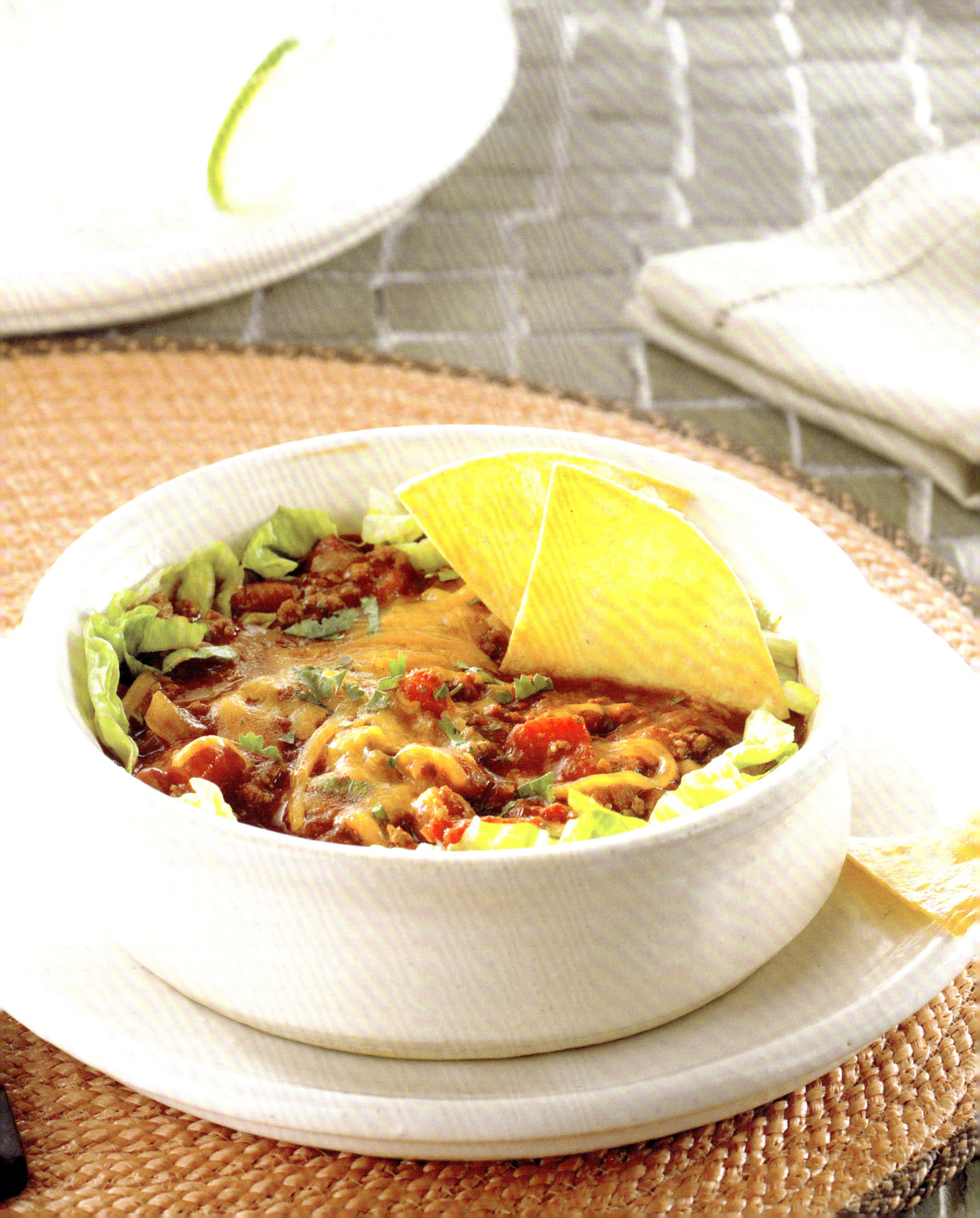

SOUPS & STEWS

SPICY PUMPKIN SOUP

- 1 can (15 ounces) pumpkin purée
- 1 can (about 14 ounces) vegetable broth
- 1 can (4 ounces) diced green chiles
- ½ cup water
- 1 teaspoon ground cumin
- ½ teaspoon chili powder
- ¼ teaspoon garlic powder
- ⅛ teaspoon ground red pepper (optional)
- ¼ cup sour cream, plus additional for garnish
- ¼ cup packed fresh cilantro leaves, finely chopped

1. Combine pumpkin, broth, chiles, water, cumin, chili powder, garlic powder and red pepper, if desired, in medium saucepan; bring to a boil over high heat. Reduce heat to medium; simmer, uncovered, 5 minutes, stirring occasionally.

2. Stir in ¼ cup sour cream and cilantro; cook over low heat 1 minute (do not boil).

3. Ladle soup into four serving bowls; top each serving with small dollops of additional sour cream, if desired. Run tip of spoon through dollops to swirl.

MAKES 4 SERVINGS

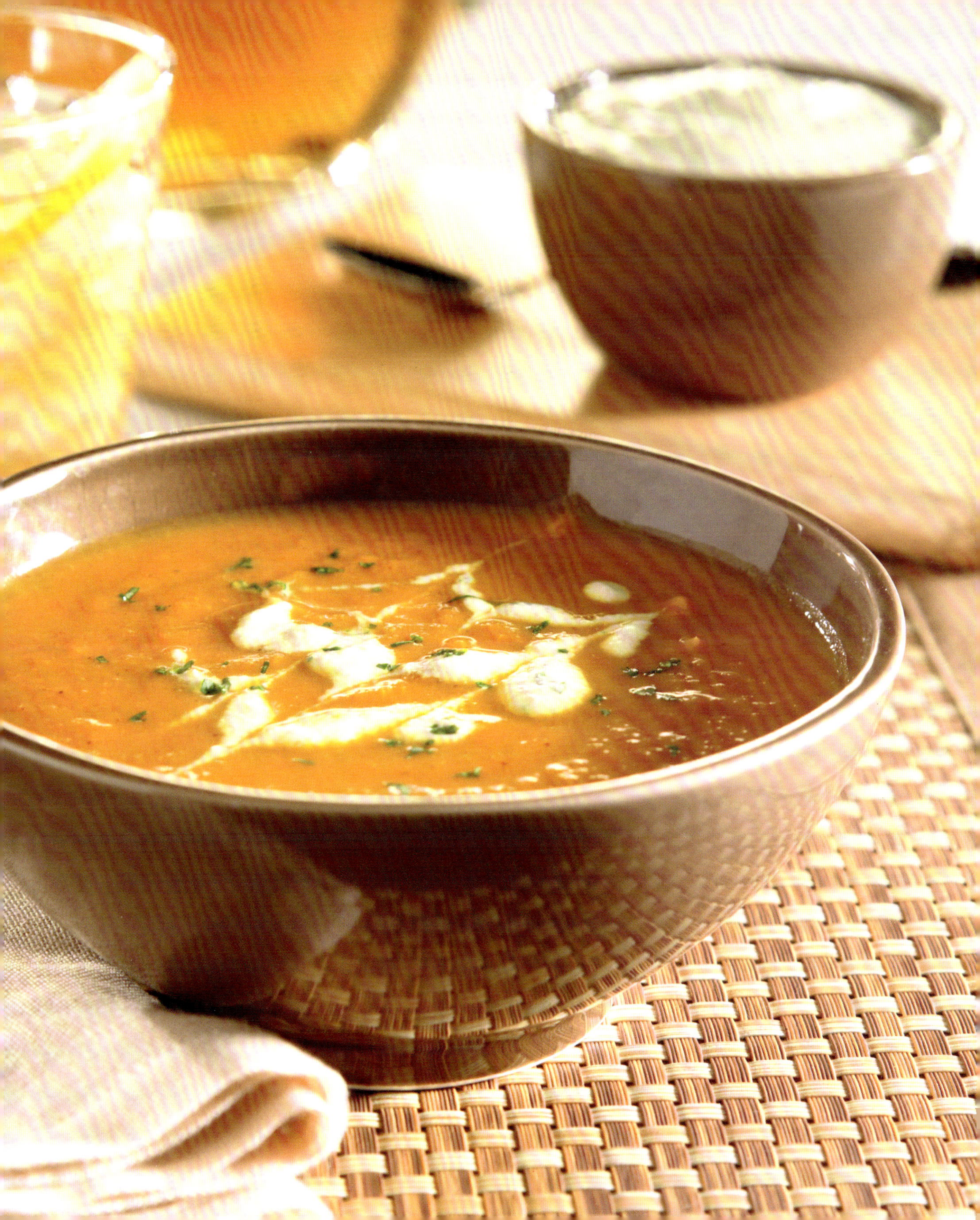

SOUPS & STEWS

MEXICAN HOT POT

- 1 tablespoon vegetable oil
- 1 medium onion, sliced
- 3 cloves garlic, minced
- 2 teaspoons red pepper flakes
- 2 teaspoons dried oregano
- 1 teaspoon salt
- 1 teaspoon ground cumin
- 1 can (28 ounces) whole tomatoes, chopped
- 2 cups thawed frozen corn
- 1 can (15 ounces) chickpeas, rinsed and drained
- 1 can (15 ounces) pinto beans, rinsed and drained
- 1 cup water
- 6 cups shredded iceberg lettuce

1. Heat oil in large saucepan or Dutch oven over medium-high heat. Add onion and garlic; cook and stir 5 minutes. Add red pepper flakes, oregano, salt and cumin. Stir in tomatoes, corn, chickpeas, pinto beans and water; bring to a boil over high heat.

2. Reduce heat to medium-low; cover and simmer 15 minutes. Ladle stew into bowls; top each bowl with 1 cup shredded lettuce.

MAKES 6 SERVINGS

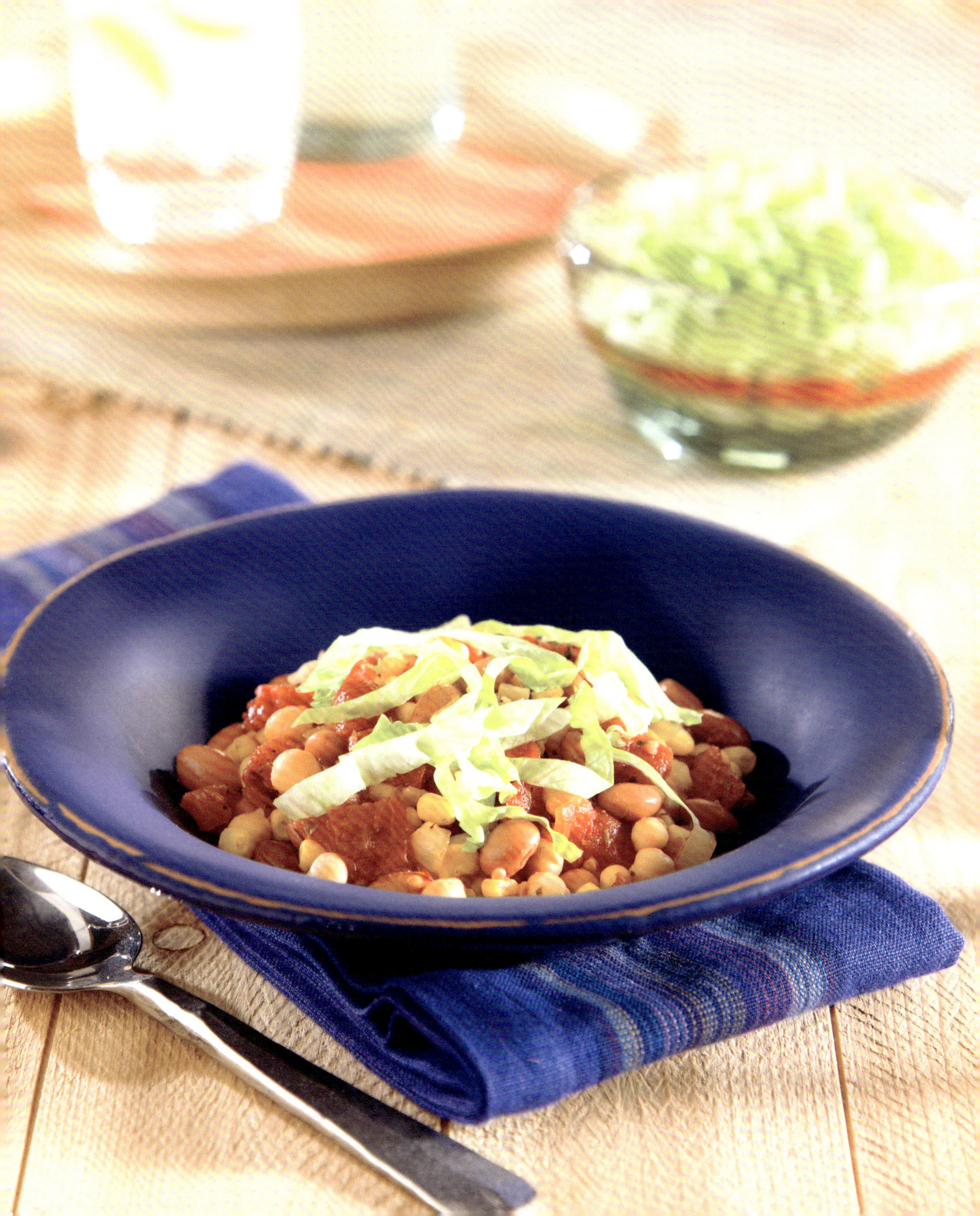

SOUPS & STEWS

CORN AND JALAPEÑO CHOWDER

- 4 cups thawed frozen corn, divided
- 2 cups vegetable broth, divided
- 2 jalapeño peppers, seeded and finely chopped
- 1½ teaspoons whole cumin seeds, crushed *or* 1 teaspoon ground cumin
- ¼ teaspoon onion salt
- 1 cup half-and-half
  Salt and black pepper
  Shredded Cheddar cheese and thinly sliced roasted red pepper (optional)

1. Combine 2 cups corn and 1 cup broth in food processor. Cover; process until almost smooth.

2. Combine blended corn mixture, remaining corn, remaining broth, jalapeños, cumin seeds and onion salt in large saucepan. Bring to a boil. Reduce heat; cover and simmer 5 minutes.

3. Stir in half-and-half; cook until heated through. Season to taste with salt and pepper. Top each serving with cheese and red pepper, if desired.

MAKES 4 SERVINGS

CHICKEN TORTILLA SOUP

- 2 cans (about 14 ounces each) chicken broth
- 1 pound boneless skinless chicken breasts
- 2 jars (16 ounces each) corn and black bean salsa
- 3 tablespoons vegetable oil
- 1 tablespoon taco seasoning mix
- 1 package (3 ounces) ramen noodles,* broken into small pieces
- 1 cup (4 ounces) shredded Monterey Jack cheese

*Use any flavor; discard seasoning packet.

1. Bring broth to a simmer in large saucepan. Add chicken; cook 12 to 15 minutes or until no longer pink in center and cooked through (165°F). Remove chicken to cutting board; set aside until cool enough to handle. Shred chicken with two forks.

2. Add salsa to saucepan with broth; cook 5 minutes or until soup comes to a simmer. Return shredded chicken to saucepan; cook 5 minutes or until heated through.

3. Combine oil and taco seasoning in small bowl. Add noodles; toss to coat. Cook and stir noodles in medium skillet over medium heat 8 to 10 minutes or until toasted. Top soup with toasted noodles and cheese.

MAKES 6 SERVINGS

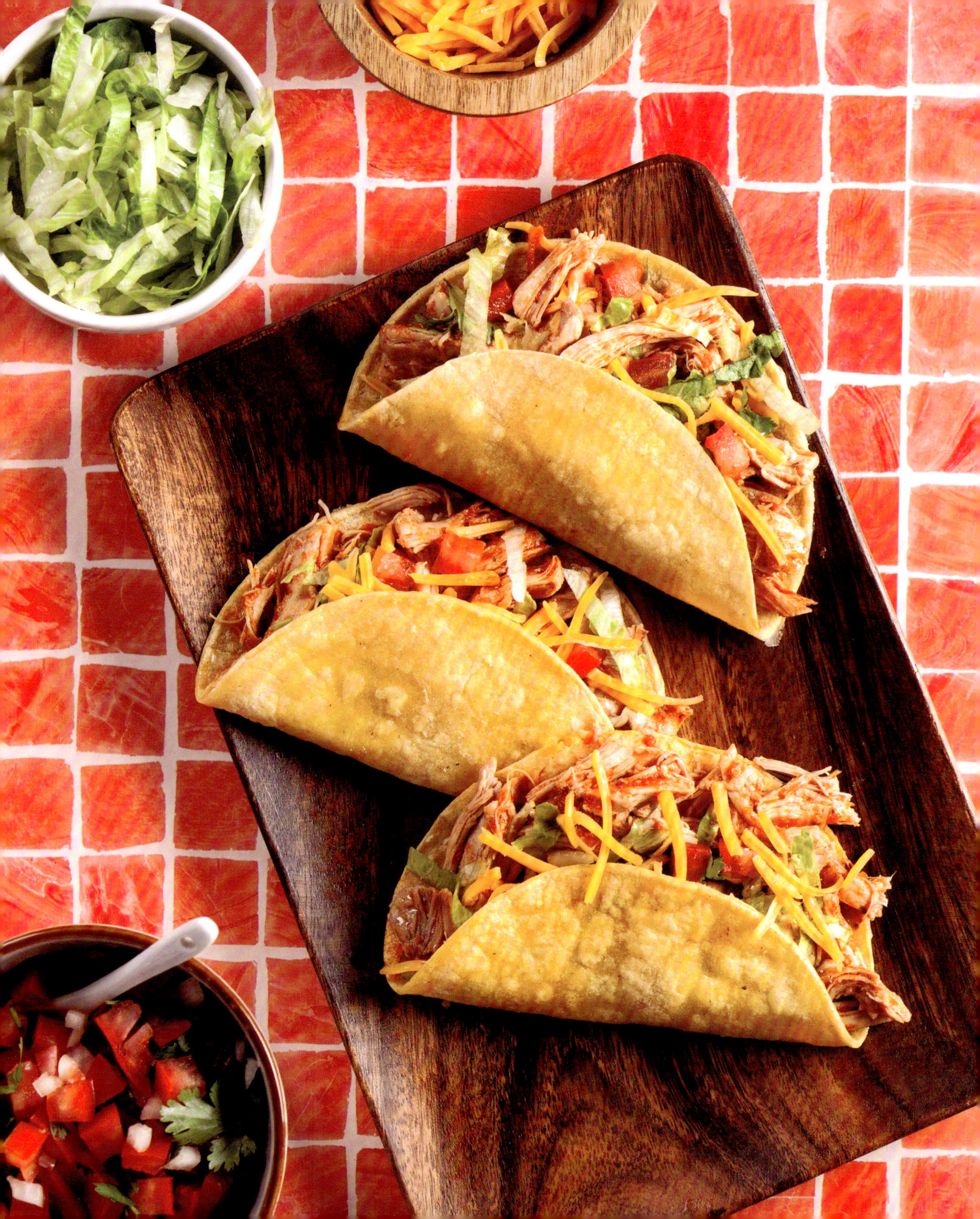

TACOS, BURRITOS & QUESADILLAS

WEEKNIGHT CHICKEN TACOS

- 2 pounds boneless skinless chicken thighs
- Salt and black pepper
- 1 tablespoon vegetable oil
- 1 cup chicken broth or water
- 1 cup chunky salsa
- Corn tortillas, warmed
- 1 cup shredded lettuce
- 1 cup pico de gallo
- 1 cup (4 ounces) shredded taco blend or Cheddar cheese
- Optional toppings: sour cream, sliced jalapeño peppers, pickled onions and/or diced avocado

1. Season chicken with salt and black pepper. Heat oil in large saucepan over medium-high heat. Add chicken; cook about 5 minutes per side or until lightly browned. Add broth and salsa; cook 1 minute, scraping up browned bits from bottom of saucepan. Bring to a boil. Reduce heat to medium-low; cover and cook about 35 minutes or until chicken is cooked through.

2. Remove chicken to plate; let stand 5 to 10 minutes or until cool enough to handle. Meanwhile, cook liquid remaining in saucepan over medium heat 5 to 10 minutes or until slightly thickened.

3. Shred chicken into bite-size pieces with two forks. Return to saucepan; stir to coat with sauce. Serve chicken mixture in tortillas with lettuce, pico de gallo, cheese and desired toppings.

MAKES 6 TO 8 SERVINGS

TACOS, BURRITOS & QUESADILLAS

GRILLED BAJA BURRITOS

- 6 tablespoons vegetable oil, divided
- 3 tablespoons lime juice, divided
- 2 teaspoons chili powder
- 1½ teaspoons lemon-pepper
- 1 pound tilapia fillets
- 3 cups coleslaw mix
- ½ cup chopped fresh cilantro
- ¼ teaspoon salt
- ¼ teaspoon black pepper
- ½ cup pico de gallo
- ½ cup guacamole
- 4 (7-inch) flour tortillas

1. Prepare grill for direct cooking or preheat broiler. Combine 2 tablespoons oil, 1 tablespoon lime juice, chili powder and lemon pepper in large resealable food storage bag. Add fish; seal bag and turn to coat. Let stand at room temperature 10 minutes.

2. Brush grid with 2 tablespoons oil. Remove fish from marinade; discard marinade. Grill fish, covered, over medium-high heat 6 to 8 minutes or until center is opaque, carefully turning once. (Or broil on baking sheet 4 inches from heat source 3 to 5 minutes per side or until center is opaque.)

3. Combine coleslaw mix, remaining 2 tablespoons oil, 2 tablespoons lime juice, cilantro, salt and pepper in medium bowl; mix well.

4. Layer fish, coleslaw mixture, pico de gallo and guacamole on tortillas; roll up tightly to enclose filling.

MAKES 4 SERVINGS

Tip

Any firm white fish such as snapper or halibut would make a great substitute for the tilapia.

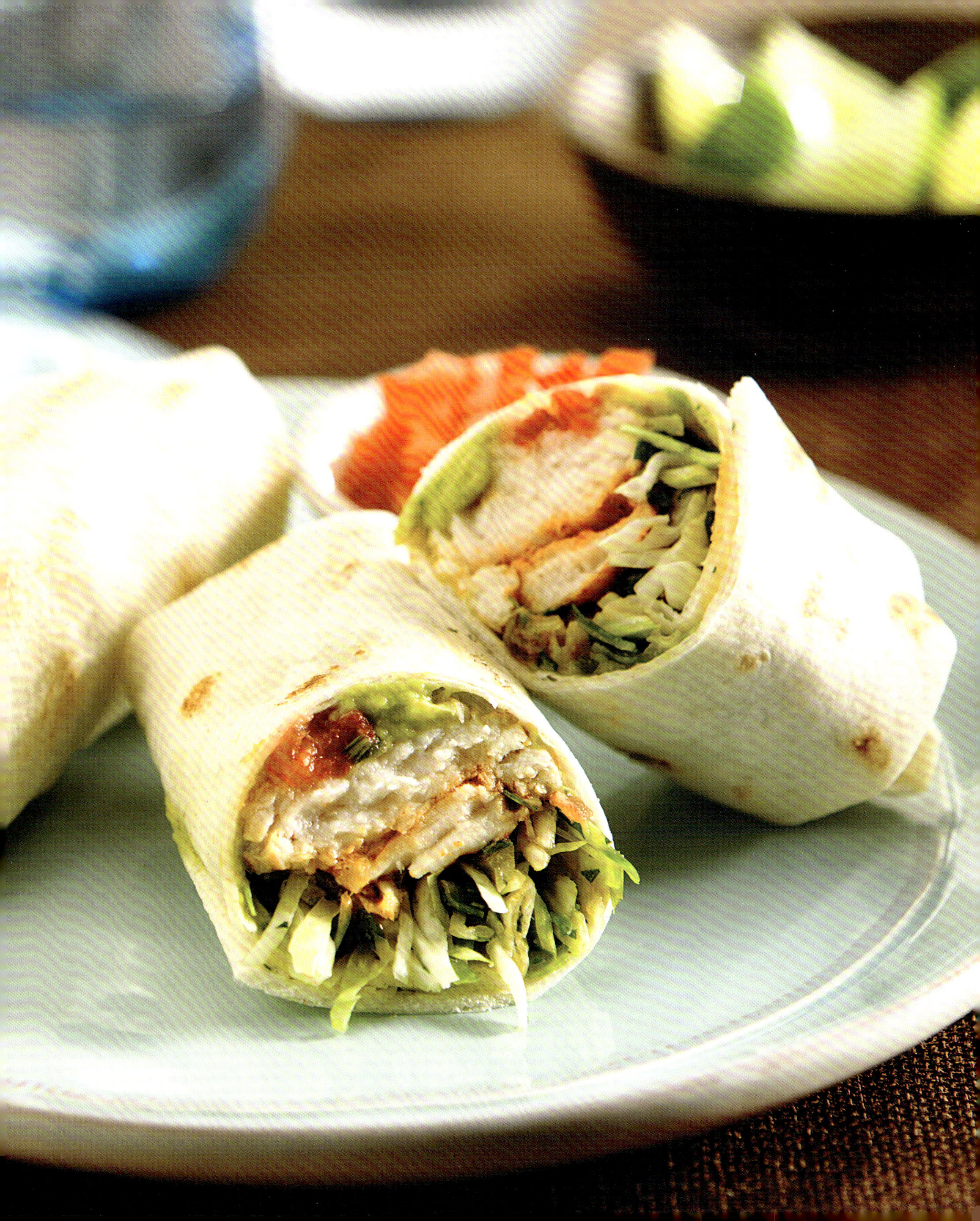

TACOS, BURRITOS & QUESADILLAS

DOUBLE DECKER TACOS

- 2 tablespoons all-purpose flour
- 2 teaspoons chili powder
- 1 teaspoon dried minced onion
- ¾ teaspoon paprika
- ½ teaspoon salt
- ½ teaspoon garlic powder
- ¼ teaspoon sugar
- 1 pound ground beef
- ⅔ cup water
- 8 hard taco shells
- 8 mini (5-inch) flour tortillas*
- 2 cups refried beans, warmed
- 1 cup shredded romaine lettuce
- 1 cup chopped tomato
- 1 cup (4 ounces) shredded Cheddar cheese
- Sour cream (optional)

*Mini flour tortillas may also be labeled as street tacos.

1. Preheat oven to 350°F. Combine flour, chili powder, onion, paprika, salt, garlic powder and sugar in small bowl; mix well.

2. Cook beef in large skillet over medium-high heat 6 to 8 minutes or until browned, stirring to break up meat. Drain fat. Add spice mixture; cook and stir 2 minutes. Stir in water; bring to a simmer. Reduce heat to medium; cook 10 minutes or until most of liquid has evaporated.

3. Meanwhile, place taco shells on baking sheet. Bake 5 minutes or until warm.

4. Wrap tortillas in damp paper towel; microwave on HIGH 25 to 35 seconds or until warm. Spread each tortilla with ¼ cup refried beans, leaving ¼-inch border around edge. Wrap flour tortillas around outside of taco shells, pressing gently to seal together.

5. Fill taco shells with beef mixture; top with lettuce, tomato and cheese. Serve immediately with sour cream, if desired.

MAKES 8 TACOS

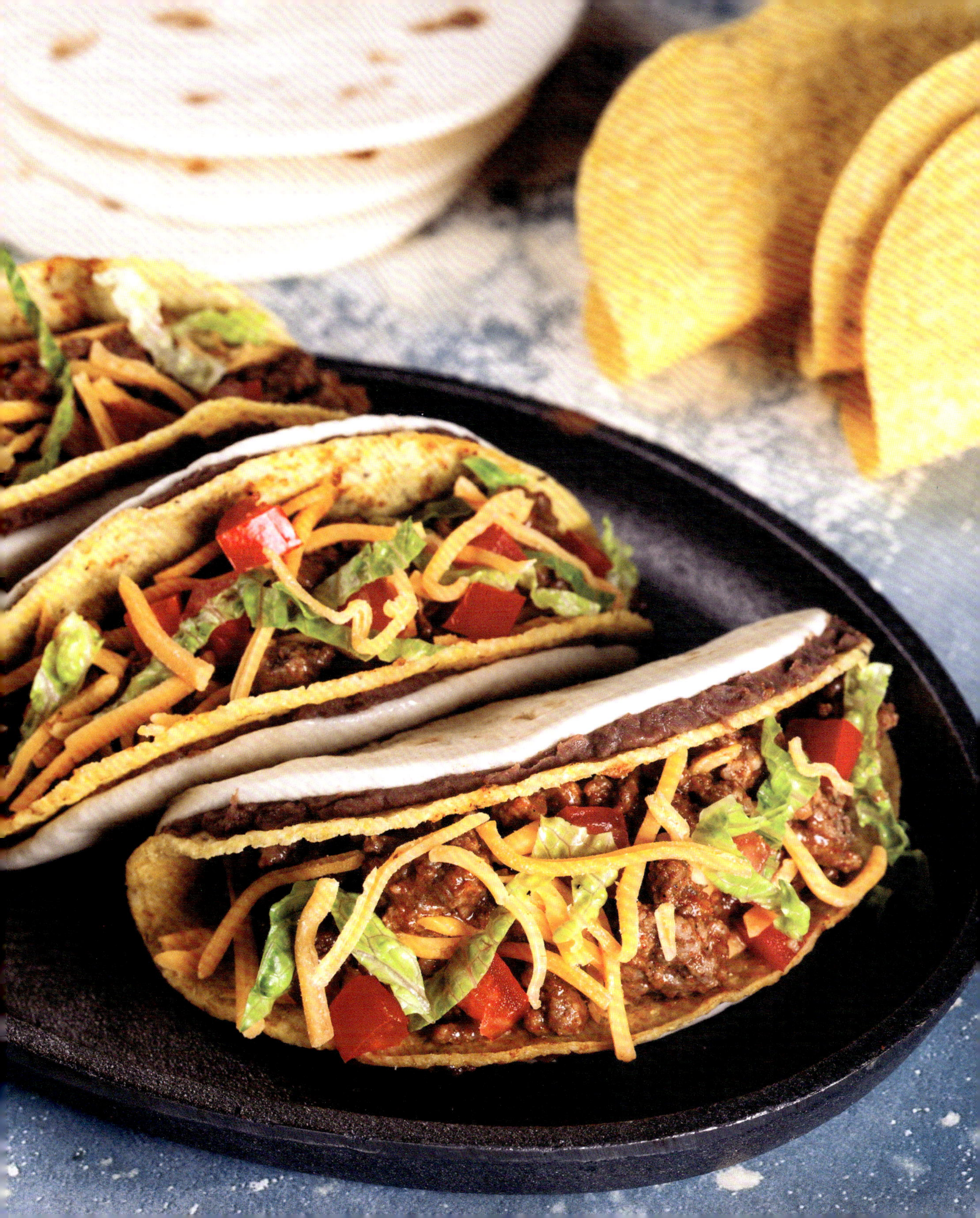

TACOS, BURRITOS & QUESADILLAS

MEXICAN PIZZA

- 1 pound ground beef
- ¾ cup water
- 1 package taco seasoning mix
- 1 to 2 tablespoons vegetable oil
- 8 (8-inch) flour tortillas
- 1 can (15 ounces) refried beans
- 1 cup taco sauce, divided
- 1⅓ cups shredded Colby Jack or Mexican blend cheese
- Optional toppings: diced fresh tomato, sliced black olives, sliced green onions, shredded lettuce

1. Preheat oven to 400°F. Line baking sheet with parchment paper.

2. Cook beef in large skillet over medium-high heat 6 to 8 minutes or until browned, stirring to break up meat. Drain fat. Stir in water and taco seasoning. Reduce heat to medium-low; cook about 10 minutes or until most of liquid is absorbed, stirring occasionally.

3. Meanwhile, heat 1 tablespoon oil in large skillet over medium-high heat. Cook tortillas in batches about 2 minutes per side or until crisp and lightly browned, adding additional oil as necessary. Drain on paper towel-lined plate. Arrange four tortillas on prepared baking sheet.

4. Heat refried beans in microwave or on stovetop according to package directions. Spread one fourth of beans (heaping ⅓ cup) on each tortilla on baking sheet. Top with one fourth of beef mixture (scant ½ cup); drizzle with 1 tablespoon taco sauce. Place remaining tortillas over beef mixture. Spread 3 tablespoons taco sauce over each tortilla; sprinkle with ⅓ cup cheese.

5. Bake 4 to 5 minutes or until cheese is melted. Immediately sprinkle with desired toppings. Cut into quarters to serve.

MAKES 4 SERVINGS

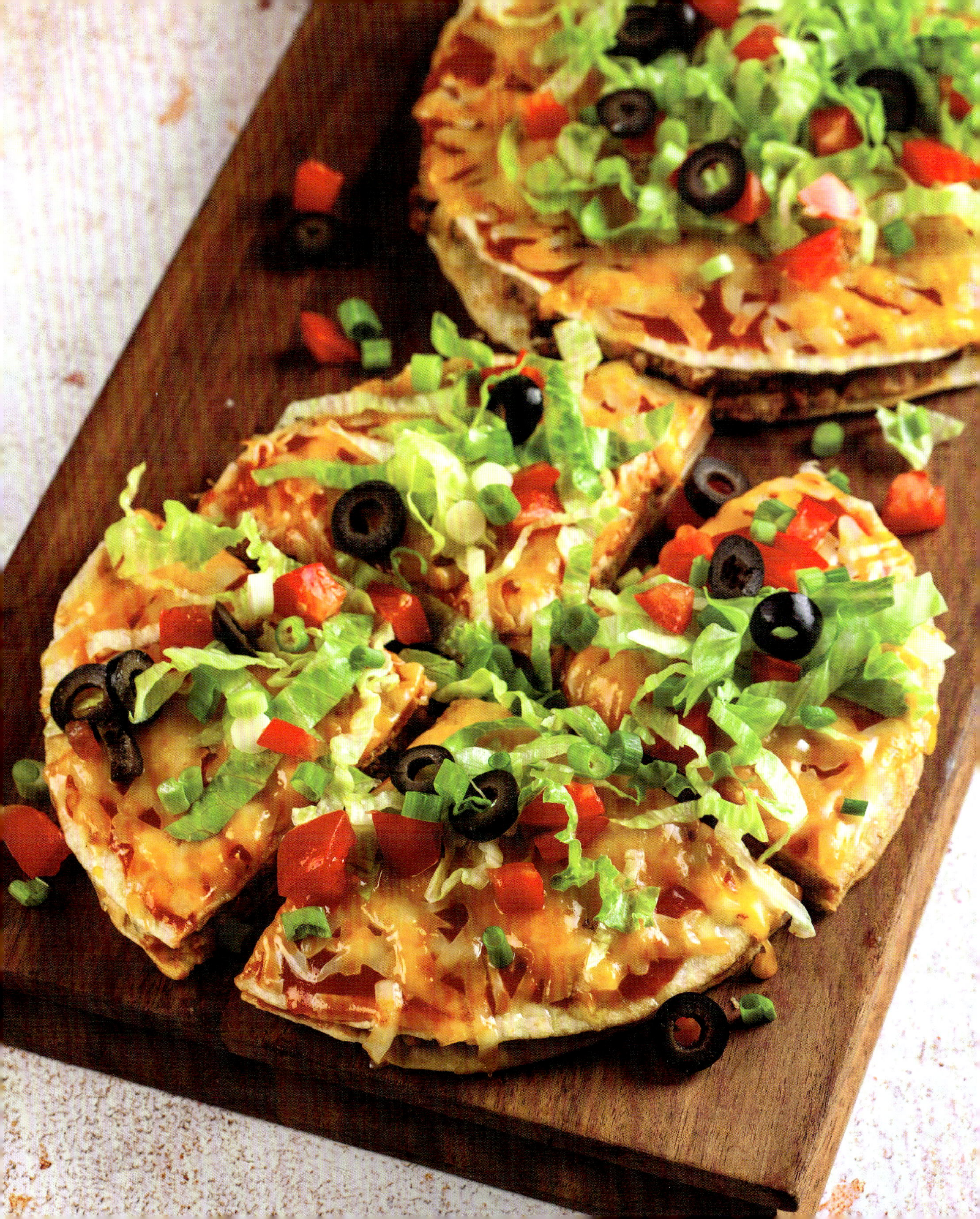

SALSA BEEF BURRITOS

- 1 boneless beef chuck shoulder roast (2 to 3 pounds)
- 1 jar (24 ounces) *or* 2 jars (16 ounces each) salsa
- Flour tortillas, warmed
- Optional toppings: shredded cheese, sour cream, salsa, lettuce, tomato, onion or guacamole

Slow Cooker Directions

1. Place roast in slow cooker; top with salsa. Cover and cook on LOW 8 to 10 hours.

2. Remove beef from slow cooker. Shred beef with two forks. Return to slow cooker. Cover and cook 1 hour or until heated through.

3. Serve shredded beef in warm tortillas with desired toppings.

MAKES 8 SERVINGS

TACOS, BURRITOS & QUESADILLAS

CHICKEN BACON QUESADILLAS

- 4 teaspoons vegetable oil, divided
- 4 (8-inch) flour tortillas
- 1 cup (4 ounces) shredded Colby-Jack cheese
- 2 cups coarsely chopped cooked chicken
- 4 slices bacon, crisp-cooked and coarsely chopped
- ½ cup pico de gallo, plus additional for serving
- Sour cream and guacamole (optional)

1. Heat large nonstick skillet over medium heat; brush with 1 teaspoon oil. Place one tortilla in skillet; sprinkle with ¼ cup cheese. Spread ½ cup chicken over one half of tortilla; top with one fourth of bacon and 2 tablespoons pico de gallo.

2. Cook 1 to 2 minutes or until cheese is melted and bottom of tortilla is lightly browned. Fold tortilla over filling, pressing with spatula. Remove to cutting board; cool slightly. Cut into wedges. Repeat with remaining ingredients. Serve with additional pico de gallo, sour cream and guacamole, if desired.

MAKES 4 SERVINGS

TACOS, BURRITOS & QUESADILLAS

CAULIFLOWER MUSHROOM TACOS

- 1 package (8 ounces) sliced cremini mushrooms
- 4 tablespoons olive oil, divided
- 1¾ teaspoons salt, divided
- 1 head cauliflower, cut into 1-inch florets
- 1 teaspoon ground cumin
- ½ teaspoon dried oregano
- ¼ teaspoon ground coriander
- ¼ teaspoon ground cinnamon
- ¼ teaspoon black pepper
- ½ cup sour cream
- 2 teaspoons lime juice
- ½ teaspoon chipotle chili powder
- ½ cup refried beans
- 8 taco-size flour or corn tortillas
-   Sliced red onion or Pickled Red Onions (recipe follows)
-   Chopped fresh cilantro (optional)

1. Preheat oven to 400°F. Toss mushrooms with 1 tablespoon oil and ¼ teaspoon salt in large bowl. Spread on small baking sheet.

2. Place cauliflower in same large bowl. Add remaining 3 tablespoons oil, 1 teaspoon salt, cumin, oregano, coriander, cinnamon and black pepper; mix well. Spread on large baking sheet in single layer.

3. Roast cauliflower 40 minutes or until browned and tender, stirring occasionally. Roast mushrooms 20 minutes or until dry and browned, stirring occasionally.

4. Combine sour cream, lime juice, chipotle chili powder and remaining ½ teaspoon salt in small bowl; mix well.

5. For each taco, spread 1 tablespoon beans over tortilla; spread 1 teaspoon crema over beans. Top with about 3 mushroom slices and ¼ cup cauliflower. Top with red onions and cilantro, if desired. Fold in half.

MAKES 8 TACOS

Pickled Red Onions

Thinly slice 1 small red onion; place in large jar or food storage container. Add ¼ cup white wine vinegar or distilled white vinegar, 2 tablespoons water, 1 teaspoon sugar and 1 teaspoon salt. Seal jar; shake well. Refrigerate at least 1 hour or up to 1 week. Makes about ½ cup.

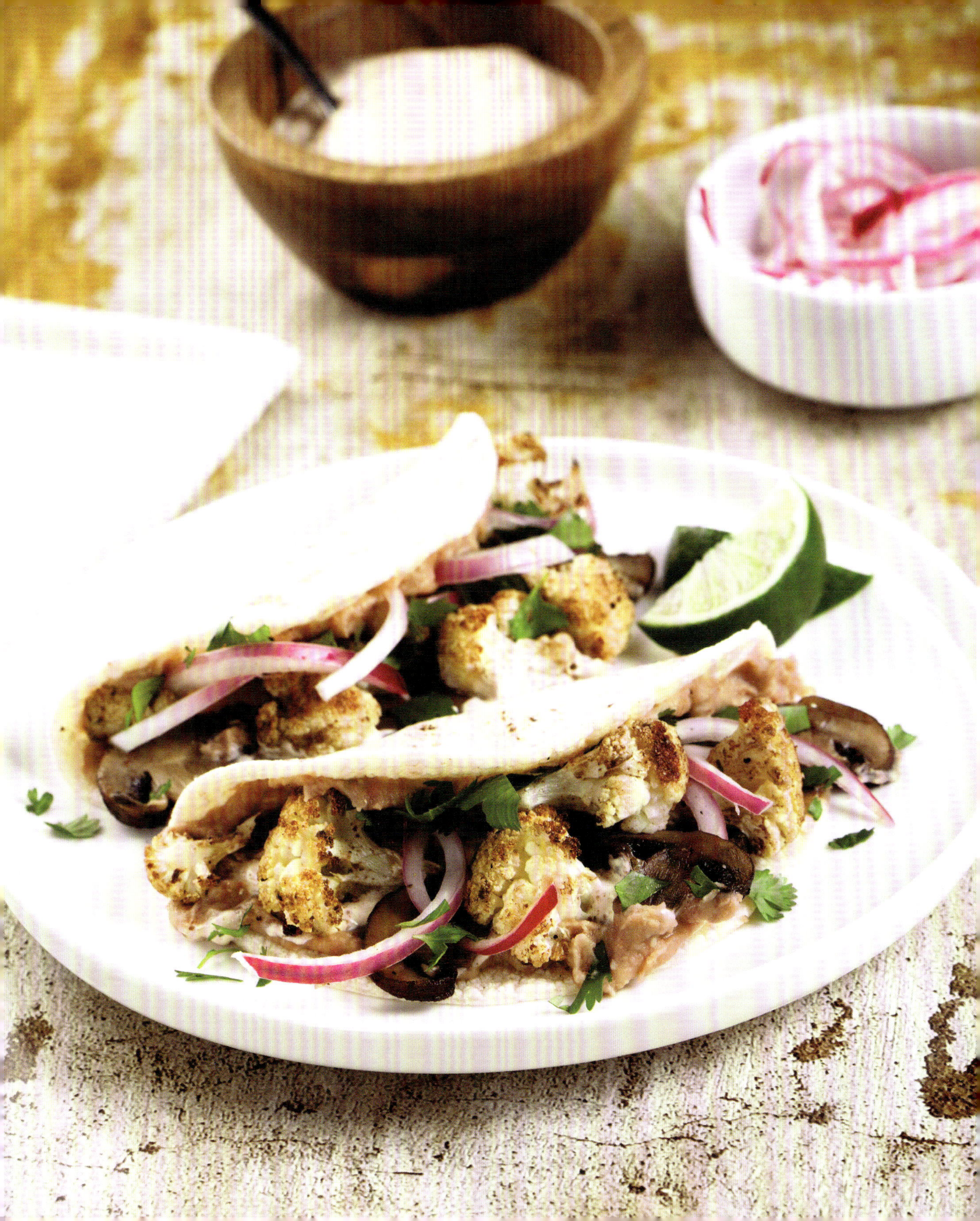

TACOS, BURRITOS & QUESADILLAS

Coleslaw

- 1 medium jicama (about 12 ounces), peeled and shredded
- 2 cups packaged coleslaw mix
- 3 tablespoons finely chopped fresh cilantro
- ¼ cup lime juice
- ¼ cup vegetable oil
- 3 tablespoons white vinegar
- 2 tablespoons mayonnaise
- 1 tablespoon honey
- 1 teaspoon salt

Tacos

- 1 to 1¼ pounds white fish such as tilapia or mahi mahi, cut into 3×1½-inch pieces
- Salt and black pepper
- 2 tablespoons vegetable oil
- 12 (6-inch) taco-size tortillas, heated
- 2 cups pico de gallo
- Guacamole (optional)

ISLAND FISH TACOS

1. For coleslaw, combine jicama, coleslaw mix and 3 tablespoons cilantro in medium bowl. Whisk ¼ cup lime juice, ¼ cup oil, vinegar, mayonnaise, honey and 1 teaspoon salt in small bowl until well blended. Pour over vegetable mixture; stir to coat. Let stand at least 15 minutes for flavors to blend.

2. For tacos, season both sides of fish with salt and black pepper. Heat 1 tablespoon oil in large skillet over medium-high heat. Add half of fish; cook 2 minutes per side or until fish is opaque and begins to flake when tested with fork. Repeat with remaining oil and fish.

3. Break fish into bite-size pieces; serve in tortillas with coleslaw, pico de gallo and guacamole, if desired.

MAKES 4 SERVINGS

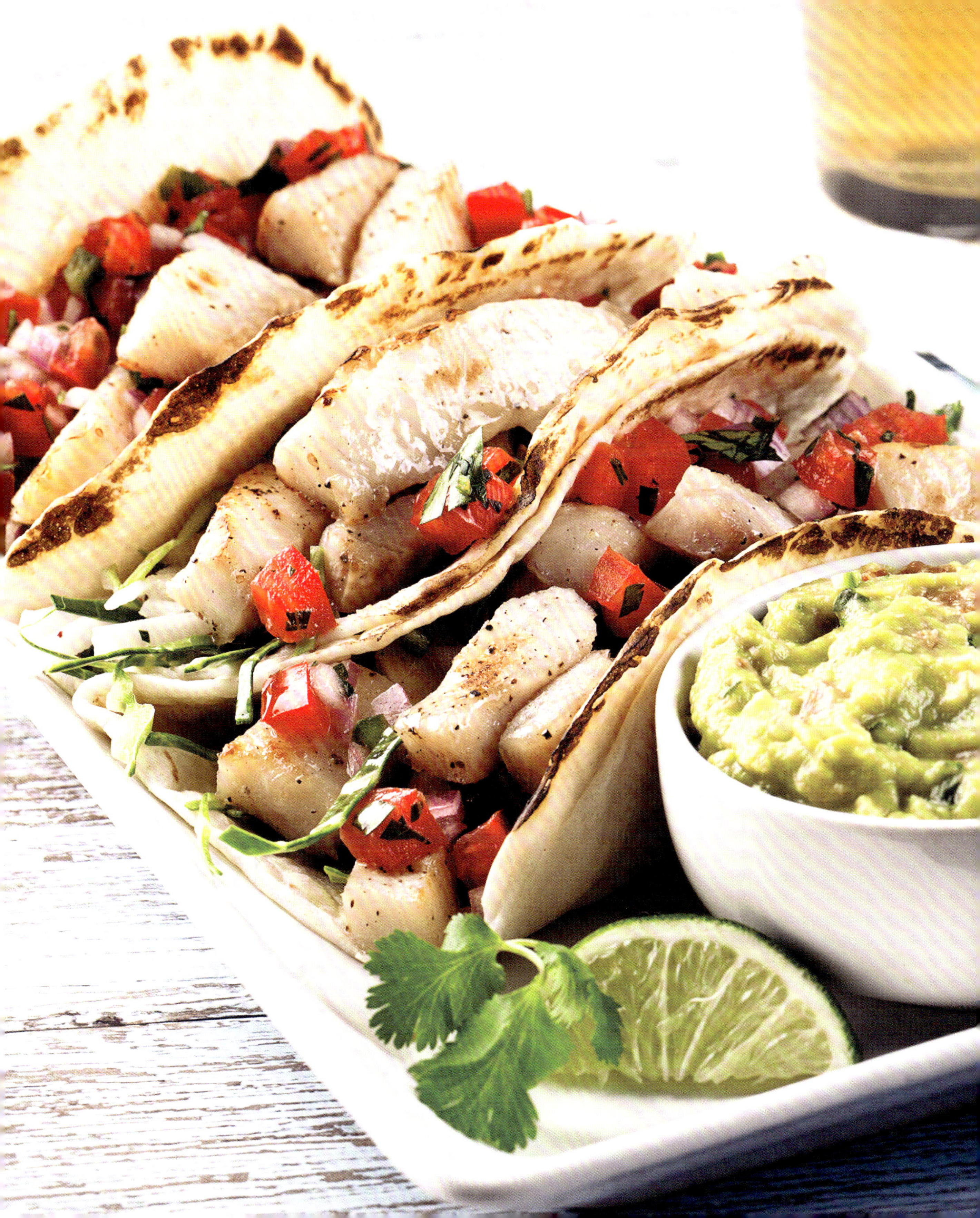

TACOS, BURRITOS & QUESADILLAS

CHICKEN FAJITA ROLL-UPS

- 1 cup ranch dressing
- 1 teaspoon chili powder
- 2 tablespoons vegetable oil, divided
- 2 teaspoons fajita seasoning mix
- 2 teaspoons lime juice
- ½ teaspoon chipotle chili powder
- ¼ teaspoon salt
- 4 boneless skinless chicken breasts (about 6 ounces each)
- 4 fajita-size flour tortillas (8 to 9 inches)
- 1 cup (4 ounces) shredded Cheddar cheese
- 1 cup (4 ounces) shredded Monterey Jack cheese
- 3 cups shredded lettuce
- 1 cup pico de gallo

1. Combine ranch dressing and chili powder in small bowl; mix well. Refrigerate until ready to serve.

2. Combine 1 tablespoon oil, fajita seasoning, lime juice, chipotle chili powder and salt in small bowl; mix well. Coat both sides of chicken with spice mixture.

3. Heat remaining 1 tablespoon oil in large nonstick skillet or grill pan over medium-high heat. Add chicken; cook 6 minutes per side or until cooked through (165°F). Remove to plate; let stand 5 minutes before slicing. Cut chicken breasts in half lengthwise, then cut crosswise into ½-inch strips.

4. Wipe out skillet with paper towel. Place one tortilla in skillet; sprinkle with ¼ cup Cheddar and ¼ cup Monterey Jack. Heat over medium heat until cheeses are melted. Remove tortilla to cutting board.

5. Sprinkle ¾ cup shredded lettuce down center of tortilla; top with ¼ cup pico de gallo and one fourth of chicken. Fold bottom of tortilla up over filling, then fold in sides and roll up. Cut in half diagonally. Repeat with remaining tortillas, cheese and fillings. Serve with ranch dipping sauce.

MAKES 4 SERVINGS

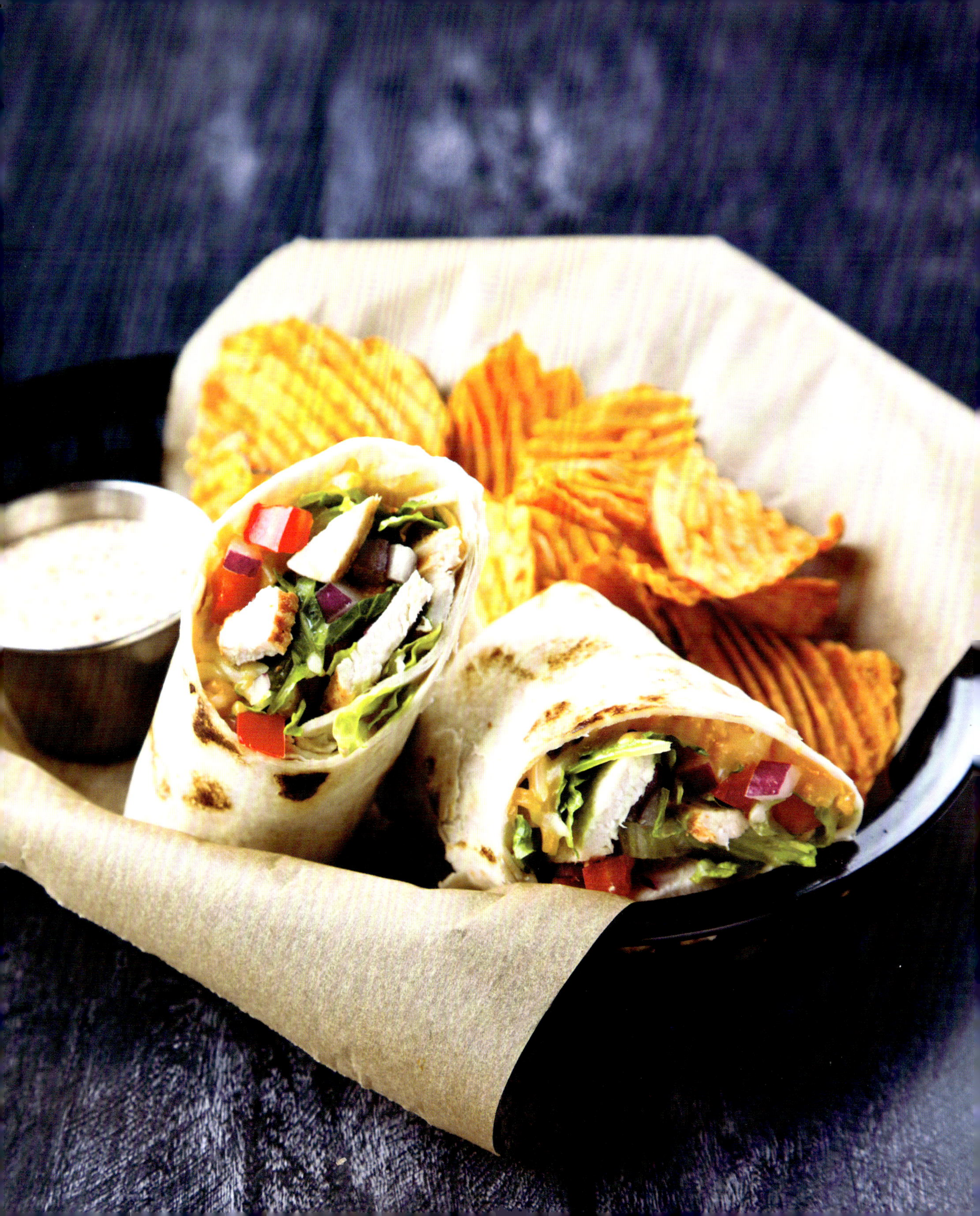

TACOS, BURRITOS & QUESADILLAS

GRILLED CHICKEN TOSTADAS

- 1 pound boneless skinless chicken breasts
- 1 teaspoon ground cumin
- Salt and black pepper
- ¼ cup orange juice
- ¼ cup plus 2 tablespoons salsa, divided
- 1 tablespoon plus 2 teaspoons vegetable oil, divided
- 2 cloves garlic, minced
- 8 green onions
- 1 can (about 15 ounces) refried beans
- 4 (10-inch) or 8 (6- to 7-inch) flour tortillas
- 2 cups chopped romaine lettuce
- 1½ cups (6 ounces) shredded pepper jack cheese
- Optional toppings: diced avocado, chopped tomatoes, chopped fresh cilantro and sour cream (optional)

1. Place chicken in single layer in shallow glass dish; sprinkle with cumin and season with salt and pepper. Combine orange juice, ¼ cup salsa, 1 tablespoon oil and garlic in small bowl; pour over chicken. Cover and marinate in refrigerator at least 2 hours or up to 8 hours, stirring occasionally.

2. Prepare grill for direct cooking.

3. Drain chicken; reserve marinade. Brush green onions with remaining 2 teaspoons oil. Grill chicken and green onions, covered, over medium-high heat 5 minutes. Brush tops of chicken with half of reserved marinade; turn and brush with remaining marinade. Turn green onions; grill, covered, 5 minutes or until chicken is cooked through (165°F) and green onions are tender.

4. Meanwhile, combine beans and remaining 2 tablespoons salsa in small saucepan; cook over medium heat until hot, stirring occasionally.

5. Place tortillas in single layer on grid. Grill, uncovered, 1 to 2 minutes per side or until golden brown. (Pierce any tortillas that puff up with tip of knife or flatten with spatula.)

6. Transfer chicken and onions to cutting board. Slice chicken crosswise into ½-inch strips. Cut onions crosswise into 1-inch pieces. Spread bean mixture over tortillas; top with lettuce, chicken, onions and cheese. Top with desired toppings.

MAKES 4 SERVINGS

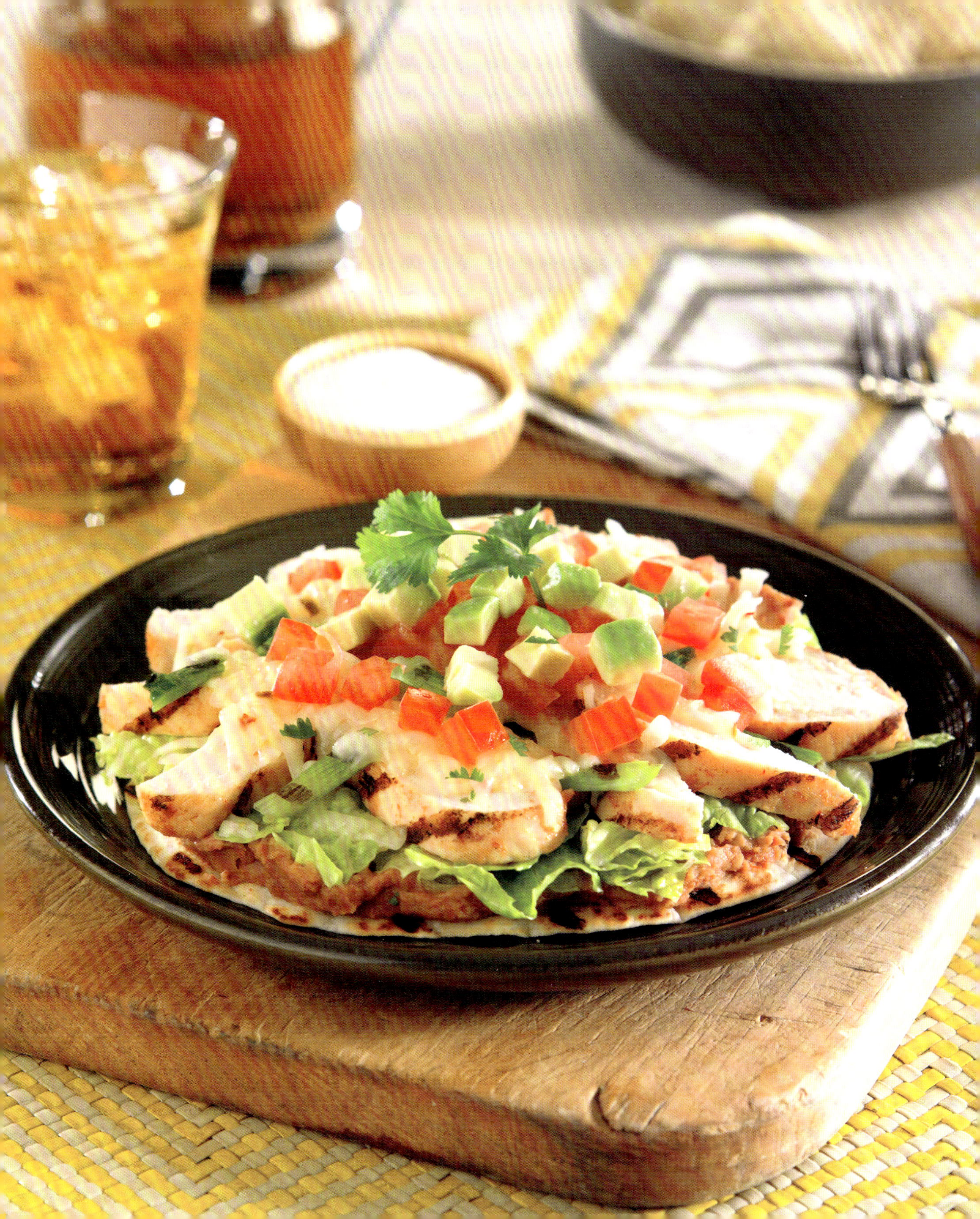

TACOS, BURRITOS & QUESADILLAS

FISH TACOS WITH CILANTRO CREAM SAUCE

- ½ cup sour cream
- ¼ cup chopped fresh cilantro
- 1¼ teaspoons ground cumin, divided
- 1 pound skinless tilapia, mahi mahi or other firm white fish fillets
- 1 teaspoon garlic salt
- 1 teaspoon chipotle hot pepper sauce, divided
- 2 teaspoons vegetable oil
- 1 red bell pepper, cut into thin strips
- 1 green bell pepper, cut into thin strips
- 8 (6-inch) corn tortillas, warmed

1. For sauce, combine sour cream, cilantro and ¼ teaspoon cumin in small bowl; mix well. Refrigerate until ready to serve.

2. Cut fish into 1-inch pieces; place in medium bowl. Add remaining 1 teaspoon cumin, garlic salt and ½ teaspoon hot pepper sauce; toss gently to coat.

3. Heat oil in large nonstick skillet over medium heat. Add fish; cook 3 to 4 minutes or until center is opaque, turning once. Remove to plate. Add bell peppers to skillet; cook 6 to 8 minutes or until tender, stirring occasionally.

4. Return fish to skillet with remaining ½ teaspoon hot pepper sauce; cook and stir just until heated through. Serve in tortillas with sauce.

MAKES 8 TACOS

MEXICAN TURKEY QUESADILLAS

- 8 (8-inch) flour tortillas
- 1 cup finely chopped cooked turkey or chicken
- ½ cup salsa, plus additional for serving
- 1 cup (4 ounces) shredded Cheddar or Chihuahua cheese
- 2 tablespoons chopped fresh cilantro
- 1 tablespoon vegetable oil
- Sour cream (optional)

1. Top four tortillas with turkey; top evenly with ½ cup salsa, cheese and cilantro. Top with remaining four tortillas.

2. Heat oil in large nonstick skillet over medium heat; tilt skillet to coat bottom. Cook quesadillas in batches 2 to 3 minutes on each side or until cheese is melted and tortillas are golden brown, pressing down with spatula. Cut quesadillas into wedges; serve with sour cream and additional salsa.

MAKES 4 SERVINGS

TACOS, BURRITOS & QUESADILLAS

- 1 teaspoon ground cumin
- 1 teaspoon chili powder
- 1 teaspoon garlic salt
- 12 ounces skirt steak, trimmed
- 3 tablespoons vegetable oil, divided
- 4 slices red onion (¼ inch thick)
- 2 cloves garlic, minced
- 1 cup canned black beans, rinsed and drained
- ½ cup salsa
- ½ cup chopped fresh tomato
- 8 corn tortillas, warmed
- ½ cup chopped fresh cilantro
- Lime wedges (optional)

GRILLED STEAK AND BLACK BEAN TACOS

1. Prepare grill for direct cooking. Combine cumin, chili powder and garlic salt in small bowl; sprinkle evenly over both sides of steak. Brush 2 tablespoons oil over steak and onion slices.

2. Grill steak and onions, covered, over medium-high heat 4 to 5 minutes per side or until steak is barely pink in center and onion is tender.

3. Heat remaining 1 tablespoon oil in large skillet over medium heat. Add garlic; cook and stir 30 seconds. Add beans, salsa and tomato; cook and stir 5 minutes or until heated through.

4. Slice steak crosswise into thin strips; separate onion slices into rings. Serve in warm tortillas with bean mixture, cilantro and lime wedges, if desired.

MAKES 8 TACOS

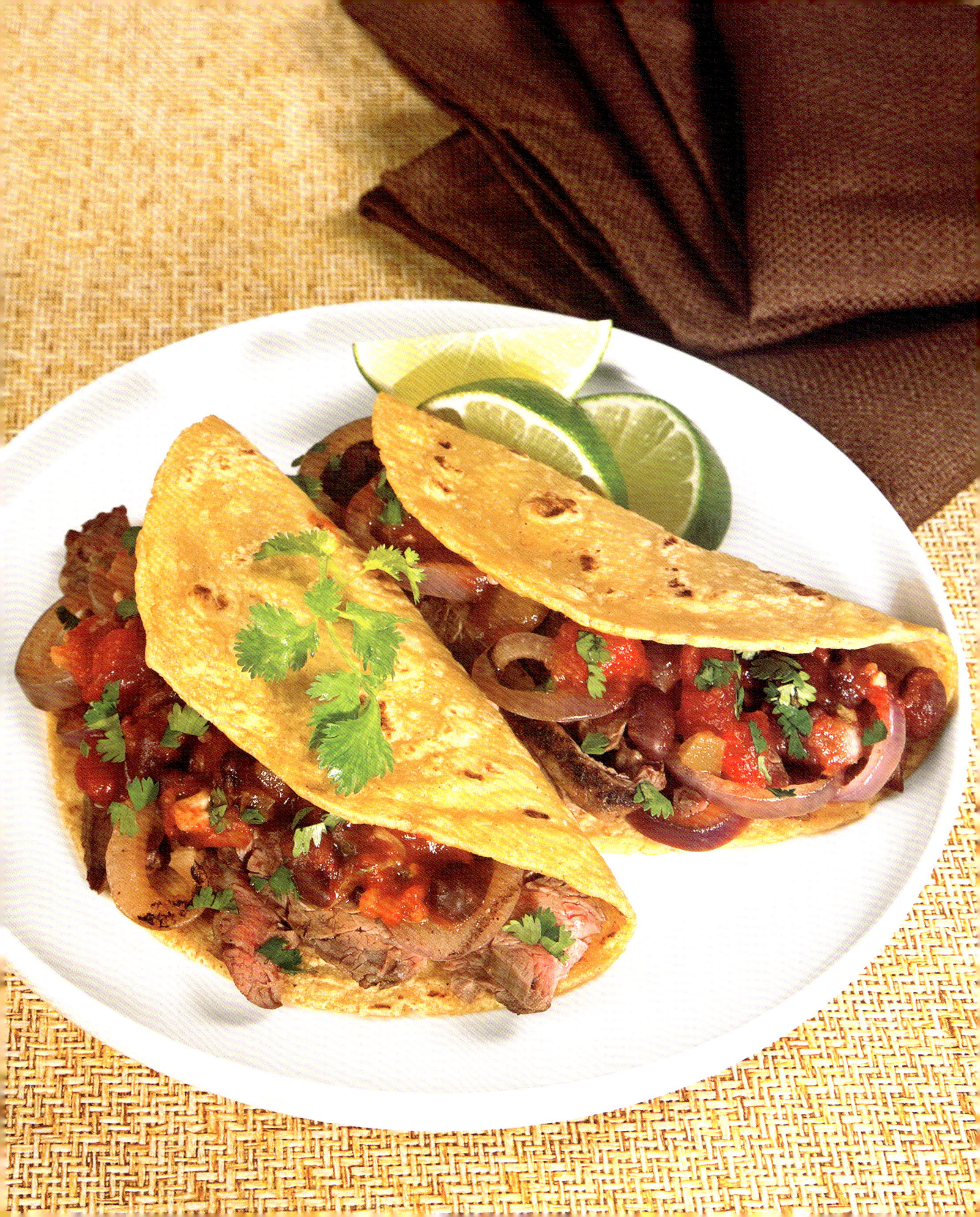

TACOS, BURRITOS & QUESADILLAS

BLACK BEAN FLAUTAS

- 1 can (about 15 ounces) black beans, undrained
- 1 cup vegetable broth
- 1 teaspoon salt, divided
- ½ teaspoon ground cumin
- ½ teaspoon chili powder
- 3 cloves garlic, minced
- ¼ cup chopped fresh cilantro
- Juice of 1 lime
- 10 (6-inch) flour tortillas
- 2½ cups (10 ounces) shredded Colby Jack or Chihuahua cheese
- 1 cup seeded and chopped tomatoes (about 2 tomatoes)
- 1 cup thinly sliced green onions
- 1 jar (16 ounces) salsa verde

1. Preheat oven to 450°F. Place beans with liquid, broth, ½ teaspoon salt, cumin, chili powder and garlic in medium saucepan. Bring to a boil over medium-high heat. Reduce heat; simmer 10 minutes or until beans are very soft. Drain; reserve liquid.

2. Purée drained bean mixture, cilantro, lime juice and remaining ½ teaspoon salt in blender or food processor until smooth. (Add reserved liquid, 1 teaspoon at a time, if beans are dry.)

3. Spread bean purée evenly on each tortilla; sprinkle with cheese, tomatoes and green onions. Roll up tightly and place, seam side down, in 13×9-inch baking dish.

4. Bake 10 to 15 minutes or until crisp and brown and cheese is melted. Serve with salsa.

MAKES 5 SERVINGS

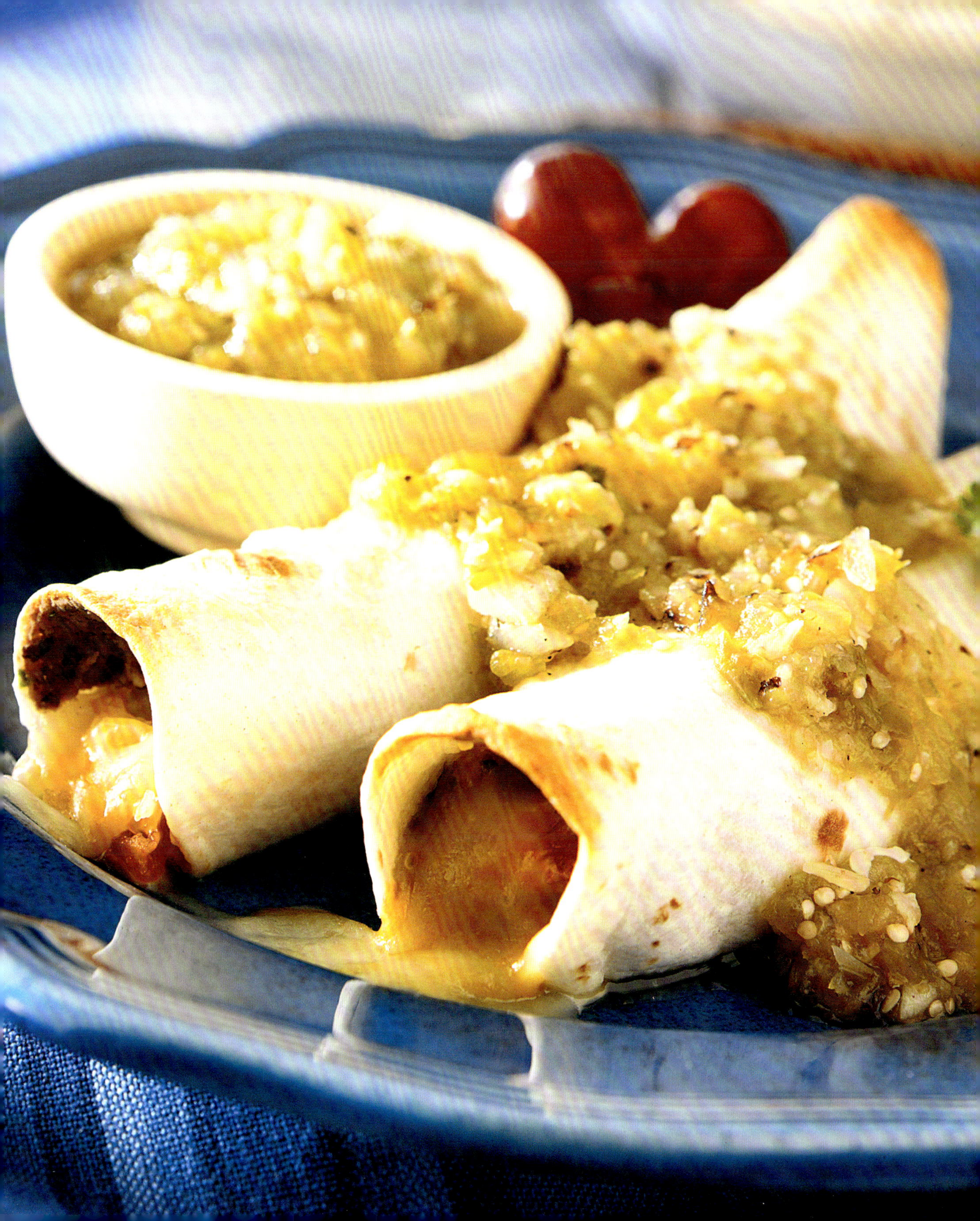

TACOS, BURRITOS & QUESADILLAS

SHREDDED BEEF TACOS

- 2 tablespoons vegetable oil
- 1 pound boneless beef chuck, cut into 1-inch cubes
- 1 to 2 teaspoons chili powder
- 1 clove garlic, minced
- ½ teaspoon salt
- ½ teaspoon ground cumin
- 1 can (about 14 ounces) diced tomatoes
- 12 (6-inch) hard taco shells
- 1 cup (4 ounces) shredded Cheddar cheese
- 2 to 3 cups shredded iceberg lettuce
- 1 large fresh tomato, seeded and chopped

1. Heat oil in large skillet over medium-high heat. Add beef; cook 10 to 12 minutes or until browned on all sides, turning occasionally. Reduce heat to low. Stir in chili powder, garlic, salt and cumin; cook and stir 30 seconds. Add diced tomatoes. Bring to a boil over high heat. Reduce heat to low. Cover and simmer 1½ to 2 hours or until beef is very tender.

2. Using two forks, pull beef into coarse shreds in skillet. Increase heat to medium. Cook, uncovered, 10 to 15 minutes or until most of liquid has evaporated. Keep warm.

3. Fill taco shells with beef, cheese, lettuce and chopped tomato.

MAKES 6 SERVINGS

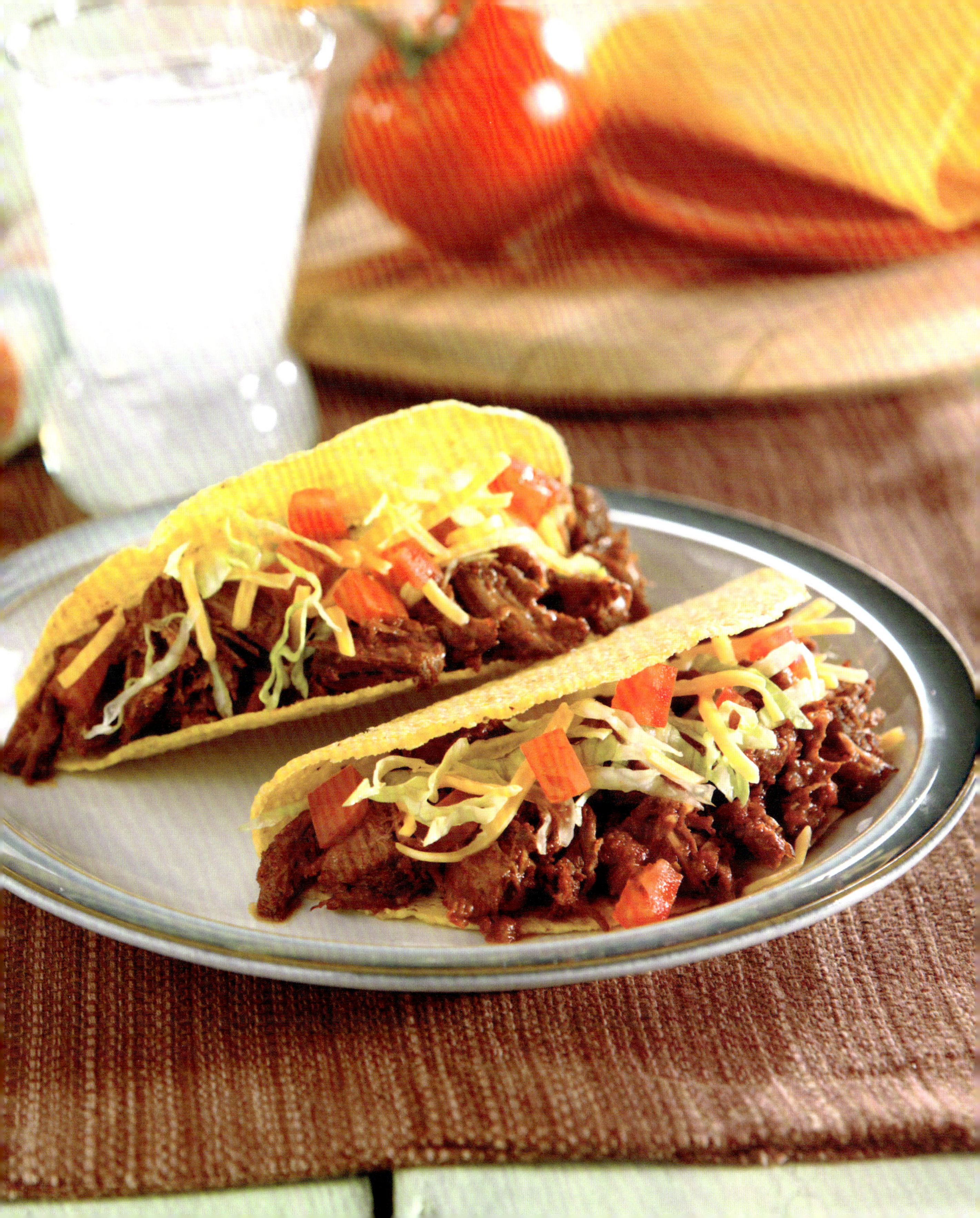

SHREDDED GREEN CHILE PORK TACOS

2 pounds boneless pork roast
1 cup salsa
1 can (4 ounces) diced mild green chiles, drained
½ teaspoon garlic salt
½ teaspoon black pepper
Corn or flour tortillas, warmed
Optional toppings: tomatillo salsa, sliced jalapeño peppers, sour cream, shredded cheese and/or shredded lettuce

Slow Cooker Directions

1 Place pork in slow cooker. Combine salsa, chiles, garlic salt and pepper in small bowl; mix well. Pour salsa mixture over pork.

2 Cover; cook on LOW 8 hours. Remove pork to cutting board; shred with two forks. Stir shredded pork back into slow cooker. Serve in warm tortillas with desired toppings.

MAKES 6 SERVINGS

TACOS, BURRITOS & QUESADILLAS

QUESADILLA GRANDE

- 2 (8-inch) flour tortillas
- 2 to 3 large fresh stemmed spinach leaves *or* ½ cup baby spinach
- 2 to 3 slices (about 3 ounces) cooked chicken
- 2 tablespoons salsa
- 1 tablespoon chopped fresh cilantro
- ¼ cup (1 ounce) shredded Monterey Jack cheese
- 2 teaspoons butter (optional)

1. Place one tortilla in large nonstick skillet; cover tortilla with spinach leaves. Place chicken in single layer over spinach. Spoon salsa over chicken. Sprinkle with cilantro; top with cheese. Place remaining tortilla on top, pressing tortilla down so filling becomes compact.

2. Cook over medium heat 4 to 5 minutes or until bottom tortilla is lightly browned. Holding top tortilla in place, gently turn over. Cook 4 minutes or until bottom tortilla is browned and cheese is melted.

3. For a crispy finish, if desired, place butter in skillet to melt. Lift quesadilla to let butter flow into center of skillet. Cook 30 seconds. Turn over; cook 30 seconds. Cut in half to serve.

MAKES 1 SERVING

TACOS, BURRITOS & QUESADILLAS

VEGETABLE FAJITAS

- 12 (10-inch) flour tortillas
- 1 tablespoon vegetable oil
- 4 medium green bell peppers, cut into thin strips
- 1 medium red onion, cut in half vertically and thickly sliced
- 1 teaspoon salt
- Black pepper
- 1 can (about 15 ounces) refried beans, heated
- 1½ cups roasted vegetable salsa

1. Heat cast iron or heavy skillet over medium-high heat. Cook tortillas one at a time 15 seconds per side until blistered and browned; keep warm.

2. Reduce heat to medium; add oil. Add bell pepper, onion, salt and black pepper; cook and stir 10 minutes or until vegetables are crisp-tender.

3. Spread about 2 tablespoons beans over each tortilla. Top with ⅓ cup vegetables and about 2 tablespoons salsa. Roll up; serve immediately.

MAKES 6 SERVINGS

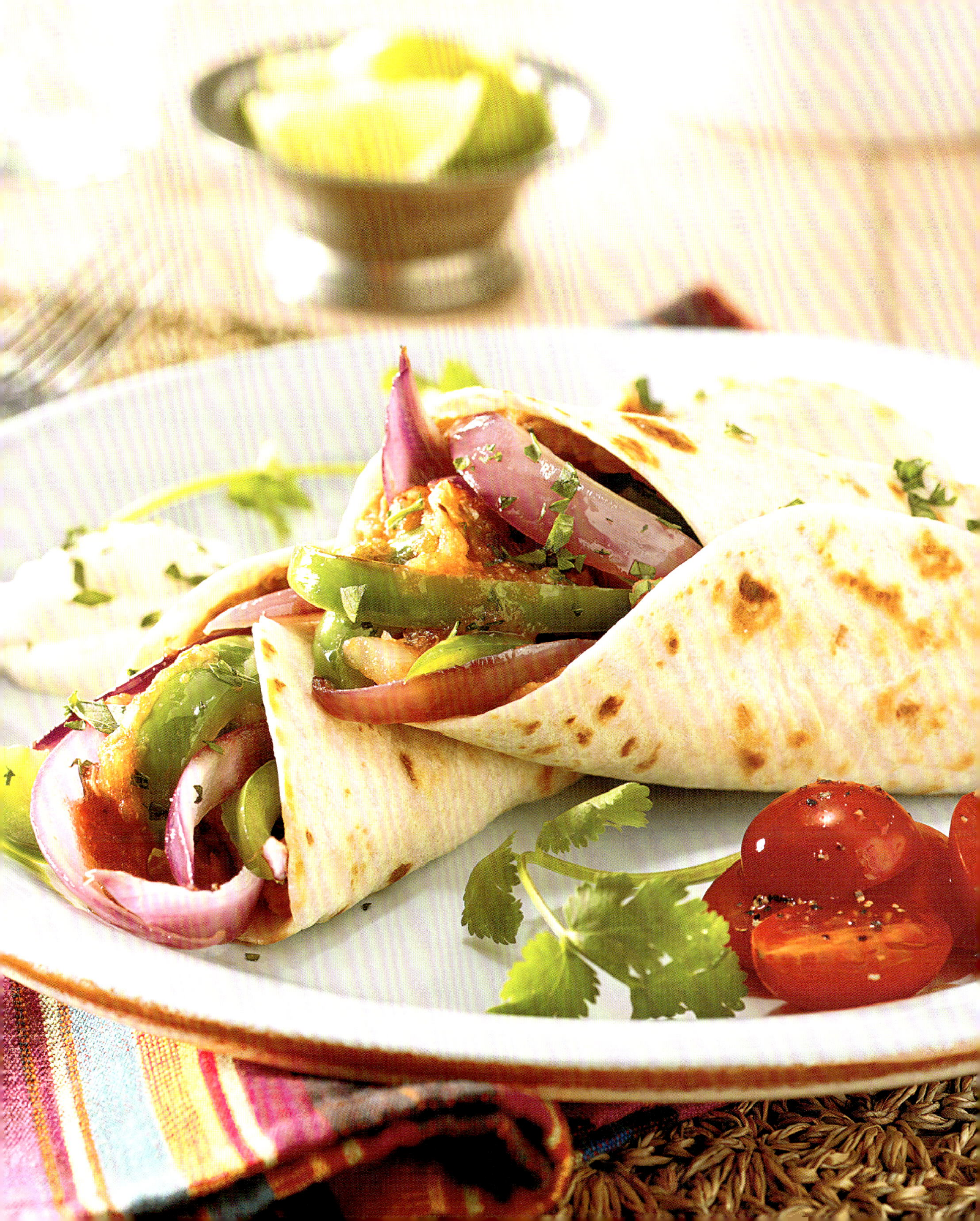

TACOS, BURRITOS & QUESADILLAS

TACOS DORADOS

2	tablespoons vegetable oil
1¾	pounds boneless skinless chicken breasts, cut into 1-inch cubes
½	cup chopped onion
1	can (about 28 ounces) diced tomatoes
2	teaspoons chili powder
1	teaspoon ground cumin
½	teaspoon salt
½	teaspoon garlic powder
½	teaspoon dried oregano
¼	teaspoon ground coriander
10	(8-inch) flour tortillas
3½	cups (14 ounces) shredded queso blanco
¼	cup chopped fresh cilantro
	Salsa or pico de gallo

1. Preheat oven to 450°F. Heat oil in large skillet over medium-high heat. Add chicken; cook and stir until cooked through (165°F). Remove from skillet; set aside.

2. Add onion to skillet; cook and stir 5 to 7 minutes until softened. Add tomatoes, chili powder, cumin, salt, garlic powder, oregano and coriander; cook and stir 15 minutes or until thickened. Stir in chicken.

3. Divide chicken mixture among tortillas; roll up tightly. Place seam-side down in 13×9-inch baking dish.

4. Bake 15 minutes or until tortillas are crisp and brown. Sprinkle with queso blanco; bake 5 minutes or until cheese is melted. Sprinkle with cilantro; serve with salsa.

MAKES 10 TACOS

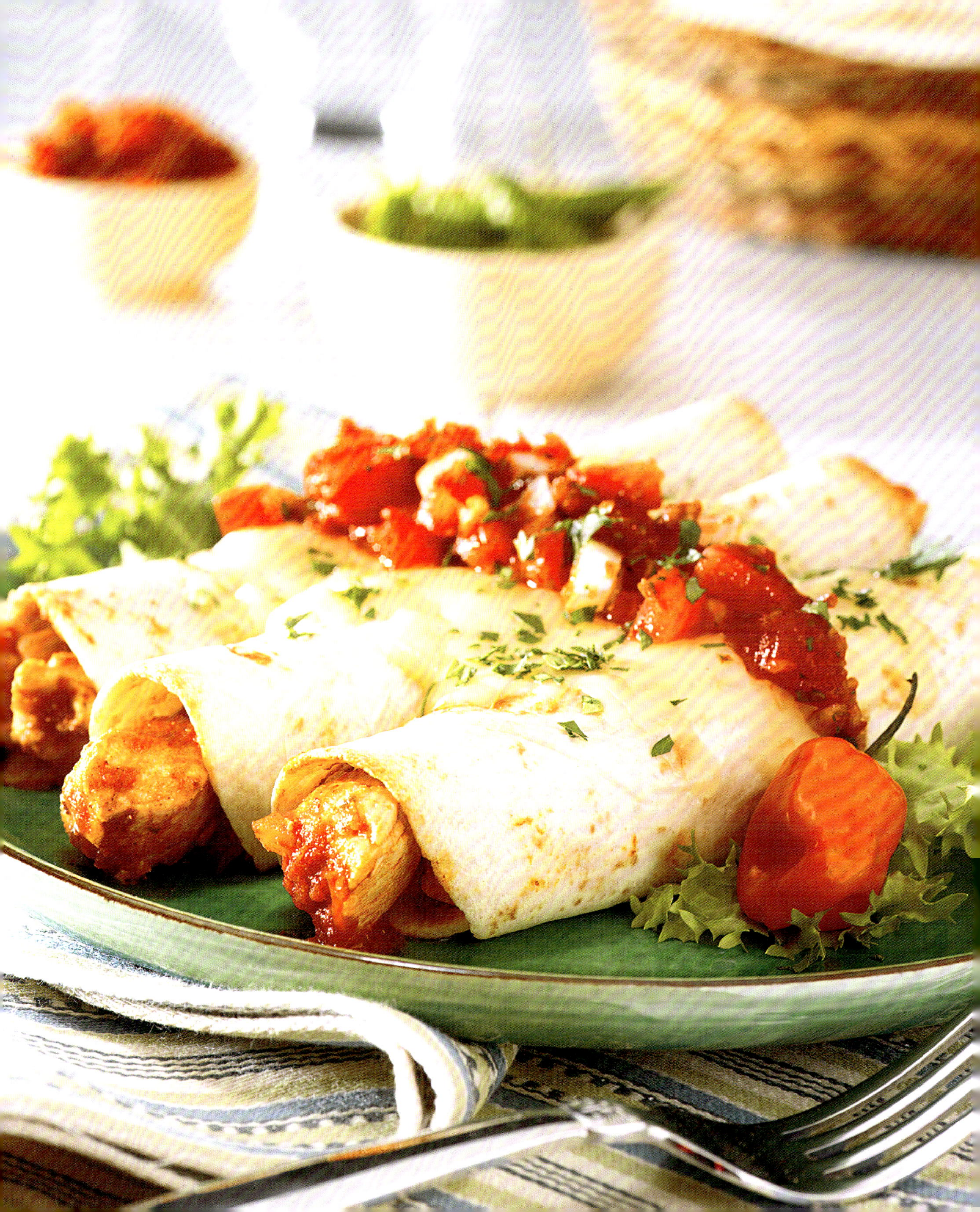

TACOS, BURRITOS & QUESADILLAS

SHRIMP TACOS

- 1 pound jumbo or colossal raw shrimp, peeled and deveined (about 16)
- 2 tablespoons lemon juice, divided
- ½ teaspoon salt, divided
- ½ teaspoon ground cumin, divided
- ¼ teaspoon black pepper
- 1 pint cherry or grape tomatoes, halved
- 1 red onion, finely chopped
- 1 serrano pepper, cored, seeded and minced
- 1 clove garlic, minced
- 1 tablespoon chopped fresh cilantro
- 1 tablespoon vegetable oil
- 8 corn tortillas or taco shells, heated
- 1 cup coarsely shredded romaine lettuce
- 1 small avocado, cut into 8 wedges

1. Cut shrimp along vein to butterfly. Place in large glass bowl with 1 tablespoon lemon juice, ¼ teaspoon salt, ¼ teaspoon cumin and black pepper; mix well. Let stand 30 minutes.

2. Meanwhile for salsa, combine tomatoes, onion, serrano pepper, garlic, cilantro, remaining 1 tablespoon lemon juice, remaining ¼ teaspoon cumin and remaining ¼ teaspoon salt in small bowl. Set aside.

3. Heat oil in large skillet over medium heat. Cook shrimp in batches 3 to 4 minutes per side or until cooked through (do not crowd pan).

4. Place two shrimp in each tortilla. Top with salsa, lettuce and avocado. Serve with remaining salsa.

MAKES 8 SERVINGS

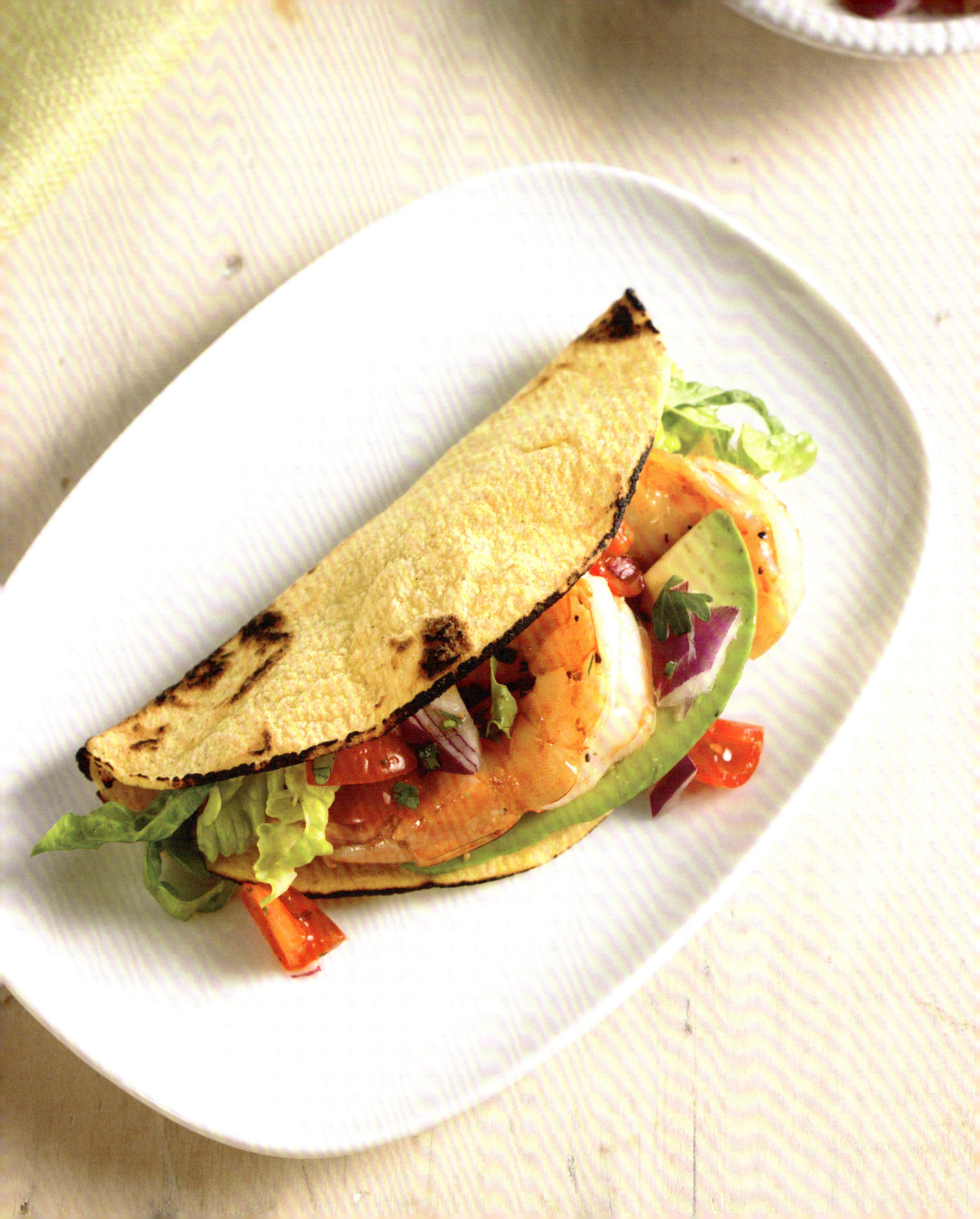

TACOS, BURRITOS & QUESADILLAS

MUSHROOM AND ZUCCHINI QUESADILLAS

- 3 tablespoons vegetable oil, divided
- 1 onion, thinly sliced
- 1 portobello mushroom, sliced
- 1 small zucchini, thinly sliced into long strips
- Salt and black pepper
- ¾ cup (3 ounces) shredded Colby Jack cheese
- 4 (6-inch) flour or whole wheat tortillas
- ½ cup salsa

1. Heat 1 tablespoon oil in large skillet over medium-high heat. Add onion, mushroom and zucchini; cook and stir 4 minutes. Transfer to bowl; season with salt and black pepper. Wipe out skillet with paper towel.

2. Heat 1 tablespoon oil in same skillet over medium heat. Spoon one fourth of cheese and one fourth of vegetable mixture onto one half of each tortilla. Fold tortillas in half.

3. Cook tortillas in batches in skillet 2 minutes per side until lightly browned on both sides, adding remaining 1 tablespoon oil if needed. Cut tortillas in half; serve with salsa.

MAKES 4 QUESADILLAS

SUPER-EASY BEEF BURRITOS

- 1 boneless beef chuck roast (2 to 3 pounds)
- 1 can (28 ounces) enchilada sauce
- 4 (8-inch) flour tortillas
- Optional toppings: shredded cheese, sour cream, salsa, lettuce and/or tomatoes

Slow Cooker Directions

1. Place beef in slow cooker; cover with enchilada sauce.
2. Cover and cook on LOW 6 to 8 hours or until beef begins to fall apart. Shred beef; serve in tortillas with desired toppings.

MAKES 4 SERVINGS

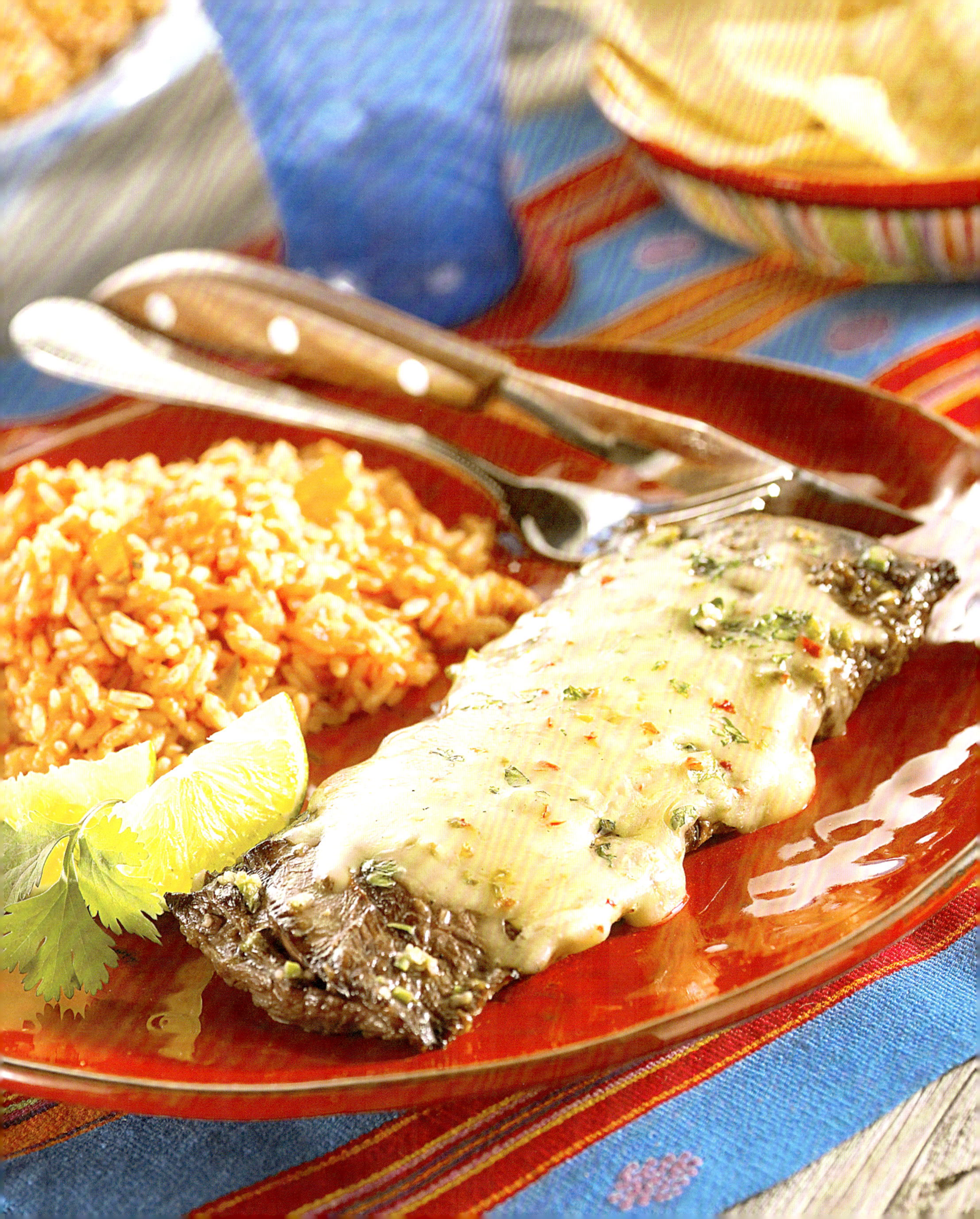

MAIN DISHES

CARNE ASADA

8 (6- to 8-ounce) thin skirt steaks
1½ teaspoons salt
¼ cup vegetable oil
2 jalapeño peppers, minced
3 tablespoons lime juice
4 cloves garlic, minced
2 cups (8 ounces) shredded Chihuahua cheese or Mexican cheese blend
½ cup chopped fresh cilantro
Hot cooked rice (optional)

1. Season steaks with salt. Combine oil, jalapeños, lime juice and garlic in large resealable food storage bag; add steaks. Seal bag; turn to coat. Refrigerate at least 2 hours or up to 24 hours.

2. Prepare grill for direct cooking. Drain steaks. Pour marinade into small saucepan; boil 2 to 3 minutes. Grill steaks, covered, over medium-high heat 5 minutes. Brush with half of marinade. Turn; brush with remaining marinade. Grill 3 to 4 minutes for medium rare or until desired doneness.

3. Combine cheese and cilantro in small bowl; sprinkle over steaks. Grill 1 minute or until cheese melts. Serve with rice, if desired.

MAKES 8 SERVINGS

MAIN DISHES

Chili

- 1 pound ground beef
- 1 medium onion, chopped
- 1 stalk celery, chopped
- 2 medium fresh tomatoes, chopped
- 1 jalapeño pepper, finely chopped
- 1½ teaspoons chili powder
- 1 teaspoon salt
- 1 teaspoon ground cumin
- ½ teaspoon black pepper
- 1 can (15 ounces) tomato sauce
- 1 can (about 15 ounces) kidney beans, rinsed and drained
- 1 can (about 15 ounces) pinto beans, rinsed and drained
- 1 cup water

Salad

- 8 cups chopped romaine lettuce (large pieces)
- 2 cups diced fresh tomatoes
- 48 small round tortilla chips
- 1 cup salsa
- ½ cup sour cream
- ½ cup (2 ounces) shredded Cheddar cheese

TACO SALAD SUPREME

1. For chili, combine beef, onion and celery in large saucepan; cook over medium-high heat 6 to 8 minutes or until beef is no longer pink, stirring to break up meat. Drain fat.

2. Add chopped tomatoes, jalapeño, chili powder, salt, cumin and black pepper; cook and stir 1 minute. Stir in tomato sauce, beans and water; bring to a boil. Reduce heat to medium-low; cook 1 hour or until most of liquid is absorbed.

3. For each salad, combine 2 cups lettuce and ½ cup diced tomatoes in serving bowl. Top with 12 tortilla chips, 1 cup chili, ¼ cup salsa and 2 tablespoons sour cream. Sprinkle with 2 tablespoons cheese. (Reserve remaining chili for another use.)

MAKES 4 SERVINGS

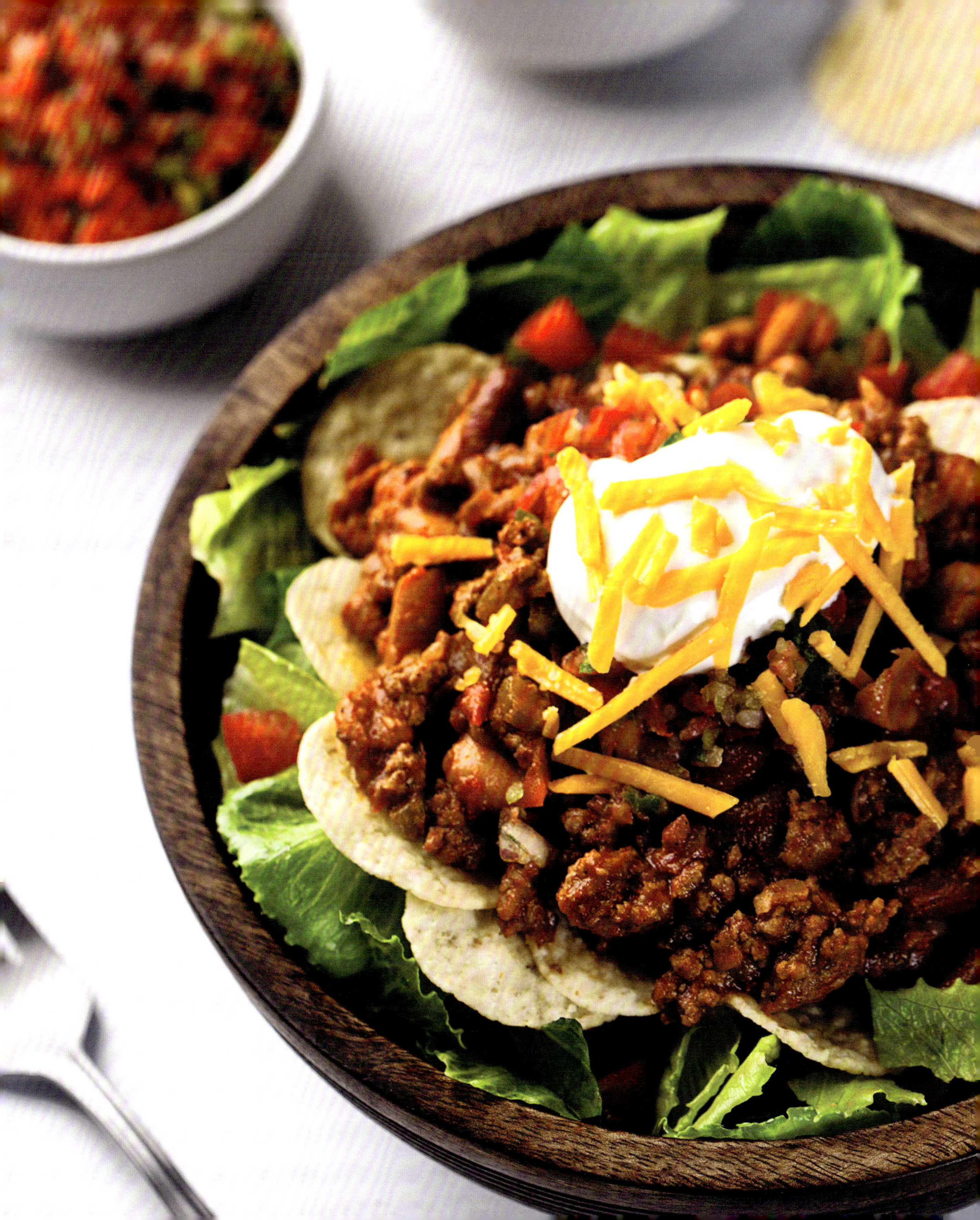

MAIN DISHES

- ¼ cup lime juice
- ¼ cup soy sauce
- 4 tablespoons vegetable oil, divided
- 2 tablespoons honey
- 2 tablespoons Worcestershire sauce
- 2 cloves garlic, minced
- ½ teaspoon ground red pepper
- 1 pound flank steak, skirt steak or top sirloin
- 1 medium yellow onion, halved and cut into ¼-inch slices
- 1 green bell pepper, cut into ¼-inch strips
- 1 red bell pepper, cut into ¼-inch strips
- Flour tortillas, warmed
- Lime wedges (optional)
- Optional toppings: pico de gallo, guacamole, sour cream, shredded lettuce and shredded Cheddar-Jack cheese

STEAK FAJITAS

1. Whisk lime juice, soy sauce, 2 tablespoons oil, honey, Worcestershire sauce, garlic and ground red pepper in medium bowl until well blended. Remove ¼ cup marinade to large bowl.

2. Place steak in large resealable food storage bag. Pour remaining marinade over steak; seal bag and turn to coat. Marinate in refrigerator at least 2 hours or overnight. Add onion and bell peppers to bowl with ¼ cup marinade; toss to coat. Cover and refrigerate until ready to cook.

3. Remove steak from marinade; discard marinade and pat steak dry with paper towels. Heat 1 tablespoon oil in large skillet (preferably cast iron) over medium-high heat. Cook steak 4 minutes per side for medium rare or to desired doneness. Remove to cutting board; tent with foil and let stand 10 minutes.

4. Meanwhile, heat remaining 1 tablespoon oil in same skillet over medium-high heat. Add vegetable mixture; cook 8 minutes or until vegetables are crisp-tender and beginning to brown in spots, stirring occasionally. (Cook in two batches if necessary; do not crowd skillet.)

5. Cut steak into thin slices across the grain. Serve with vegetables, tortillas, lime wedges and desired toppings.

MAKES 2 SERVINGS

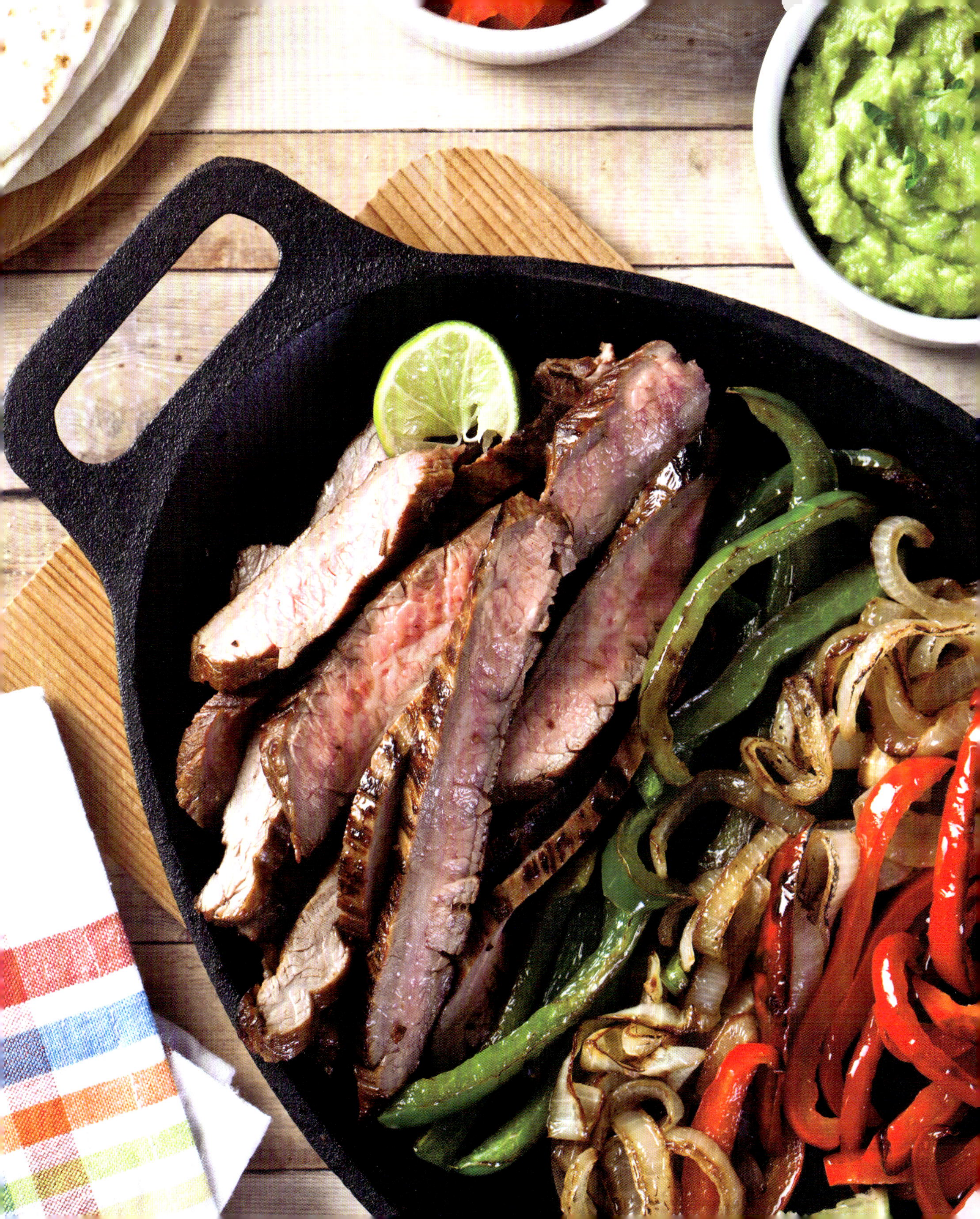

MAIN DISHES

GREEN ENCHILADAS WITH CHICKEN

Vegetable oil for frying
12 (6- or 7-inch) corn tortillas
1 can (28 ounces) green enchilada sauce
3 cups shredded cooked chicken
2½ cups (10 ounces) shredded Monterey Jack cheese
1 cup sour cream
4 green onions, thinly sliced

1 Preheat oven to 350°F. Heat ¼ inch of oil in small skillet over medium-high heat. Place one tortilla in hot oil; cook 2 seconds per side or just until limp. Drain briefly on paper towels, then dip softened tortilla into enchilada sauce. Transfer sauced tortilla to plate or cutting board.

2 Place about ¼ cup chicken and 2 tablespoons cheese across center of tortilla; roll to enclose. Place seam side down in 15×10-inch baking pan. Repeat until all tortillas are filled. Spoon remaining sauce over enchiladas, making sure all ends are moistened; reserve remaining cheese. Cover with foil.

3 Bake 20 to 30 minutes or until hot in center. Uncover and top with reserved cheese. Continue baking, uncovered, 10 minutes or until cheese is melted. Serve with sour cream and green onions.

MAKES 6 SERVINGS

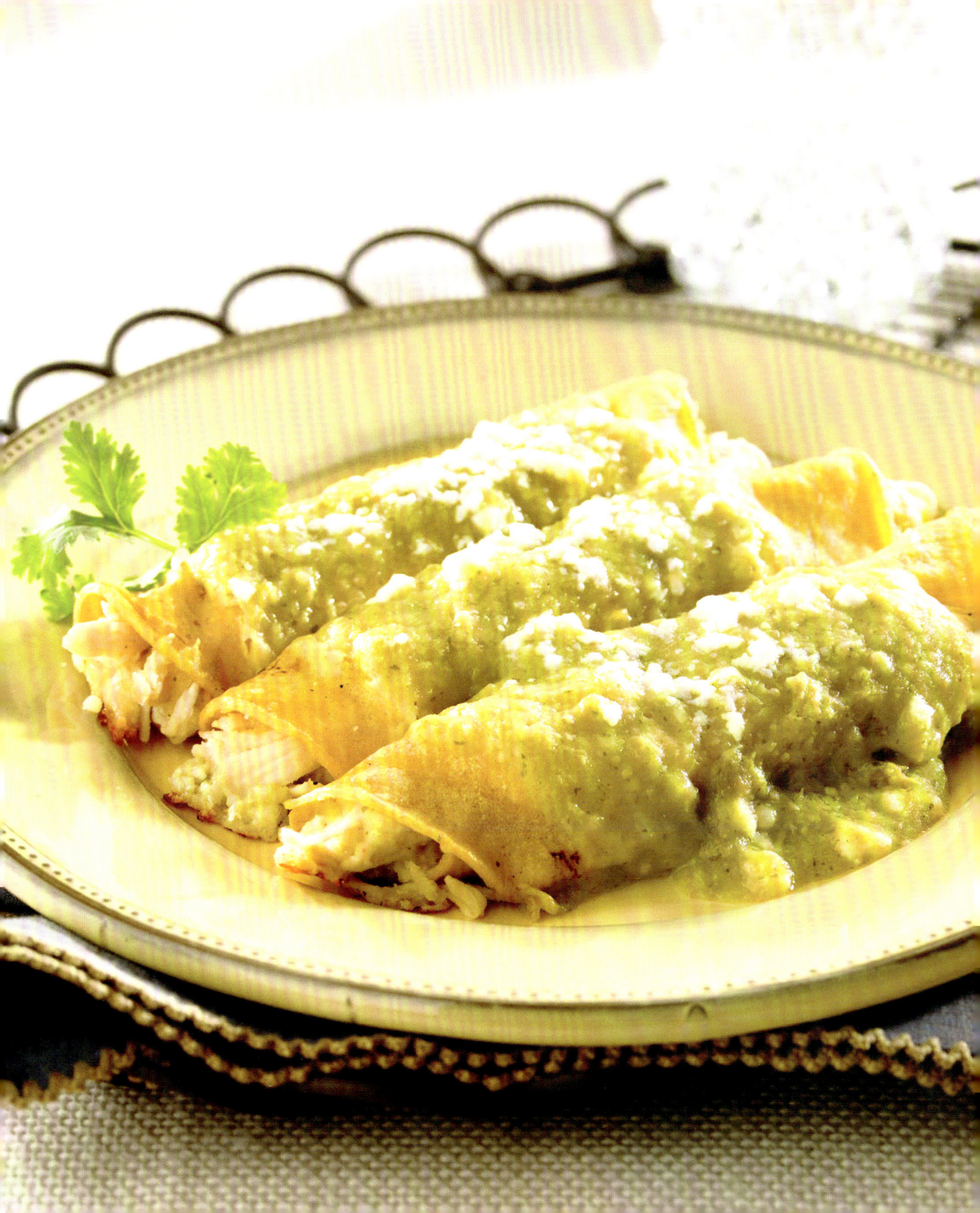

MAIN DISHES

LIME-POACHED FISH WITH CORN SALSA

- 4 swordfish steaks, 1 inch thick (about 1½ pounds)*
- 1 cup baby carrots, cut lengthwise into halves
- 2 green onions, cut into 1-inch pieces
- 3 tablespoons lime juice
- ½ teaspoon salt, divided
- ½ teaspoon chili powder
- 1½ cups chopped tomatoes
- 1 cup thawed frozen corn
- 1 can (4 ounces) chopped green chiles, drained
- 2 tablespoons chopped fresh cilantro
- 1 tablespoon butter

*Tuna or halibut steaks can be substituted.

1. Place fish and carrots in saucepan just large enough to hold them in single layer. Add onions, lime juice, ¼ teaspoon salt and chili powder. Add enough water to just cover fish.

2. Bring to a simmer over medium heat. Cook 8 minutes or until center of fish begins to flake when tested with fork. Transfer to serving plates with spatula.

3. Meanwhile, for salsa, combine tomatoes, corn, chilies, cilantro and remaining ¼ teaspoon salt in medium bowl; toss well.

4. Drain carrots; add butter. Transfer to serving plates; serve with salsa.

MAKES 4 SERVINGS

Tip

If you have time, prepare the salsa in advance so the flavors have more time to develop. Do not add salt until ready to serve. Cover and refrigerate salsa up to 1 day before serving.

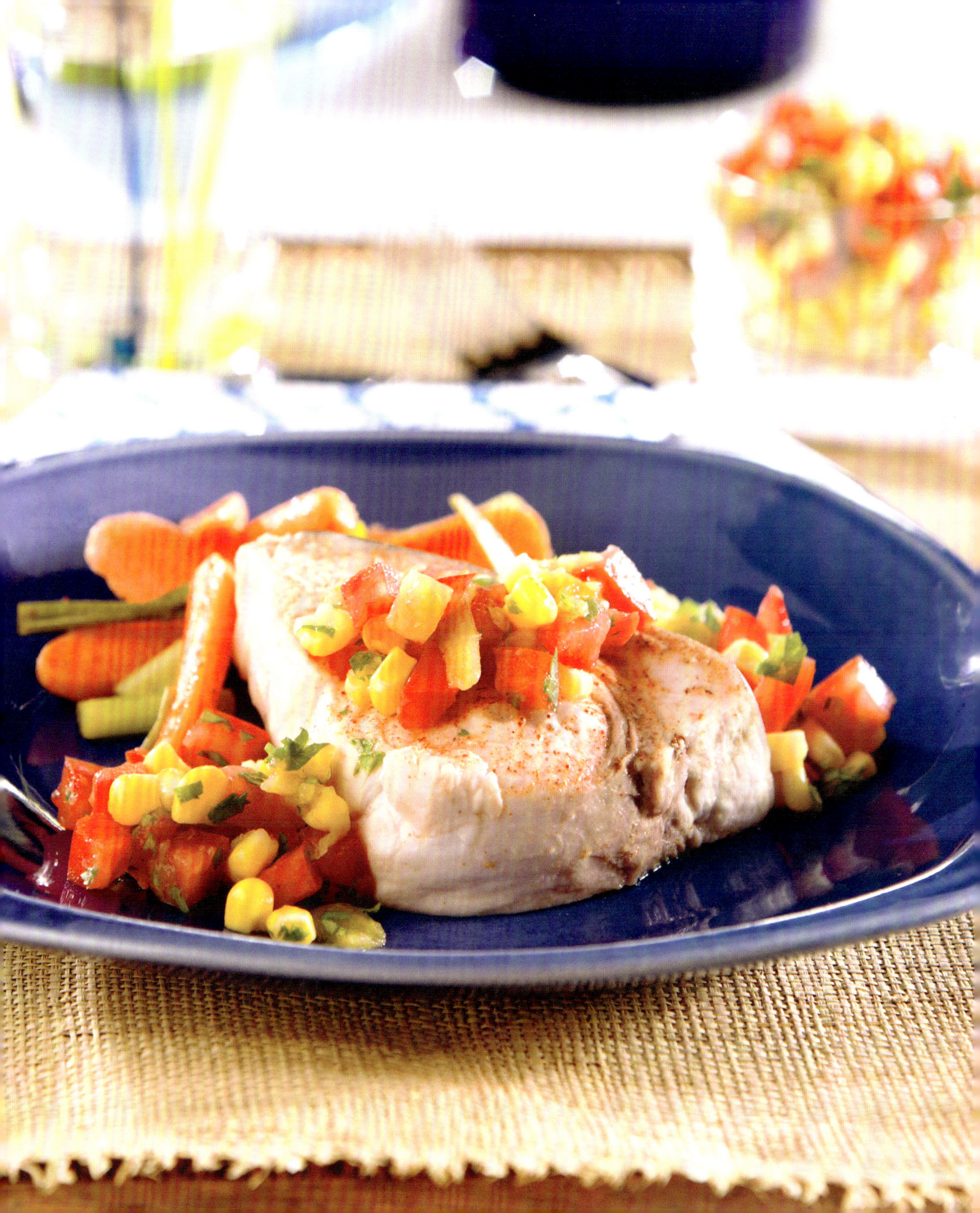

MAIN DISHES

FIESTA BEEF ENCHILADAS

- 8 ounces ground beef
- ¼ cup sliced green onions
- 1 teaspoon minced garlic
- ½ cup mild or hot red or green enchilada sauce
- 1 cup (4 ounces) shredded Mexican cheese blend or Cheddar cheese, divided
- ¾ cup chopped tomato, divided
- ½ cup thawed frozen corn
- ½ cup cooked black beans
- ⅓ cup cooked white or brown rice
- ¼ cup salsa or picante sauce
- 6 (6-inch) corn tortillas
- 2 sheets (20×12 inches each) heavy-duty foil, generously sprayed with nonstick cooking spray
- ½ cup sliced romaine lettuce

1. Preheat oven to 375°F. Brown beef in large nonstick skillet over medium-high heat 6 to 8 minutes or until no longer pink, stirring to break up meat. Drain fat. Add green onions and garlic; cook and stir 2 minutes.

2. Combine meat mixture, enchilada sauce, ¾ cup cheese, ½ cup tomato, corn, beans, rice and salsa in large bowl; mix well. Spoon mixture down center of tortillas. Roll up; place three enchiladas, seam side down, on each foil sheet.

3. Double fold sides and ends of foil to seal packets, leaving head space for heat circulation. Place packets on large baking sheet.

4. Bake 15 minutes. Remove from oven; open packets. Sprinkle with remaining ¼ cup cheese; reseal packets. Bake 10 minutes or until cheese is melted. Serve with lettuce and remaining ¼ cup tomato.

MAKES 2 SERVINGS

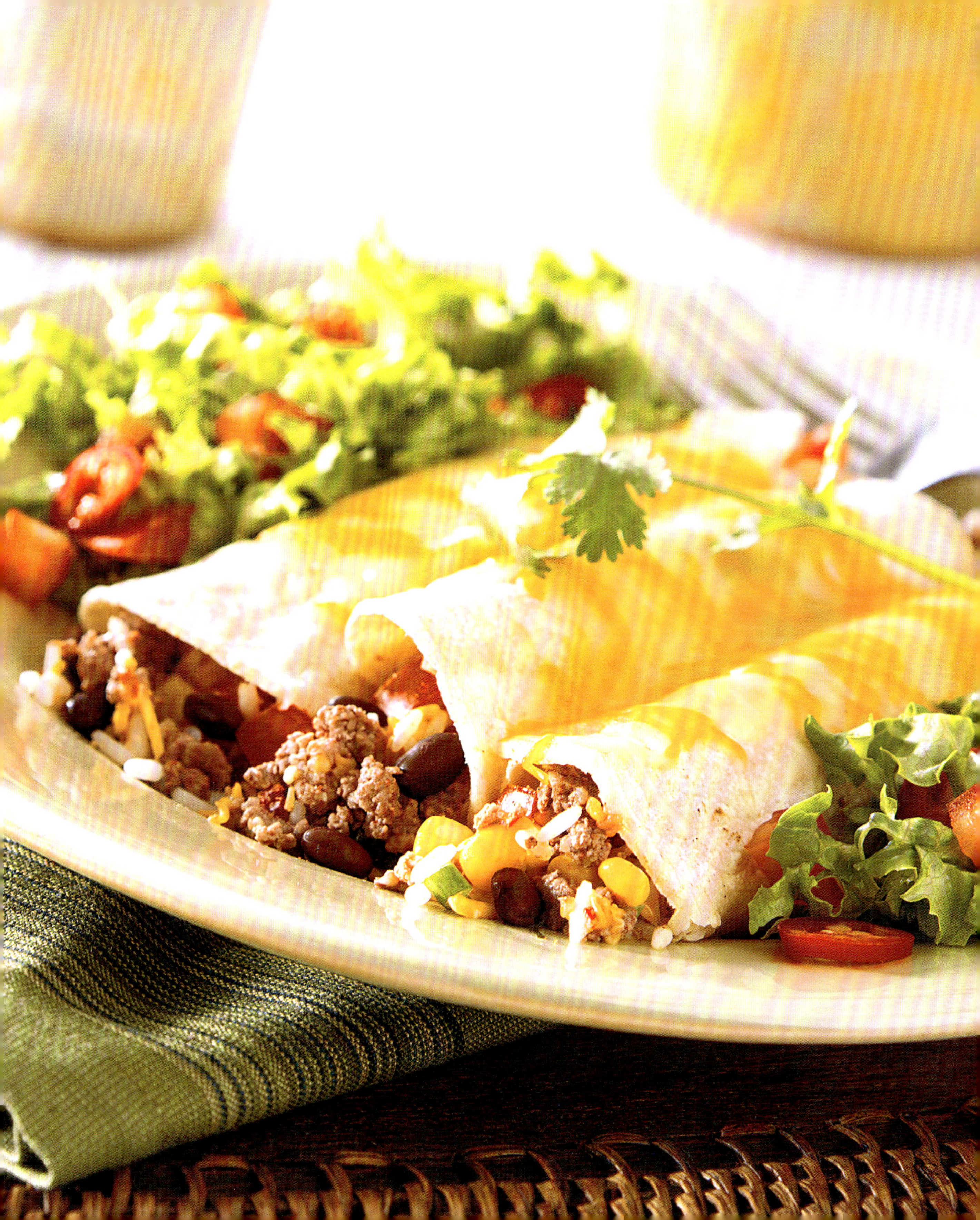

MAIN DISHES

TAMALES

- 1 package dried corn husks (8 husks)
- 4 ounces quesadilla cheese or mozzarella cheese
- 1 can (about 7 ounces) pickled jalapeños
- 1 can (about 15 ounces) yellow corn, drained, liquid reserved
- 1 cup plus 3 tablespoons cornmeal
- 2 tablespoons butter, softened
- 1 teaspoon salt
  Salsa, pico de gallo or guacamole

1. Soak corn husks in warm water 1 hour or until softened.

2. Cut cheese into 4-inch-long strips. Cut jalapeños into strips. Tear narrow strips of corn husk to use as ties for tamales.*

3. Combine corn and 2 tablespoons reserved corn liquid in food processor; pulse until paste forms. Add 1 cup cornmeal, butter and salt; pulse 1 minute or until dough forms. Add more cornmeal gradually until dough is soft and moist, but not sticky. Transfer dough to work surface and keep covered to prevent drying out.

4. Pat corn husk dry. Place 2 tablespoons cornmeal mixture in center of husk. Pat dough into rectangle about 4×2 inches. Arrange 1 strip of cheese and 1 strip of jalapeño in center of dough.

5. Lift sides of husk to enclose filling in dough and wrap gently around tamale. Fold bottom of husk over tamale; tie closed with strip of husk. Tie top closed or leave open. Transfer tamales to steamer basket.

6. Fill large saucepan with water to a depth that will not touch bottom of steamer basket. Bring to a boil. Place steamer basket over water. Cover; steam 45 minutes to 1 hour or until tamale no longer sticks to corn husk, adding additional water to saucepan as needed.

7. Serve tamales with salsa. Tamales may also be refrigerated or frozen and reheated in steamer or microwave.

MAKES 8 TAMALES

*You can also secure tamales with kitchen twine, if desired.

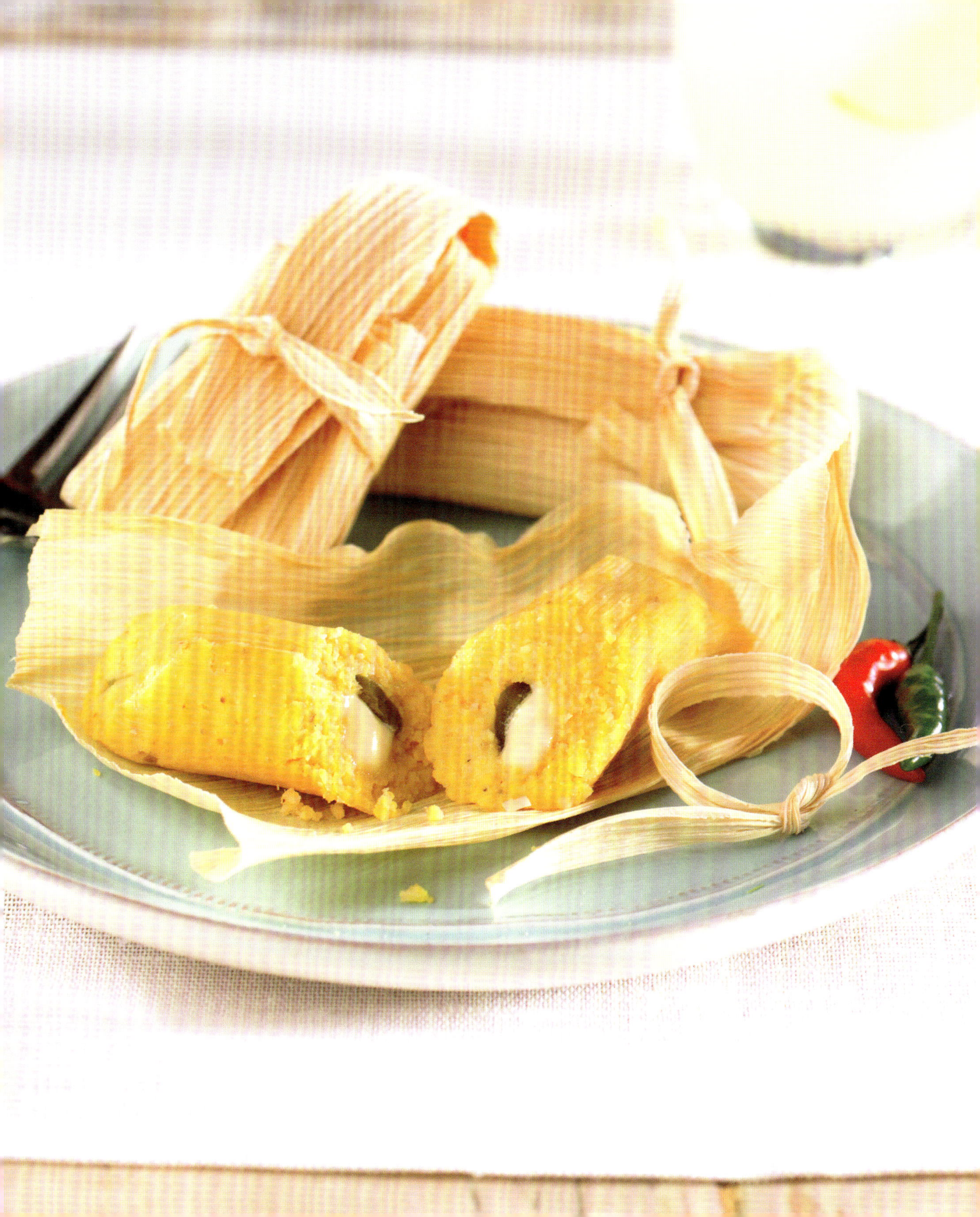

MAIN DISHES

BEEF AND BEAN ENCHILADAS

- 8 ounces ground beef
- 1 can (about 15 ounces) pinto beans, rinsed and drained
- ½ teaspoon ground cumin
- ½ teaspoon salt, divided
- ¼ teaspoon black pepper, divided
- 1 tablespoon vegetable oil
- 1 onion, chopped
- 1 green bell pepper, chopped
- 1 jalapeño pepper, minced (optional)
- 1 clove garlic, minced
- 1 can (about 14 ounces) crushed tomatoes
- 1½ teaspoons chili powder
- 8 (5-inch) corn tortillas, softened according to package directions

1. Preheat oven to 350°F. Brown beef in large skillet over medium-high heat 6 to 8 minutes, stirring to break up meat. Drain fat.

2. Mash beans in large bowl. Stir in cumin, ¼ teaspoon salt and ⅛ teaspoon black pepper. Add beef; mix well.

3. Heat oil in same skillet over medium heat. Add onion, bell pepper, jalapeño, if desired, and garlic; cook and stir 8 to 10 minutes or until vegetables are softened.

4. Stir tomatoes, chili powder, remaining ¼ teaspoon salt and ⅛ teaspoon black pepper into skillet. Reduce heat to low; simmer 5 minutes.

5. Spoon ¼ cup bean mixture down center of each tortilla. Fold ends to center to enclose filling. Place in 9-inch square baking dish. Top evenly with tomato sauce. Bake 20 minutes or until heated through.

MAKES 4 SERVINGS

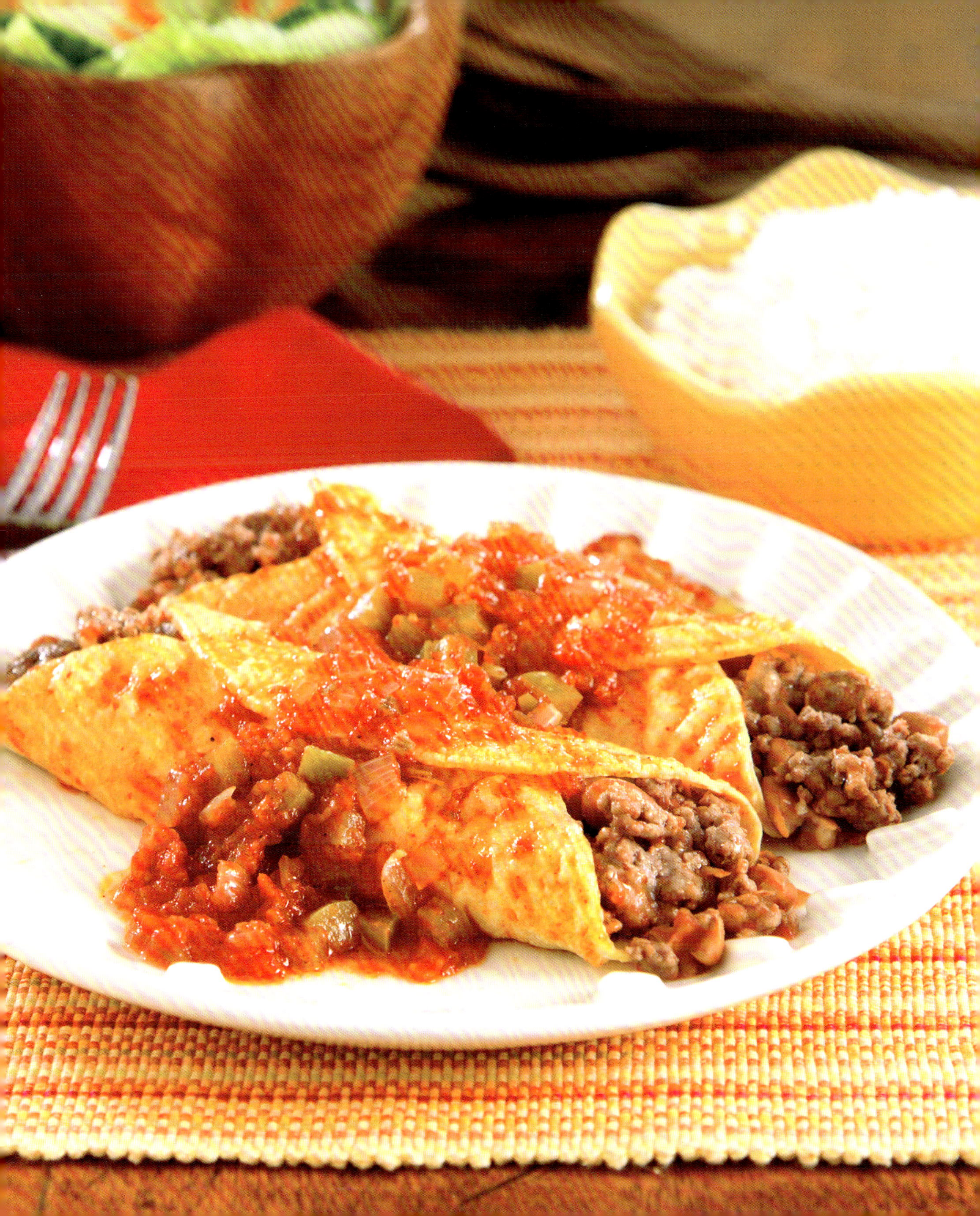

MAIN DISHES

MEXICAN SHRIMP WITH HOT CHILI BUTTER

- 2 tablespoons extra virgin olive oil
- 2 cloves garlic, minced
- 1 cup chopped onion
- 2 pounds large shrimp, peeled and deveined
- ¼ cup chili powder
- ¼ teaspoon ground red pepper
- ½ cup (1 stick) butter
- ¼ cup lime juice
- ¾ teaspoon salt
- 3 cups hot cooked white rice or yellow Spanish rice
- Lime wedges

1. Heat 1 tablespoon oil in large nonstick skillet or wok over medium-high heat. Add 1 clove garlic; cook 15 seconds. Add ½ cup onion and 1 pound shrimp. Sprinkle with half of chili powder and red pepper; cook 5 minutes or until shrimp are opaque. Remove to large bowl; repeat with remaining oil, garlic, shrimp, chili powder and red pepper.

2. Return reserved shrimp mixture to skillet. Add butter, lime juice and salt; cook and stir until butter is melted.

3. Place rice on serving platter. Spoon shrimp mixture over rice. Garnish with lime wedges.

MAKES 4 SERVINGS

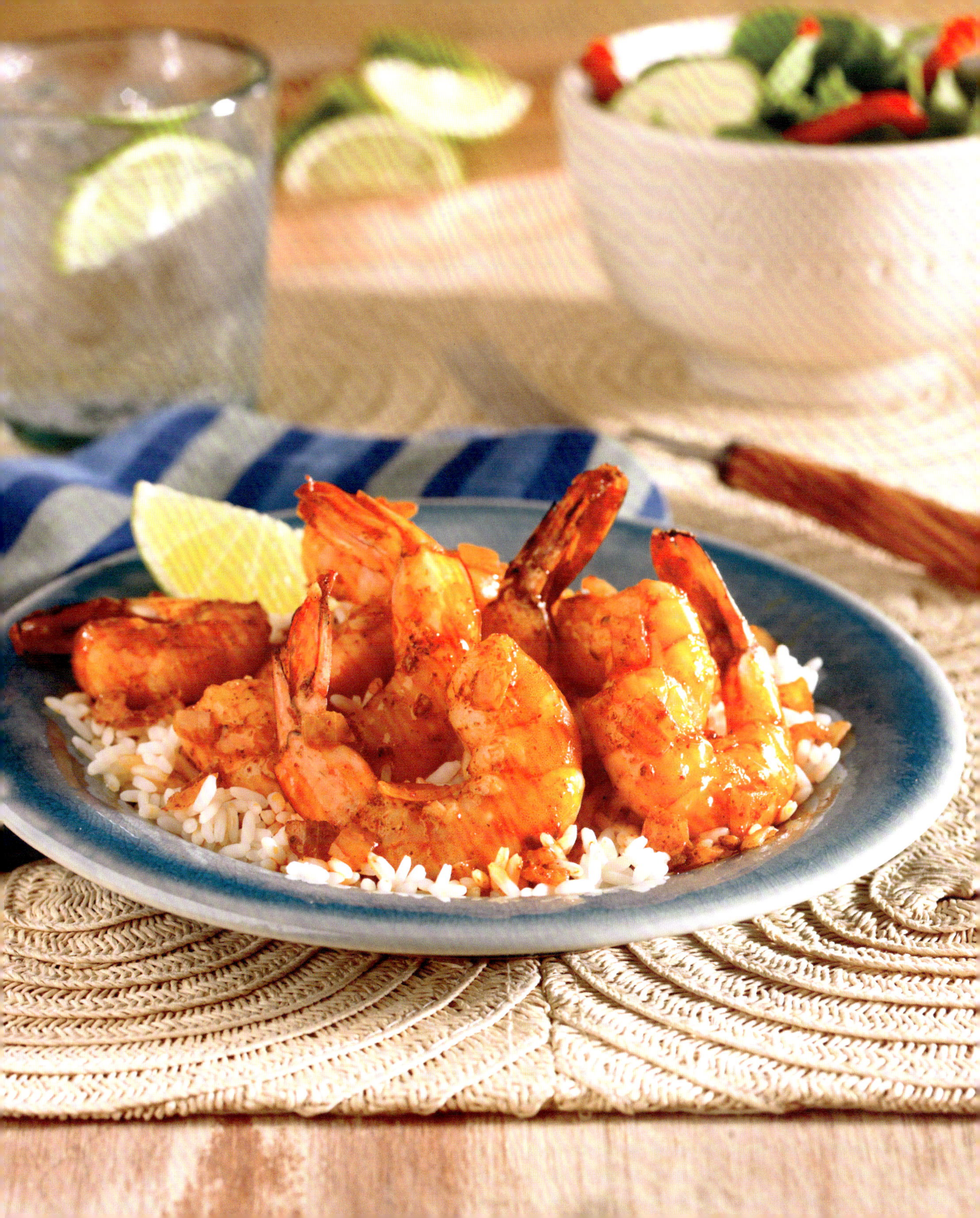

MAIN DISHES

MOLE CHICKEN

- 4 tablespoons vegetable oil, divided
- 1 onion, chopped
- 1 green bell pepper, chopped
- 3 cloves garlic, chopped
- 2 tablespoons chili powder
- 2 teaspoons ground cumin
- ½ teaspoon ground cinnamon
- 1 can (about 14 ounces) diced tomatoes
- 1 cup chicken broth
- 1 cup dark Mexican beer
- ¼ cup raisins
- 2 canned chipotle peppers in adobo sauce, chopped
- 2 tablespoons peanut butter
- 1 tablespoon sugar
- 1 teaspoon salt
- 2 ounces unsweetened chocolate, chopped
- 1 cut-up whole chicken (4 pounds)
- Hot cooked rice (optional)
- Lime wedges and chopped fresh cilantro (optional)

1. Preheat oven to 350°F.

2. Heat 1 tablespoon oil in medium saucepan. Add onion, bell pepper and garlic; cook and stir 5 minutes or until vegetables are softened. Stir in chili powder, cumin and cinnamon; cook 5 minutes. Add tomatoes, broth, beer, raisins, chipotle peppers, peanut butter, sugar and salt; bring to a simmer. Cook 20 minutes, stirring frequently. Pour vegetable mixture into food processor or blender. Add chocolate; process until smooth.

3. Meanwhile, heat remaining 3 tablespoons oil in large skillet over medium heat. Add chicken pieces in batches; brown on all sides. Place in large baking pan.

4. Pour sauce over browned chicken pieces. Cover pan loosely with foil; bake 45 minutes or until chicken is cooked through (165°F) and sauce is bubbly.

5. Serve with rice, if desired; garnish with lime wedges and cilantro.

MAKES 4 SERVINGS

Tip

This recipe makes plenty of sauce. Drizzle extra sauce around the plate or serve over side dishes.

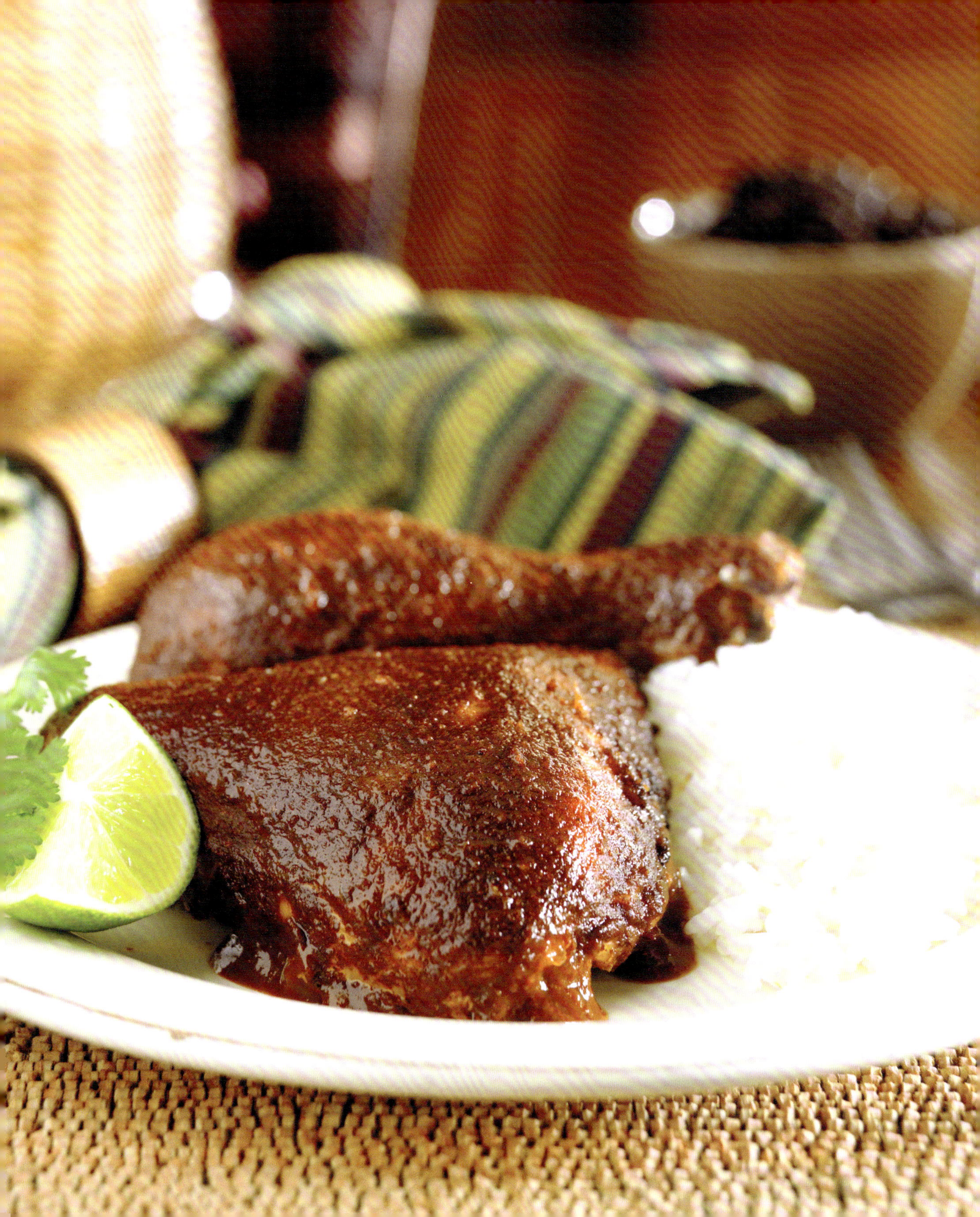

MAIN DISHES

GUADALAJARA BEEF

- 1 bottle (12 ounces) dark beer
- ¼ cup reduced-sodium soy sauce
- 3 cloves garlic, minced
- 1 teaspoon ground cumin
- 1 teaspoon chili powder
- ½ teaspoon ground red pepper
- 1 beef flank steak (about 1 pound)
- 6 medium yellow, red and green bell peppers, cut lengthwise into quarters
- 8 (6- to 8-inch) flour tortillas
- Sour cream and salsa

1 Combine beer, soy sauce, garlic, cumin, chili powder and ground red pepper in large resealable food storage bag; add beef. Seal bag; turn to coat. Refrigerate up to 24 hours, turning occasionally.

2 Prepare grill for direct cooking over medium heat. Lightly oil grate. Remove beef from marinade; discard marinade. Grill beef, uncovered, 17 to 21 minutes to at least 145°F or to desired degree of doneness, turning once. Meanwhile, grill bell peppers 7 to 10 minutes or until tender, turning once.

3 Remove steak to cutting board. Cut steak across grain into thin slices; serve with bell peppers, tortillas, sour cream and salsa.

MAKES 4 SERVINGS

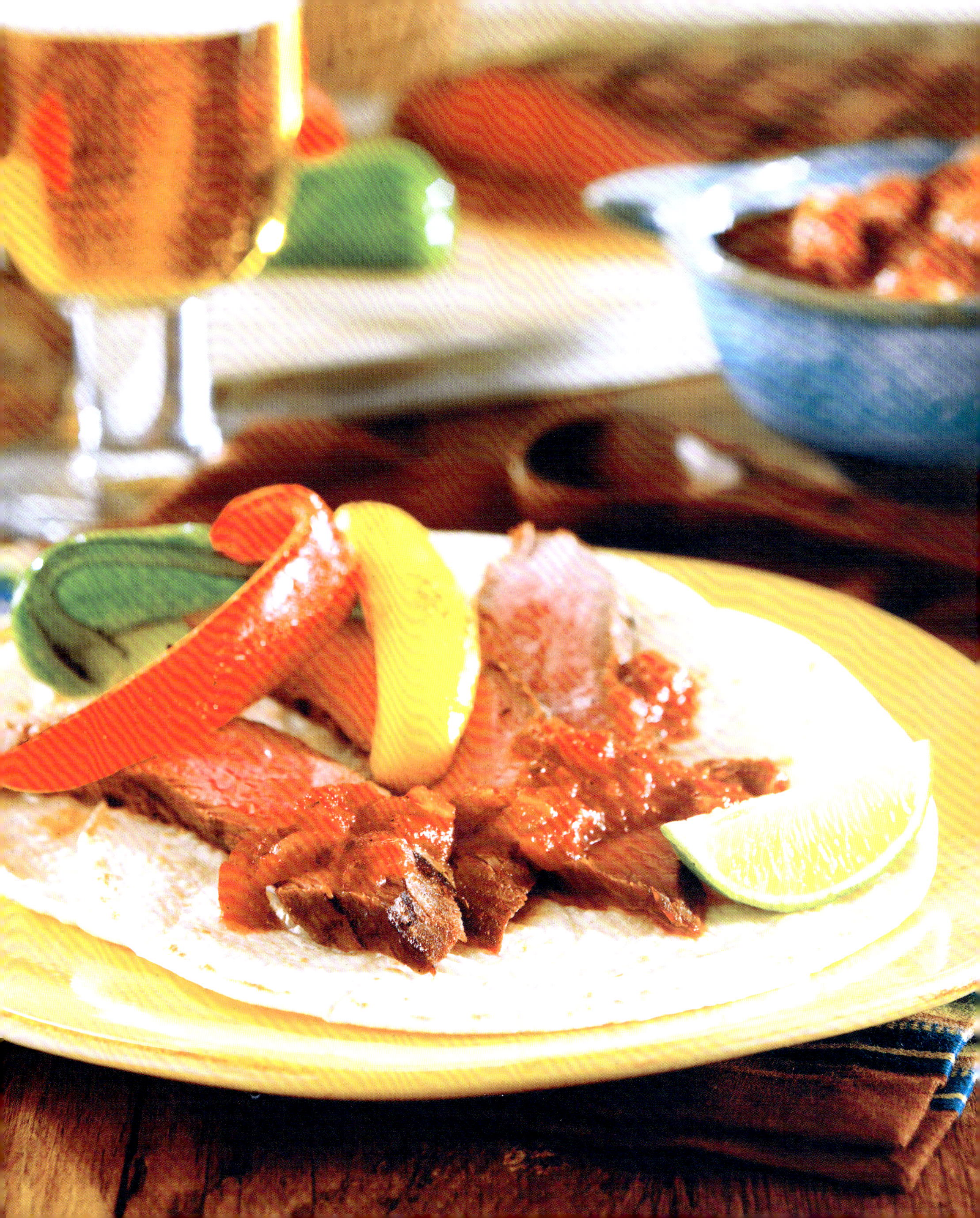

MAIN DISHES

PUERCO SABROSAS (SAVORY PORK)

- 3 tablespoons vegetable oil
- 1½ pounds pork, cut into 1×1½-inch strips
- Salt and black pepper
- 1 green bell pepper, finely chopped
- 1 medium onion, finely chopped
- 2 mild green chile peppers (Hatch or Anaheim), seeded and minced
- 1 clove garlic, minced
- 1 can (about 14 ounces) whole stewed tomatoes, crushed
- 2 tablespoons chopped fresh cilantro
- 1 teaspoon chopped fresh oregano
- 1 teaspoon ground cumin
- 1 cup Mexican beer or water
- Hot cooked rice

1. Preheat oven to 350°F.

2. Heat oil in Dutch oven over medium-high heat. Add pork; cook and stir 5 to 6 minutes or until browned on both sides. Season with salt and black pepper.

3. Add bell pepper, onion, chile peppers and garlic to Dutch oven; cook and stir 5 minutes or until onion and peppers are tender. Add tomatoes, cilantro, oregano and cumin; mix well.

4. Cover; bake 30 minutes. Stir well; add beer. Bake about 1½ hours or until pork is very tender. Serve over rice.

MAKES 6 SERVINGS

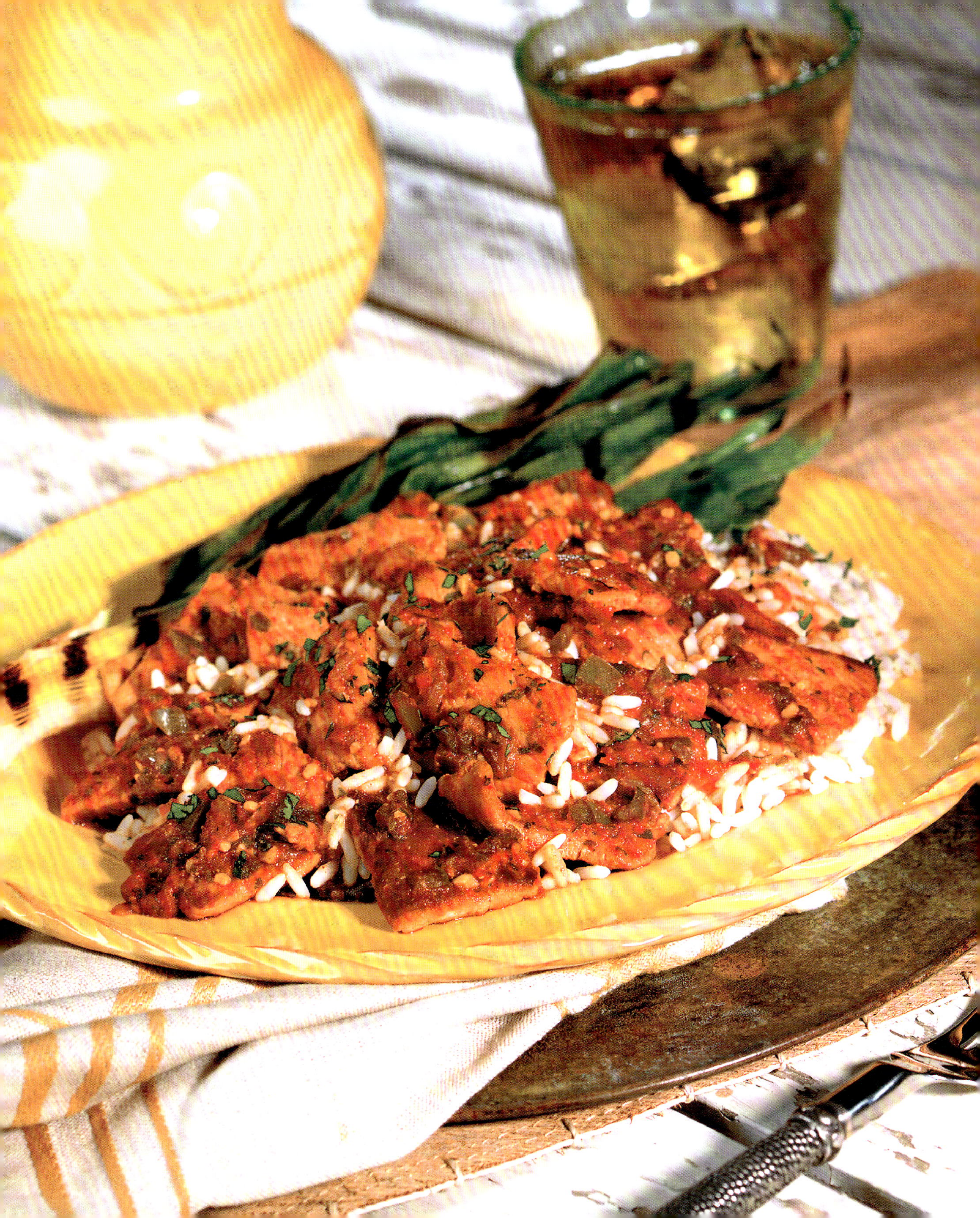

CHIPOTLE STRIP STEAKS

- 1 tablespoon olive oil
- ⅓ cup finely chopped onion
- ¾ cup Mexican beer
- 1 teaspoon Worcestershire sauce
- ⅓ cup ketchup
- 1 tablespoon red wine vinegar
- 1 teaspoon sugar
- ⅛ to ¼ teaspoon chipotle chili powder
- 4 bone-in strip steaks (8 to 9 ounces each)
- 1 teaspoon salt

1. Heat oil in small saucepan over medium-high heat. Add onion; cook 3 minutes or until softened, stirring occasionally. Add beer and Worcestershire sauce; bring to a boil. Cook until reduced to about ⅓ cup, stirring occasionally. Stir in ketchup, vinegar, sugar and chipotle chili powder; simmer over medium-low heat 3 minutes or until thickened, stirring occasionally. Keep warm.

2. Prepare grill for direct cooking over medium-high heat. Spray grate with nonstick cooking spray. Sprinkle steaks with salt.

3. Grill steaks 4 to 5 minutes per side for medium rare (145°F) or until desired doneness. Serve with chipotle sauce.

MAKES 4 SERVINGS

MAIN DISHES

RED SNAPPER VERA CRUZ

- 4 red snapper fillets (about 1 pound)
- ¼ cup lime juice
- 1 tablespoon lemon juice
- 1 teaspoon chili powder
- ½ teaspoon salt
- 4 green onions, sliced into ½-inch pieces
- 1 tomato, coarsely chopped
- ½ cup chopped Anaheim or green bell pepper
- ½ cup chopped red bell pepper
- Black pepper

1. Place fish in shallow 9- to 10-inch round microwavable baking dish. Combine lime juice, lemon juice, chili powder and salt in small bowl; pour over snapper. Marinate 10 minutes, turning once or twice.

2. Sprinkle green onions, tomato, Anaheim and bell pepper over snapper. Season with black pepper. Cover dish loosely with vented plastic wrap. Microwave on HIGH 5 to 6 minutes or just until fish flakes in center when tested with fork. Let stand, covered, 4 minutes before serving.

MAKES 4 SERVINGS

MAIN DISHES

BEEFY TORTILLA PIE

2 teaspoons vegetable oil
1½ cups chopped onion
2 pounds ground beef
1 teaspoon chili powder
1 teaspoon ground cumin
1 teaspoon salt
2 cloves garlic, minced
1 can (15 ounces) tomato sauce
1 cup sliced black olives
7 (6-inch) flour tortillas
4 cups (16 ounces) shredded Cheddar cheese
Optional toppings: sour cream, salsa and/or chopped green onion

Slow Cooker Directions

1 Heat oil in large skillet over medium heat. Add onion; cook and stir 3 to 5 minutes or until tender. Add beef, chili powder, cumin, salt and garlic; cook 6 to 8 minutes or until beef is no longer pink, stirring to break up meat. Stir in tomato sauce; heat through. Stir in olives.

2 Prepare foil handles.* Place in slow cooker. Lay one tortilla on foil strips. Spread with one seventh of meat sauce and one seventh of cheese. Repeat layers of tortillas, meat sauce and cheese layers six times.

3 Cover and cook on HIGH 1½ hours. To serve, lift out of slow cooker using foil handles and place on serving platter. Discard foil. Cut into wedges. Serve with desired toppings.

MAKES 4 TO 6 SERVINGS

*Prepare foil handles by tearing off four 18×2-inch strips of heavy-duty foil (or use regular foil folded to double thickness). Crisscross foil strips in spoke design.

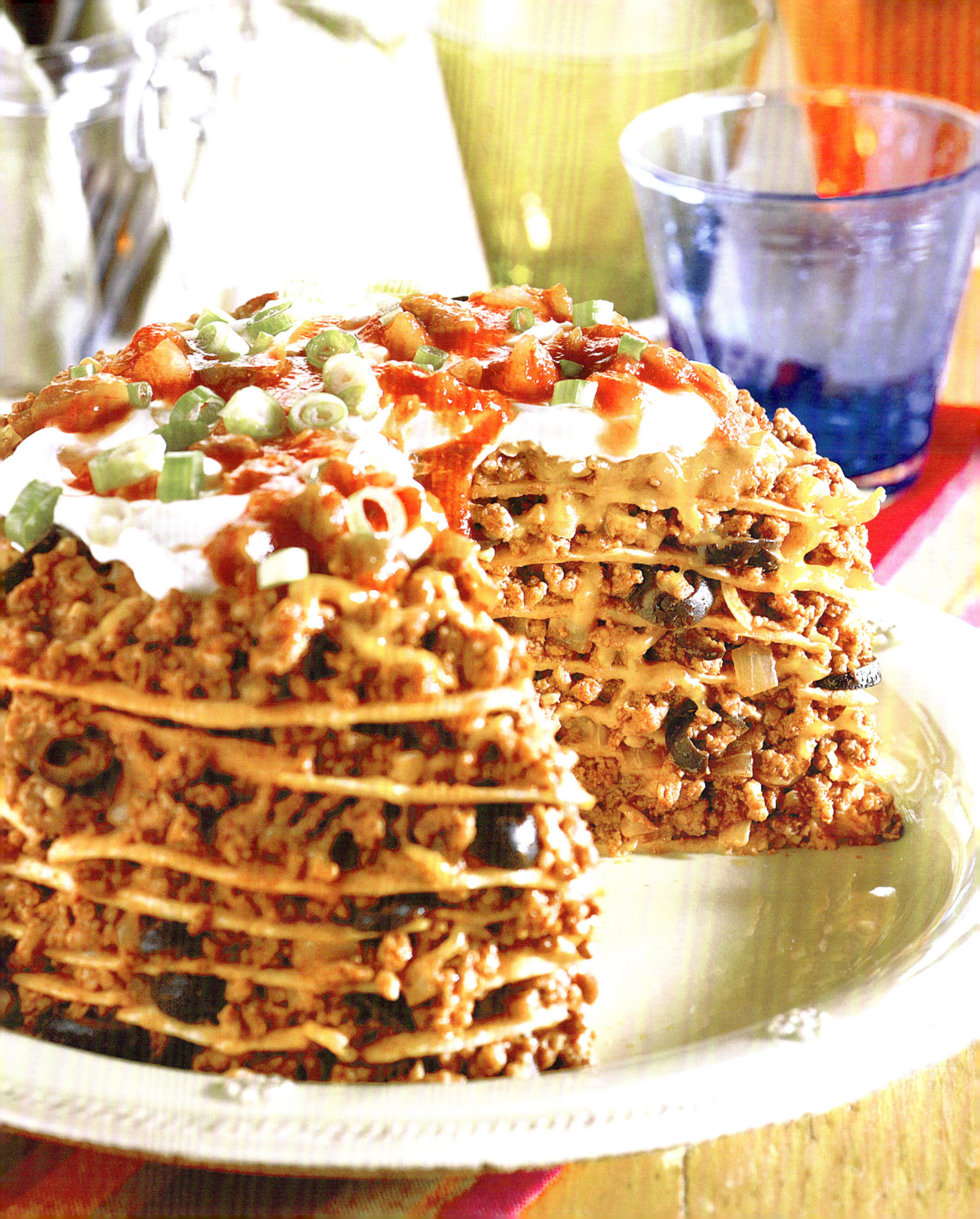

MAIN DISHES

- 1 pound ground beef
- 1 small onion, chopped
- 1 clove garlic, minced
- 1 can (about 14 ounces) diced tomatoes, undrained
- ¼ cup golden raisins
- 1 tablespoon chili powder
- 1 tablespoon cider vinegar
- 1 teaspoon salt
- ½ teaspoon ground cumin
- ½ teaspoon dried oregano
- ½ teaspoon ground cinnamon
- ¼ teaspoon red pepper flakes
- ¼ cup slivered almonds (optional)

PICADILLO

Slow Cooker Directions

1. Cook beef, onion and garlic in large nonstick skillet over medium-high heat 6 to 8 minutes or until beef is no long pink, stirring to break up meat; drain fat. Transfer mixture to slow cooker.

2. Stir tomatoes, raisins, chili powder, vinegar, salt, cumin, oregano, cinnamon and pepper flakes into beef in slow cooker.

3. Cover and cook on LOW 6 to 7 hours. Garnish with almonds, if desired.

MAKES 4 SERVINGS

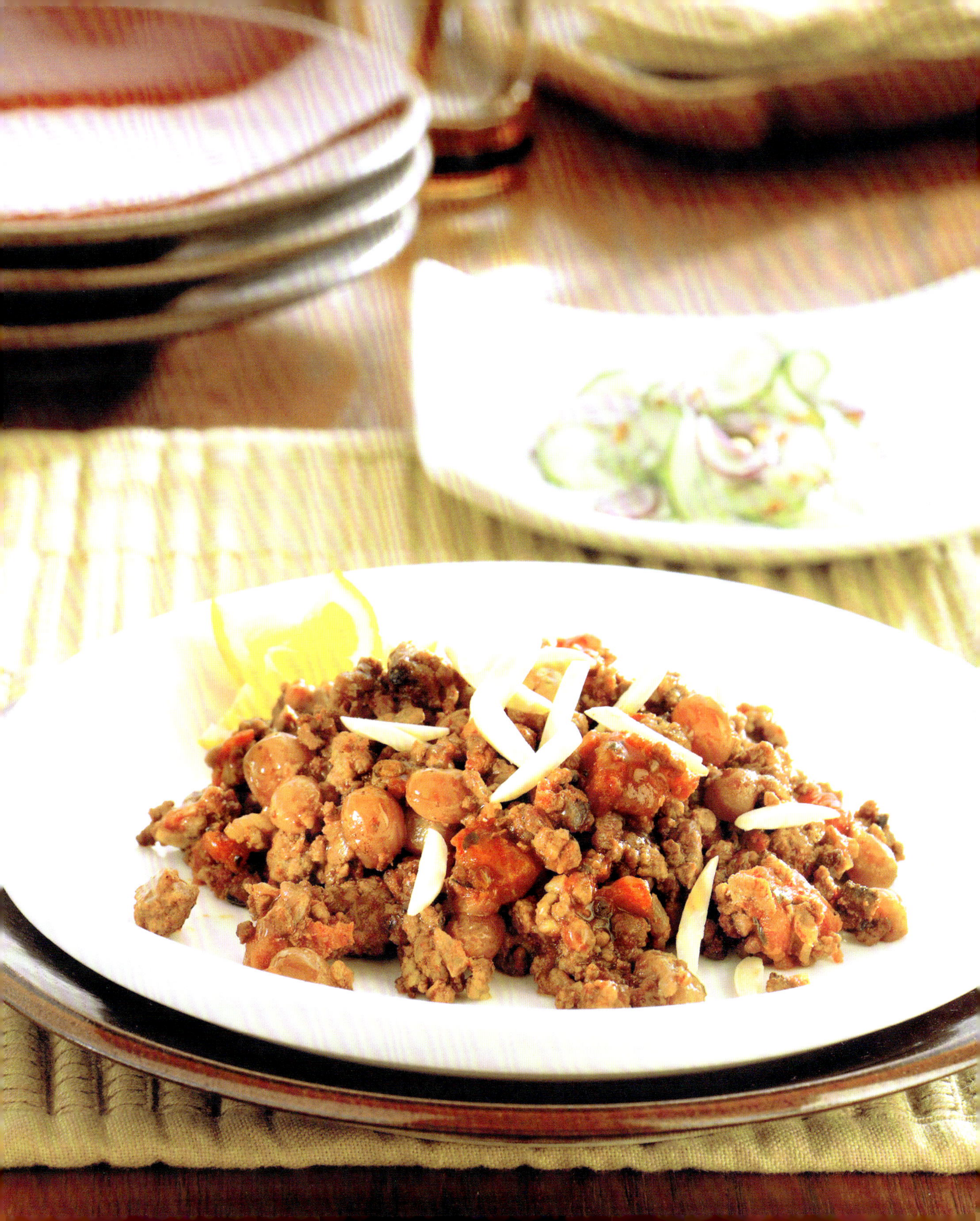

MAIN DISHES

CHICKEN CHILE RELLENO CASSEROLE

- 3 cups diced cooked chicken
- 1 can (about 7 ounces) chopped green chiles
- 1½ cups (6 ounces) shredded pepper jack or Mexican cheese blend, divided
- 1½ cups salsa, divided
- ¾ cup milk
- 3 eggs
- ¼ cup all-purpose flour
- 1 teaspoon chili powder
- 2 tablespoons minced fresh cilantro

1. Preheat oven to 350°F. Spray 2-quart baking dish with nonstick cooking spray.

2. Spread chicken in baking dish; top with chiles and ¾ cup cheese. Whisk ½ cup salsa, milk, eggs, flour and chili powder in medium bowl. Stir in ¼ cup cheese; pour over chicken. Sprinkle with remaining ½ cup cheese.

3. Bake 25 to 30 minutes or until top is set and cheese is lightly browned. Sprinkle with cilantro and serve with remaining 1 cup salsa.

MAKES 6 SERVINGS

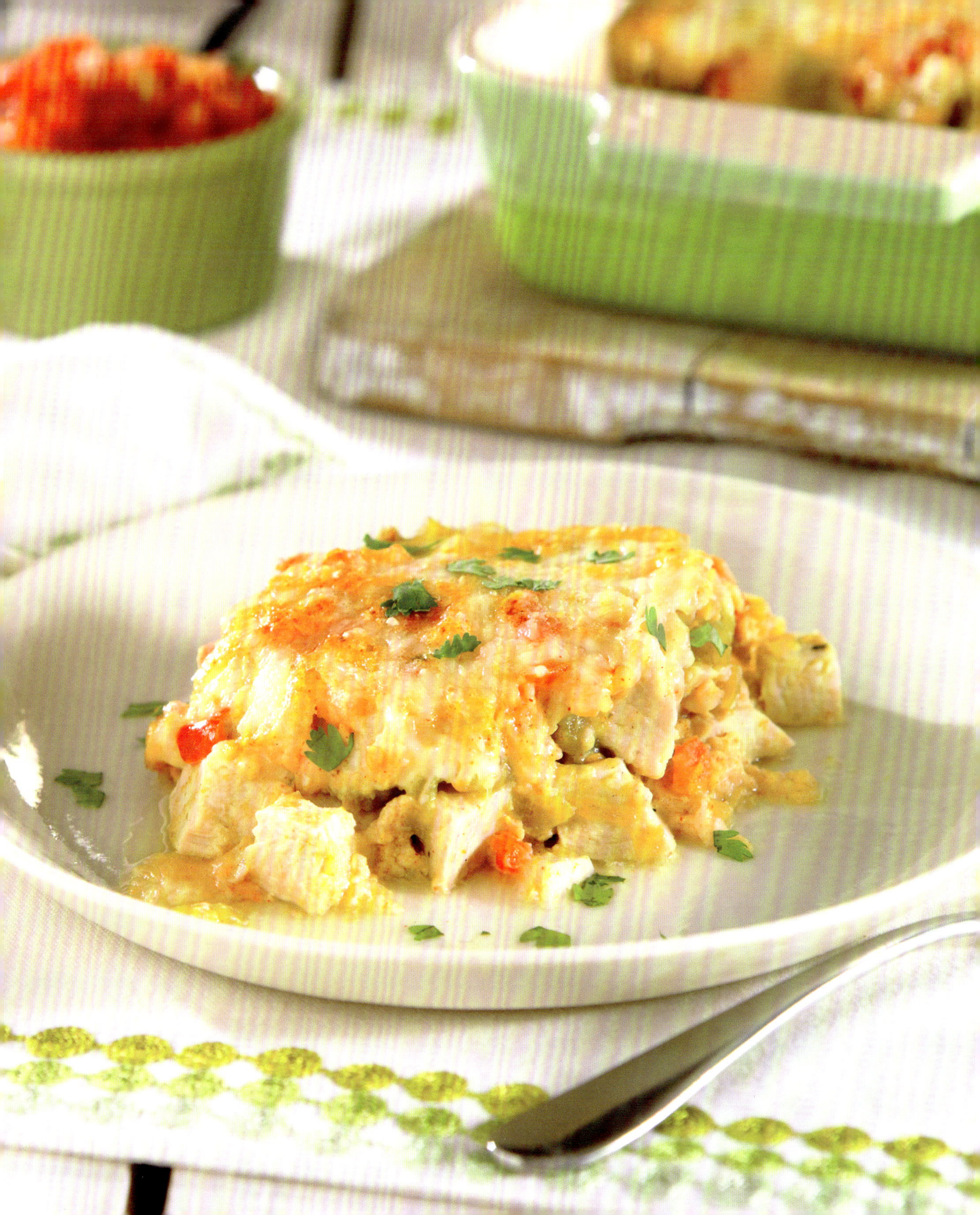

MAIN DISHES

GRILLED FISH WITH CHILE-CORN SALSA

- 1 cup thawed frozen corn
- 1 large tomato, seeded and diced
- ¼ cup thinly sliced green onions
- ¼ cup canned diced mild green chiles, drained
- 1 tablespoon chopped fresh cilantro
- 1 tablespoon lime juice
- 4 teaspoons olive oil, divided
- ⅛ teaspoon ground cumin
- Salt and black pepper
- 1½ pounds firm-textured fish steaks or fillets such as halibut, salmon, sea bass or swordfish (each 1 inch thick)

1 Combine corn, tomato, green onions, chiles, chopped cilantro, lime juice, 2 teaspoons oil and cumin in small bowl; mix well. Season with salt and pepper. Let stand at room temperature 30 minutes for flavors to blend.

2 Brush fish with remaining 2 teaspoons oil; season with salt and pepper. Lightly oil grill grate. Prepare grill for direct cooking. Grill fish over medium-high heat 4 to 5 minutes per side or until fish just begins to flake when tested with fork. Serve with salsa.

MAKES 4 SERVINGS

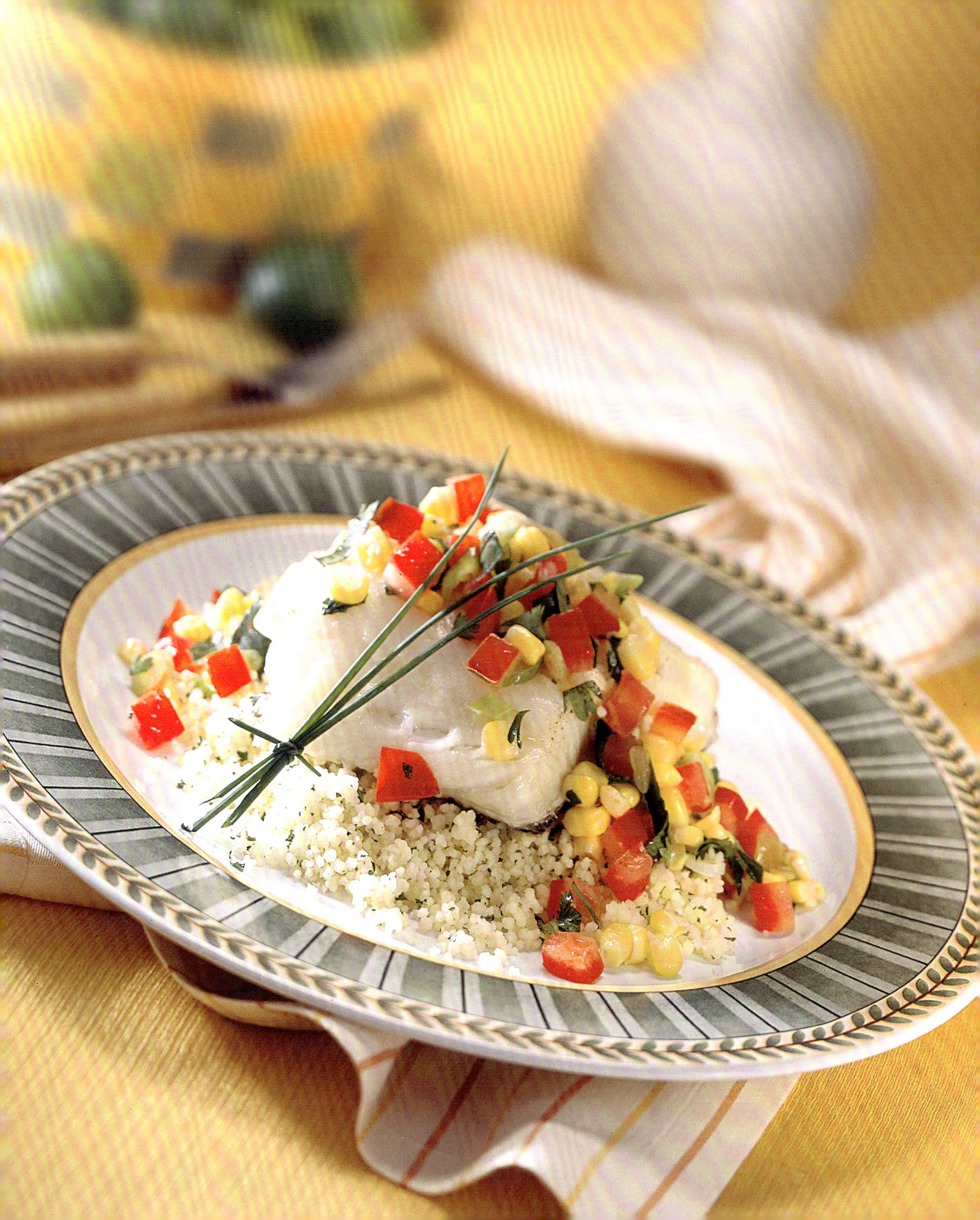

MAIN DISHES

- 1 package (about 6 ounces) corn bread mix
- ⅓ cup milk
- 1 egg
- 1 tablespoon vegetable oil
- 1 pound ground beef
- ¾ cup chopped onion
- 1 cup thawed frozen corn
- 1 can (about 14 ounces) Mexican-style diced tomatoes
- 2 teaspoons cornstarch
- ¾ cup (3 ounces) shredded sharp Cheddar cheese

TAMALE BEEF SQUARES

1. Preheat oven to 400°F. Spray 12×8-inch baking dish with nonstick cooking spray.

2. Stir together corn bread mix, milk, egg and oil in medium bowl. Spread in prepared baking dish.

3. Brown beef and onion in large skillet over medium-high heat 6 to 8 minutes, stirring to break up meat. Drain fat. Stir in corn.

4. Stir tomatoes and cornstarch in medium bowl. Stir into beef mixture in skillet. Bring to a boil, stirring frequently. Spoon beef mixture over corn bread mixture in baking dish.

5. Cover with foil; bake 15 minutes. Remove foil; bake 10 minutes. Sprinkle with cheese. Bake 2 to 3 minutes or until cheese is melted. Remove from oven; let stand 5 minutes. Cut into squares.

MAKES 6 SERVINGS

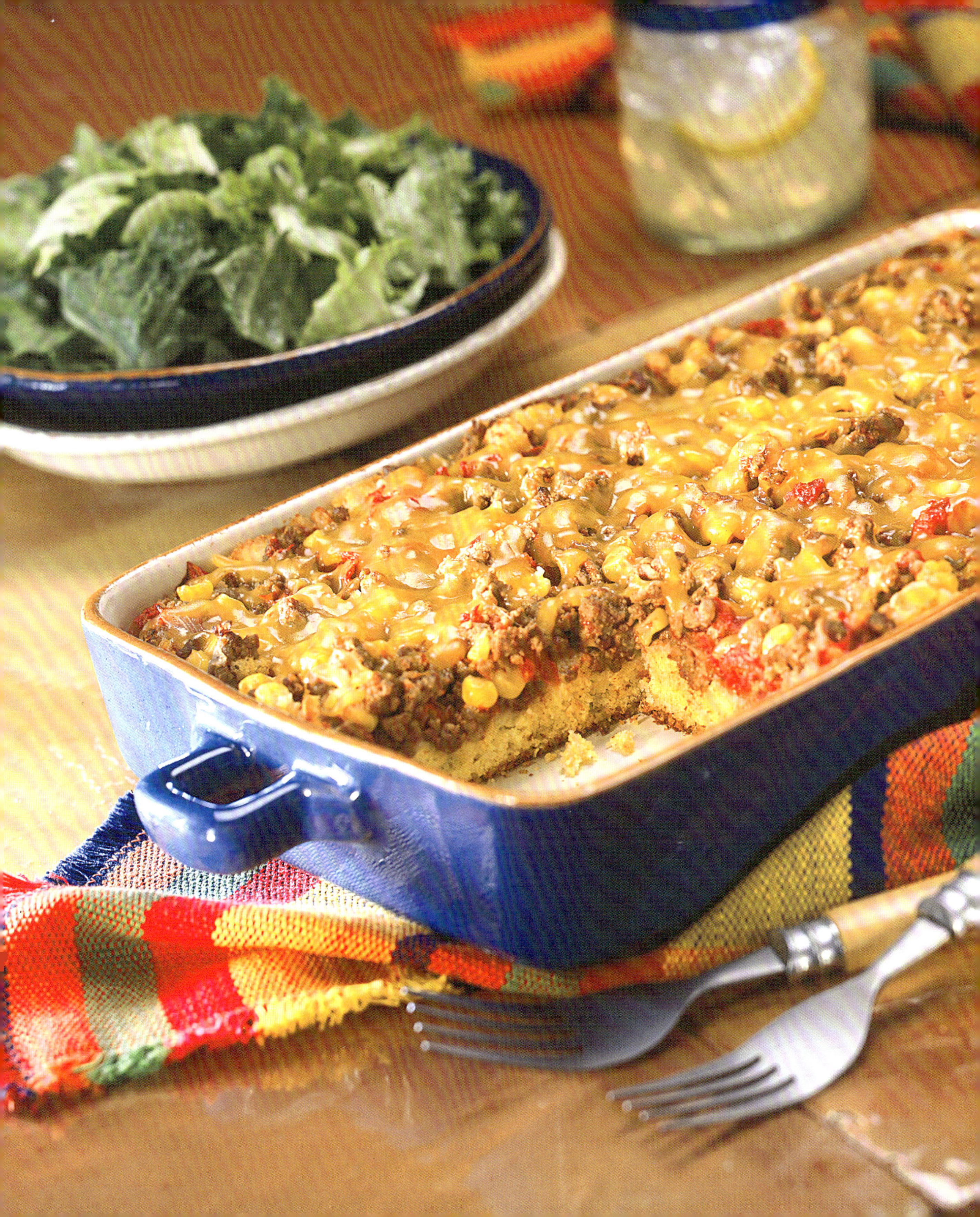

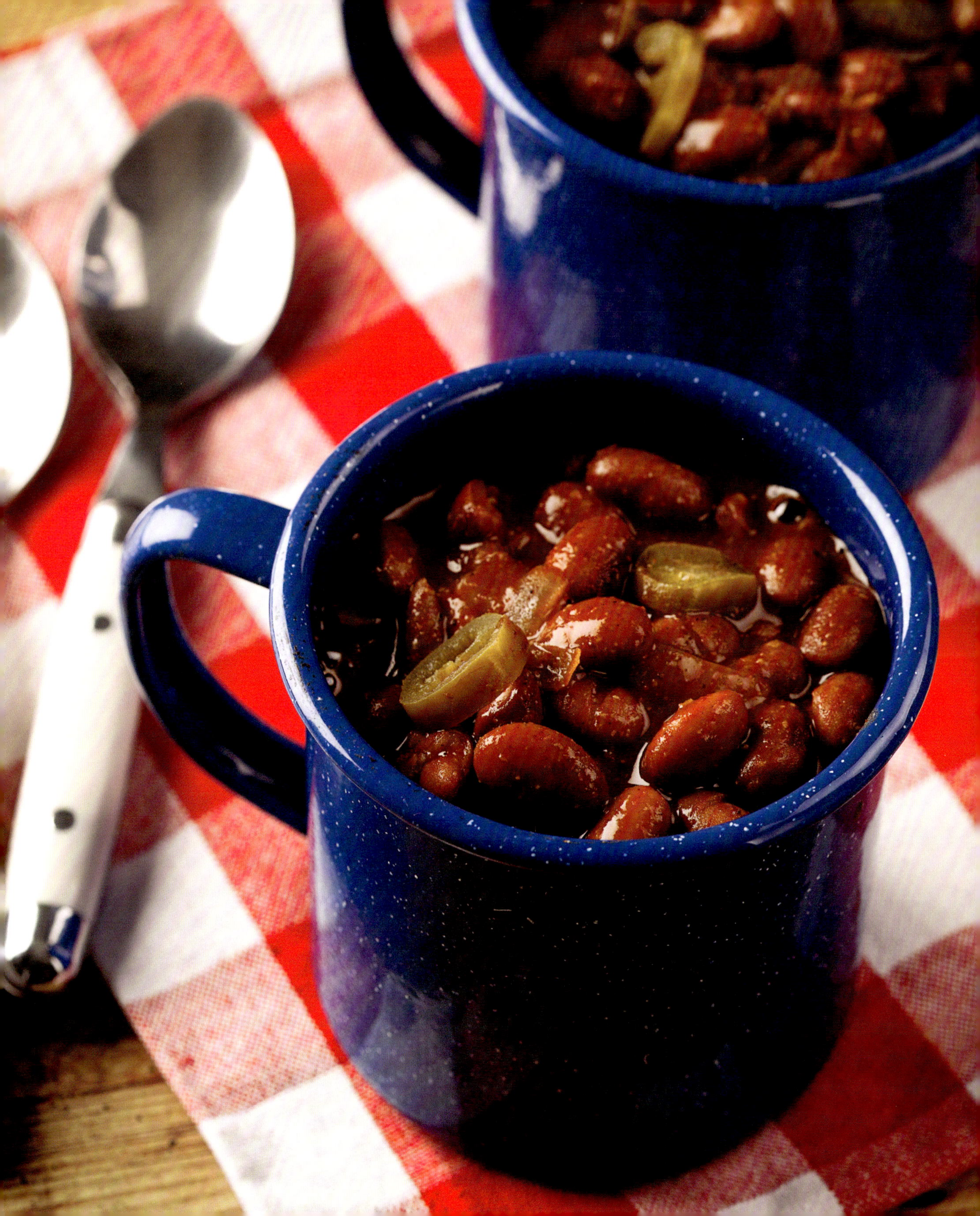

SIDE DISHES & SALADS

JALAPEÑO BEANS

- 1 tablespoon vegetable oil
- 1 small onion, finely chopped
- 1 teaspoon ground cumin
- 1 teaspoon garlic powder
- ½ teaspoon smoked paprika
- ¼ teaspoon ground red pepper
- 3 tablespoons chopped pickled jalapeño peppers
- 2 cans (about 15 ounces each) chili beans (made with pinto beans)
- ⅓ cup dark lager beer
- 1 tablespoon white vinegar
- 1 teaspoon sugar
- ½ teaspoon hot pepper sauce
- Salt and black pepper

1. Heat oil in large saucepan over medium-high heat. Add onion; cook and stir 2 minutes or until translucent. Add cumin, garlic powder, paprika and red pepper; cook and stir 1 minute. Add jalapeños; cook and stir 30 seconds.

2. Stir in beans, beer, vinegar, sugar and hot pepper sauce; bring to a boil. Reduce heat to medium-low; cook 15 minutes, stirring occasionally. Season with salt and black pepper. Beans will thicken upon standing.

MAKES 4 TO 6 SERVINGS

SIDE DISHES & SALADS

FIESTA CORN SALAD

- 5 large ears fresh corn, husks and silks removed
- 1 cup plain yogurt or sour cream
- 3 tablespoons minced onion
- 1½ tablespoons fresh lime juice
- 1 clove garlic, minced
- 1 teaspoon ground cumin
- 1 teaspoon chili powder
- ½ teaspoon salt
- 1½ cups shredded red cabbage
- 1 large tomato, chopped
- 1 green bell pepper, seeded and chopped
- 5 slices bacon, cooked and crumbled (optional)
- 1 cup coarsely crushed tortilla chips
- 1 cup (4 ounces) shredded Cheddar cheese

1. Bring large saucepan of water to a boil. Add corn; cover and cook 6 minutes or until tender. Drain and cool completely.

2. Meanwhile for dressing, combine yogurt, onion, lime juice, garlic, cumin, chili powder and salt in large bowl.

3. Cut corn from cob using sharp knife. Add corn, cabbage, tomato and bell pepper to dressing; mix lightly. Cover and refrigerate until ready to serve. Stir in bacon just before serving, if desired, and sprinkle with chips and cheese.

MAKES 4 TO 6 SERVINGS

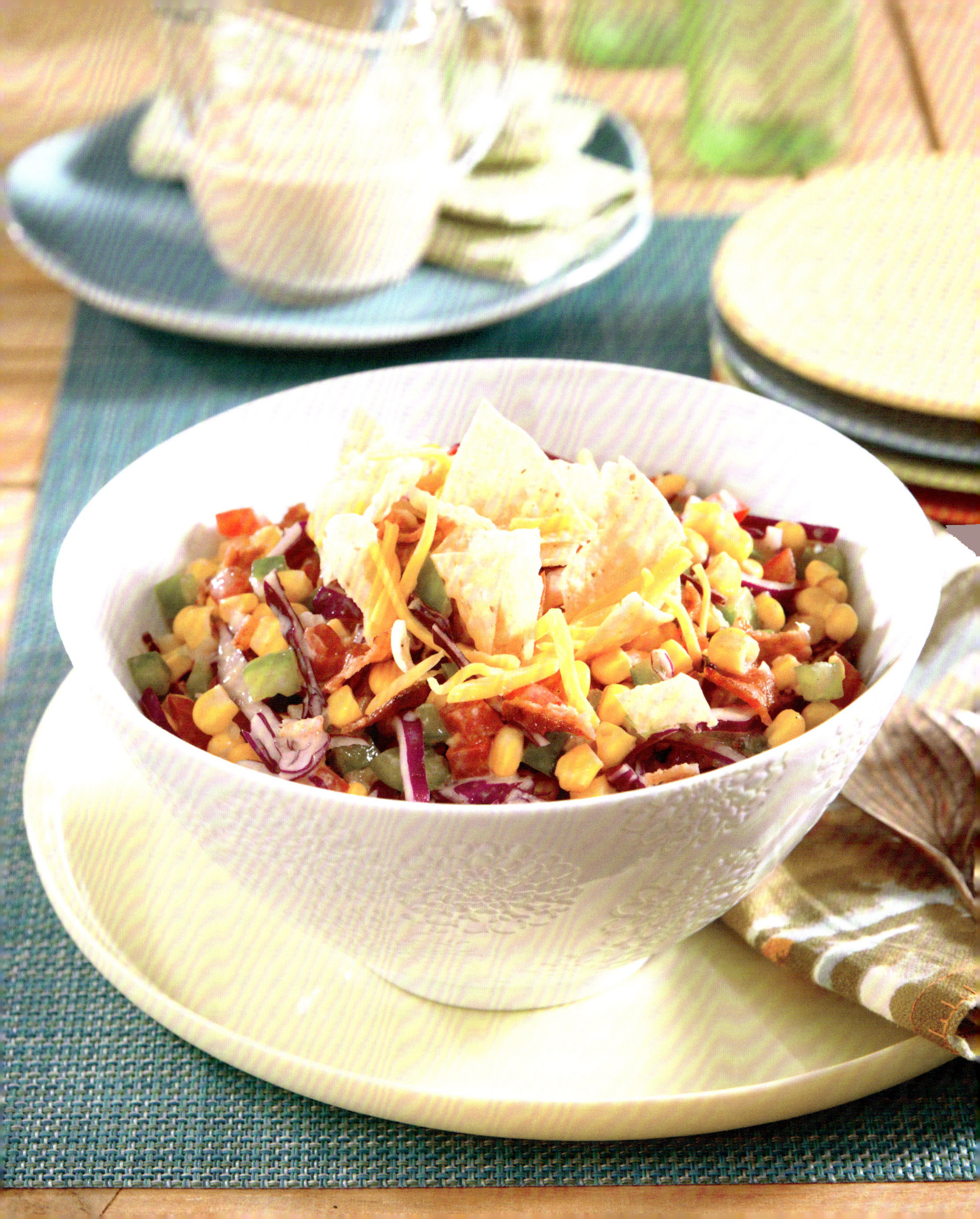

SIDE DISHES & SALADS

PICANTE PINTOS AND RICE

- 2 cups dried pinto beans, rinsed and sorted
- 2 cups water
- 1 can (about 14 ounces) stewed tomatoes
- 1 cup coarsely chopped onion
- ¾ cup coarsely chopped green bell pepper
- ¼ cup sliced celery
- 4 cloves garlic, minced
- ½ small jalapeño pepper, seeded and chopped
- 2 teaspoons dried oregano
- 2 teaspoons chili powder
- ½ teaspoon ground red pepper
- 2 cups chopped kale
- 3 cups hot cooked brown rice

1. Place beans in large saucepan; add water to cover by 2 inches. Bring to a boil over high heat; boil 2 minutes. Remove from heat; let stand, covered, 1 hour. Drain beans; discard water. Return beans to saucepan.

2. Add 2 cups water, tomatoes, onion, bell pepper, celery, garlic, jalapeño pepper, oregano, chili powder and red pepper to saucepan; bring to a boil over high heat. Reduce heat to low. Simmer, covered, 1½ hours or until beans are tender, stirring occasionally.

3. Gently stir kale into bean mixture. Simmer, uncovered, 30 minutes. (Beans will be very tender.) Serve over rice.

MAKES 8 SERVINGS

Tip

Instead of using dried beans, use two cans (28 ounces each) canned beans. Omit step 1 and combine all ingredients except for kale in Dutch oven; bring to a boil. Reduce heat to low; simmer 30 minutes. Stir in kale; simmer, uncovered, 30 minutes.

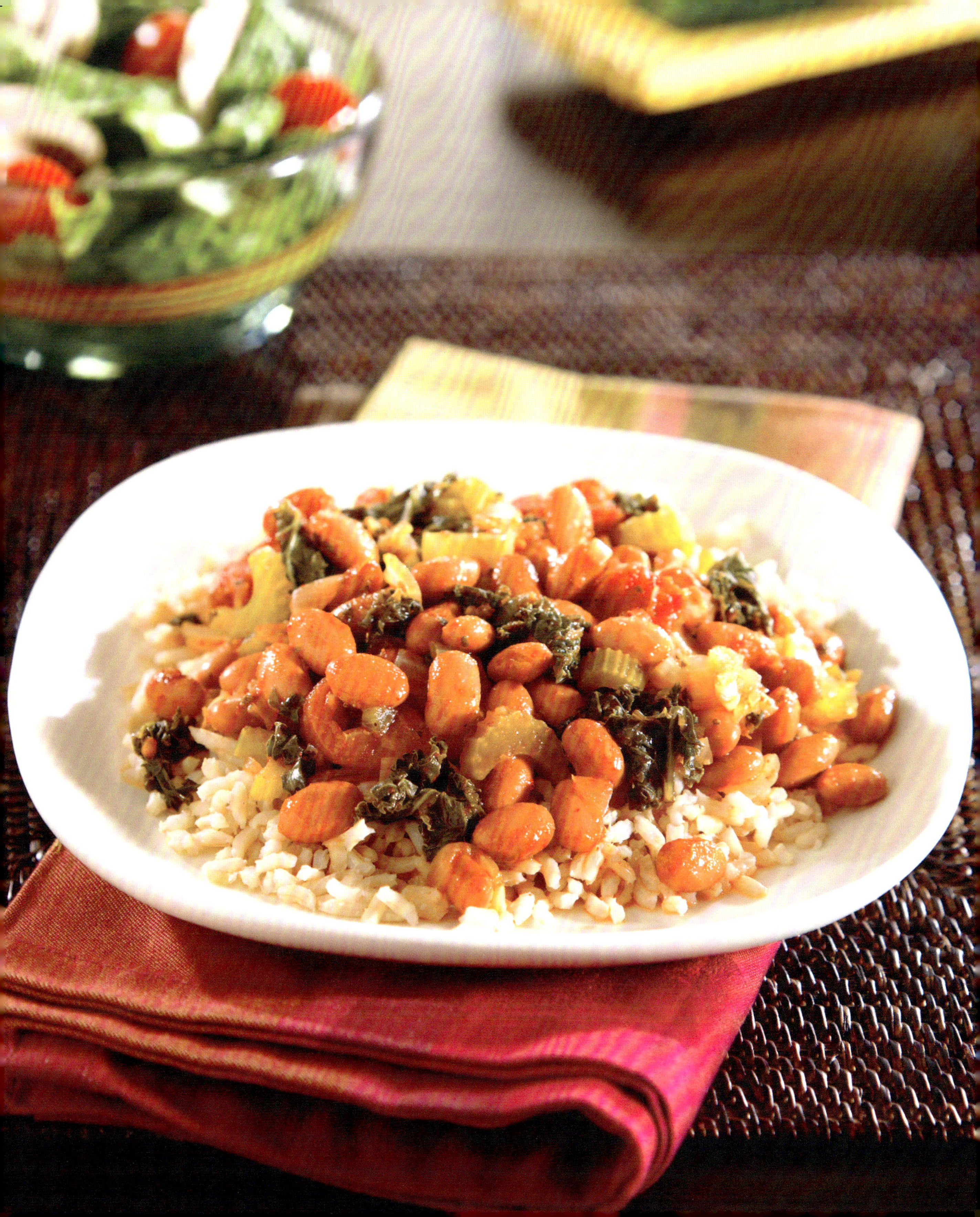

SOUTHWEST GAZPACHO SALAD

- 1 can (about 15 ounces) black beans, rinsed and drained
- 1 cup diced tomato
- ⅔ cup thawed frozen corn
- ½ cup diced cucumber
- 2 tablespoons diced red onion
- 1 tablespoon finely chopped fresh cilantro
- 3 tablespoons tomato juice
- 1 tablespoon lime juice
- 2 teaspoons extra virgin olive oil
- ½ teaspoon salt
- ½ teaspoon chili powder
- Pinch black pepper
- Lime wedges (optional)

1. Combine beans, tomato, corn, cucumber, onion and cilantro in large bowl; toss to blend.

2. Whisk tomato juice, lime juice, oil, salt, chili powder and pepper in small bowl. Pour over salad; toss to blend. Serve with lime wedges, if desired.

MAKES 4 SERVINGS

SIDE DISHES
& SALADS

GREEN CHILE RICE

- 1 cup uncooked white rice
- 3 cups water
- 1 can (4 ounces) diced mild green chiles
- ½ medium yellow onion, diced
- 1 teaspoon dried oregano
- ½ teaspoon salt
- ½ teaspoon cumin seeds
- 3 green onions, thinly sliced
- ⅓ to ½ cup chopped fresh cilantro

1. Combine water, rice, chiles, yellow onion, oregano, salt and cumin in large saucepan. Bring to a boil over high heat.

2. Reduce heat to low; cover and simmer 18 minutes or until liquid is absorbed and rice is tender. Stir in green onions and cilantro.

MAKES 6 SERVINGS

SIDE DISHES & SALADS

SAVORY CORN CAKES

- 1 cup all-purpose flour
- 1 cup yellow cornmeal
- 1 teaspoon baking powder
- 1 teaspoon salt
- 2 cups thawed frozen corn
- 1 cup (4 ounces) shredded smoked Cheddar cheese
- 1 cup buttermilk
- 2 eggs
- 3 green onions, finely chopped
- 2 cloves garlic, minced
- 2 tablespoons chili powder
- 2 tablespoons vegetable oil
- Salsa (optional)

1. Combine flour, cornmeal, baking powder and salt in large bowl; mix well. Stir in corn, cheese, buttermilk, eggs, green onions, garlic and chili powder until well combined.

2. Heat oil in large nonstick skillet over medium-high heat. Drop batter by ¼ cupfuls into skillet. Cook 3 minutes per side or until golden brown. Serve with salsa, if desired.

MAKES 12 CAKES

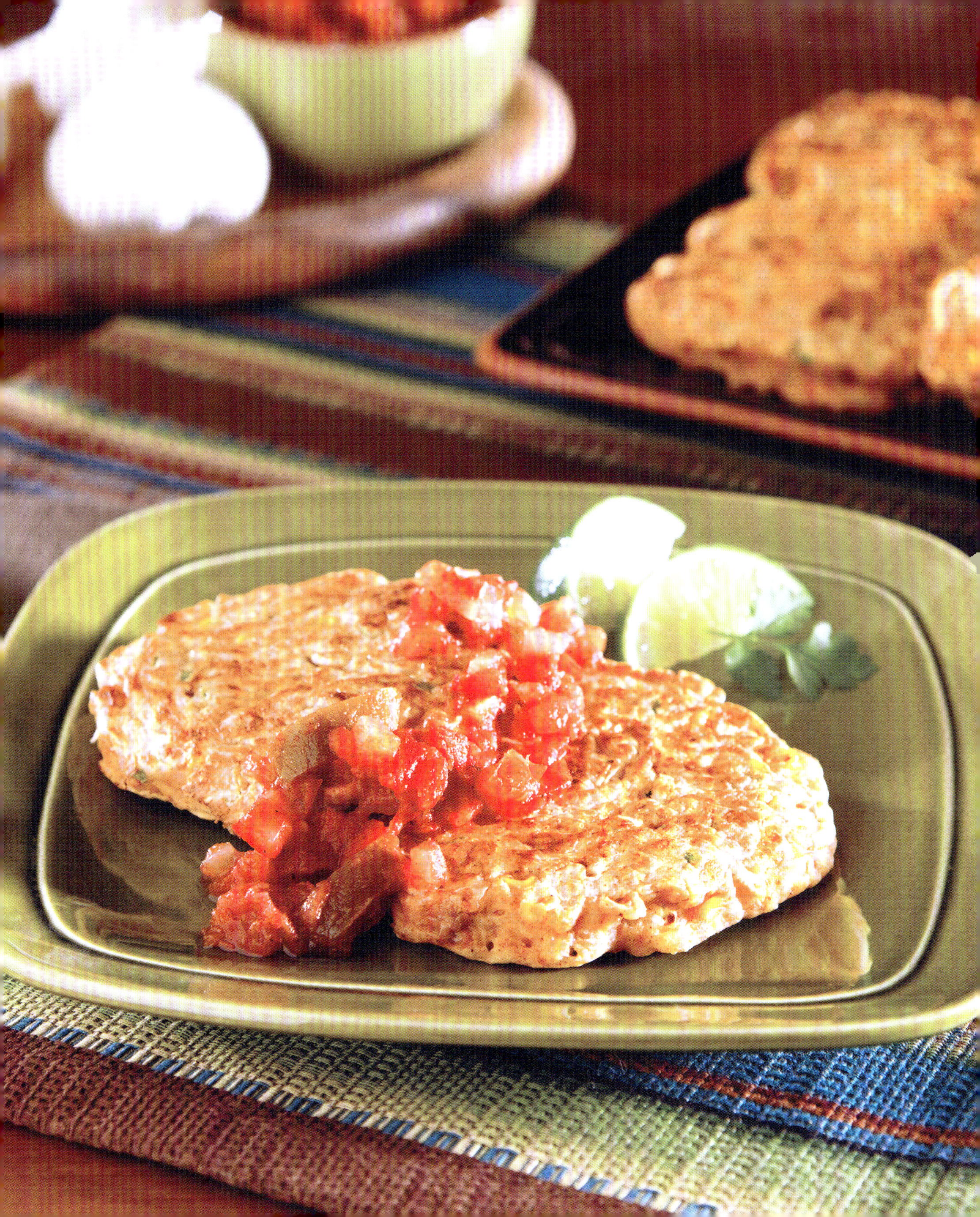

SIDE DISHES & SALADS

CHILI CORN BREAD

- 1 tablespoon vegetable oil
- ¼ cup chopped red bell pepper
- ¼ cup chopped green bell pepper
- 2 small jalapeño peppers, minced
- 2 cloves garlic, minced
- ¾ cup thawed frozen corn
- 1½ cups yellow cornmeal
- ½ cup all-purpose flour
- 2 tablespoons sugar
- 2 teaspoons baking powder
- ½ teaspoon baking soda
- ½ teaspoon ground cumin
- ½ teaspoon salt
- 1½ cups buttermilk
- 2 eggs
- ¼ cup (½ stick) butter, melted

1. Preheat oven to 375°F. Spray 8-inch square baking pan with cooking spray.

2. Heat oil in small skillet over medium heat. Add bell peppers, jalapeño peppers and garlic; cook and stir 3 to 4 minutes or until peppers are tender. Stir in corn; cook 1 to 2 minutes. Remove from heat.

3. Combine cornmeal, flour, sugar, baking powder, baking soda, cumin and salt in large bowl. Add buttermilk, eggs and butter; mix until blended. Stir in corn mixture. Pour batter into prepared baking pan.

4. Bake 25 to 30 minutes or until golden brown. Cool slightly on wire rack; serve warm.

MAKES 12 SERVINGS

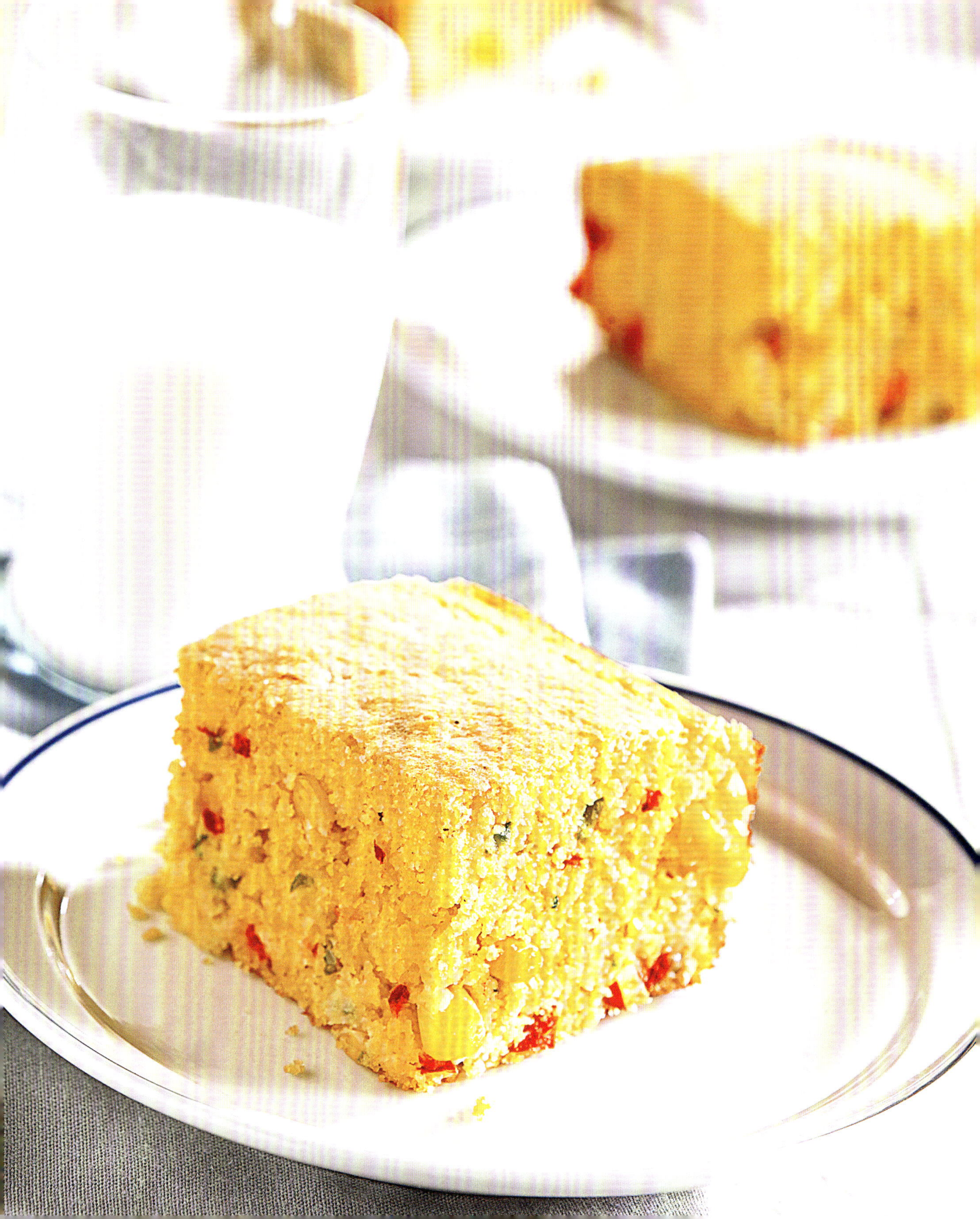

SIDE DISHES & SALADS

TURKEY TACO SALAD

- 2 tablespoons vegetable oil
- 1 tablespoon red wine vinegar
- 1 clove garlic, minced
- 1 pound ground turkey
- 1¾ teaspoons chili powder
- ½ teaspoon salt
- ¼ teaspoon ground cumin
- 1 can (about 14 ounces) Mexican-style diced tomatoes, drained
- 1 cup canned chickpeas or pinto beans, rinsed and drained
- ⅔ cup chopped peeled cucumber
- ⅓ cup thawed frozen corn
- ¼ cup chopped red onion
- 1 to 2 jalapeño peppers, seeded and finely chopped (optional)
- 3 cups chopped lettuce
- Tortilla chips
- Fresh cilantro

1. Whisk oil, vinegar and garlic in small bowl until well blended.

2. Heat large nonstick skillet over medium heat. Add turkey, chili powder, salt and cumin; cook 5 minutes or until turkey is no longer pink, stirring to break up meat.

3. Combine turkey, tomatoes, chickpeas, cucumber, corn, onion and jalapeño, if desired, in large bowl. Add dressing; stir to coat. Stir in lettuce. Serve with tortilla chips; garnish with cilantro.

MAKES 4 SERVINGS

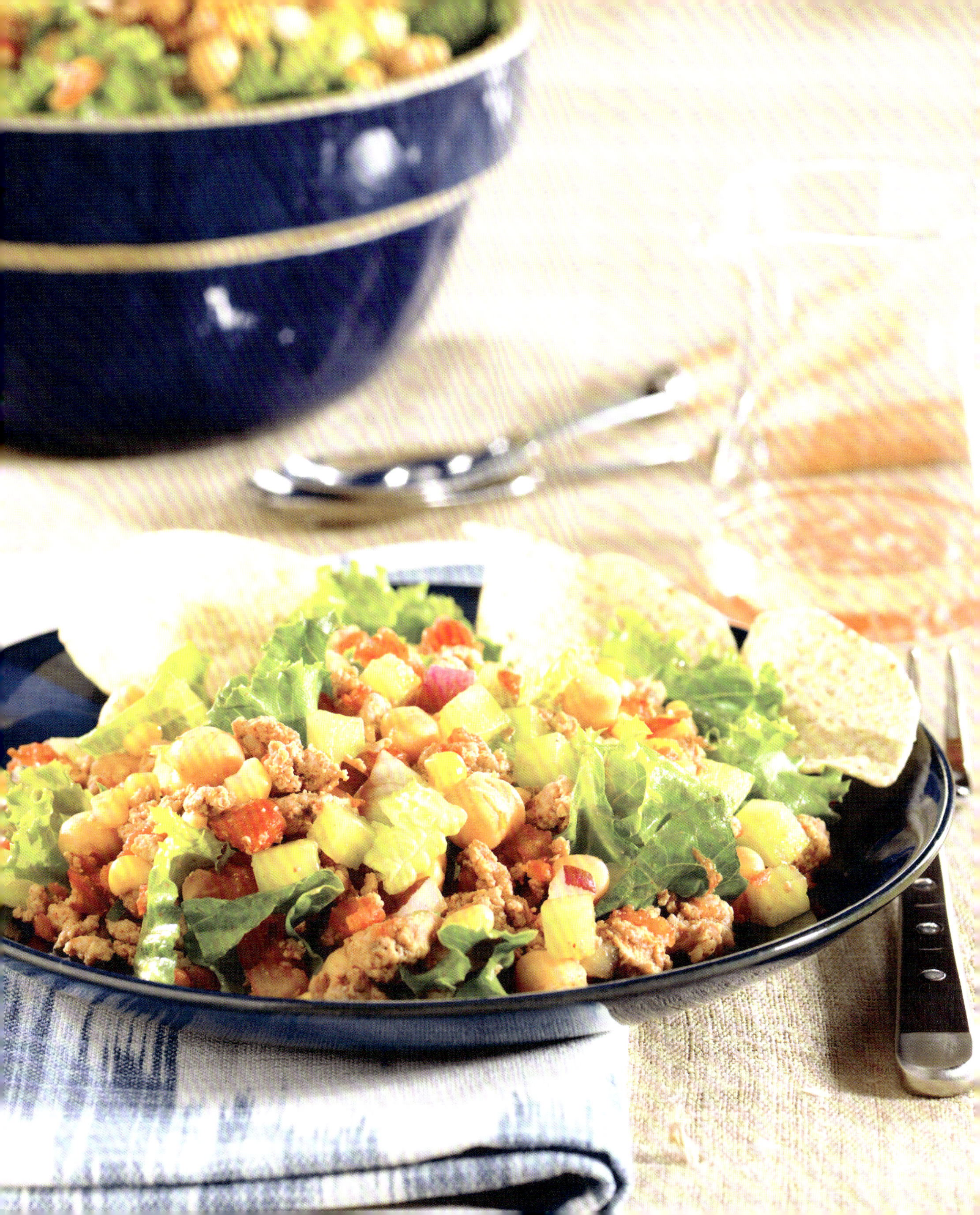

SIDE DISHES & SALADS

GREEN CHILI VEGETABLE SALAD

- 4 cups torn romaine lettuce leaves
- 1 green bell pepper, cut into thin strips
- 1 cup halved cherry tomatoes
- ¼ cup (1 ounce) shredded Cheddar cheese
- ¼ cup mayonnaise or ranch dressing
- 2 tablespoons plain yogurt
- 1 can (4 ounces) diced mild green chiles, drained
- ¼ teaspoon ground cumin

1. Combine lettuce, bell pepper, tomatoes and cheese in large bowl. Combine mayonnaise, yogurt, green chiles and cumin in small bowl.
2. Add dressing to salad; toss to coat.

MAKES 4 SERVINGS

CONFETTI BLACK BEANS

- 1 tablespoon olive oil
- 1 medium onion, chopped
- ¼ cup chopped red bell pepper
- ¼ cup chopped yellow bell pepper
- 2 cloves garlic, minced
- 1 jalapeño pepper, finely chopped
- 1 large tomato, seeded and chopped
- ½ teaspoon salt
- ⅛ teaspoon black pepper
- 2 cans (about 15 ounces each) black beans, rinsed and drained
- Hot pepper sauce

1. Heat oil in large nonstick skillet over medium heat. Add onion, bell peppers, garlic and jalapeño pepper; cook and stir 8 to 10 minutes or until onion is translucent. Add tomato, salt and black pepper; cook and stir 5 minutes.

2. Add beans; cook 15 to 20 minutes or until flavors are blended and beans are heated through, stirring occasionally. Season with hot pepper sauce.

MAKES 6 SERVINGS

SIDE DISHES & SALADS

MEXICAN RICE OLÉ

- 1 teaspoon vegetable oil
- 1 cup uncooked long grain rice
- 1 teaspoon salt
- 1 clove garlic, minced
- 2 cups broth or water
- 1 can (10½ ounces) condensed cream of celery soup
- ¾ cup sour cream
- 1 can (4 ounces) chopped mild green chiles, undrained
- ⅓ cup salsa
- 1 teaspoon ground cumin
- 1 cup (4 ounces) shredded Cheddar cheese
- 1 can (about 2 ounces) sliced pitted black olives, drained

1. Preheat oven to 350°F. Spray 3-quart baking dish with nonstick cooking spray.

2. Heat oil in large skillet over medium heat. Add rice, salt and garlic; cook and stir 2 to 3 minutes or until rice is well coated. Pour broth into skillet; cook about 15 minutes or until rice is tender, stirring occasionally.

3. Remove skillet from heat. Stir in condensed soup, sour cream, chiles, salsa and cumin; mix well. Transfer to prepared baking dish.

4. Bake 20 minutes. Top with cheese and olives; bake 5 to 10 minutes or until cheese is melted and casserole is heated through.

MAKES 4 SERVINGS

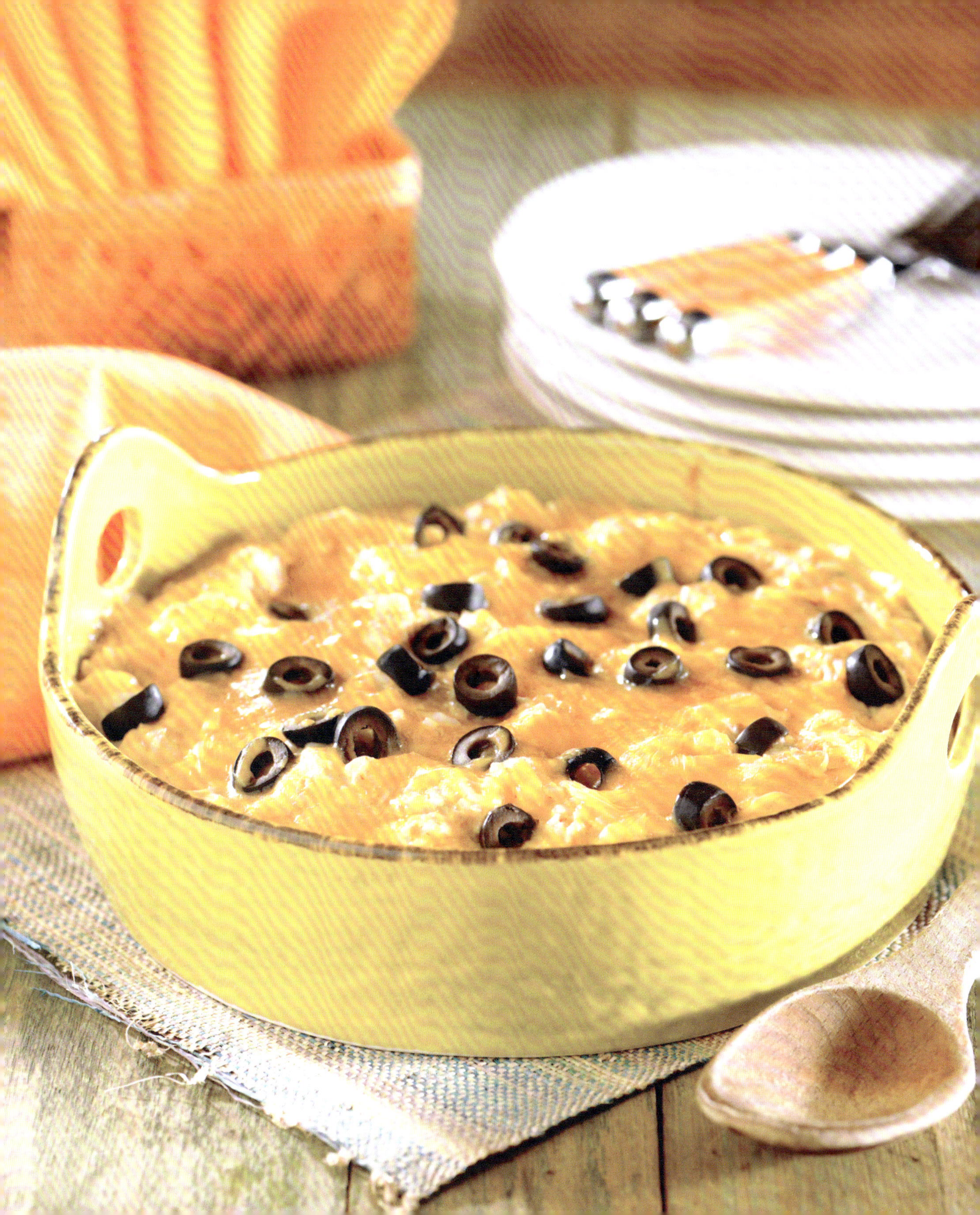

SIDE DISHES & SALADS

LAYERED TACO SALAD

- 8 ounces ground beef
- 1½ teaspoons chili powder
- 1½ teaspoons ground cumin, divided
- ½ teaspoon salt
- ½ cup picante sauce
- 1 teaspoon sugar
- 6 cups shredded romaine lettuce
- 2 plum tomatoes, seeded and diced
- ½ cup chopped green onions
- ¼ cup chopped fresh cilantro
- 28 nacho-flavored tortilla chips, crumbled (2 ounces)
- ½ cup sour cream
- ½ cup (2 ounces) shredded sharp Cheddar cheese or Mexican cheese blend

1. Brown beef in medium nonstick skillet over medium-high heat 6 to 8 minutes stirring to break up meat. Drain fat. Stir in chili powder, 1 teaspoon cumin and salt. Let cool.

2. Combine picante sauce, sugar and remaining ½ teaspoon cumin in small bowl.

3. Place lettuce in 11×7-inch baking dish. Layer with beef, tomatoes, green onions, cilantro and chips. Dollop with sour cream; sprinkle with cheese. Spoon picante sauce mixture on top.

MAKES 4 SERVINGS

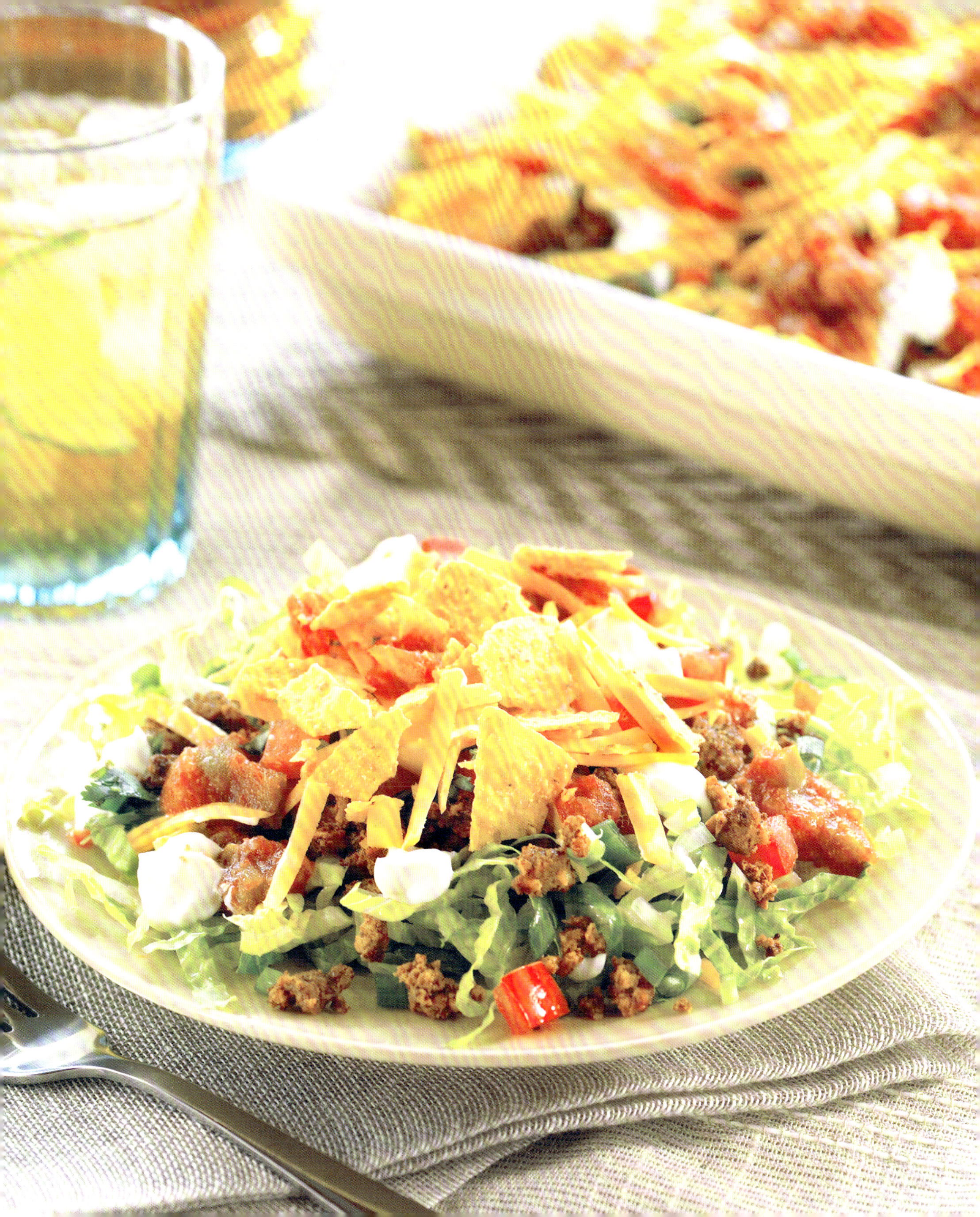

SIDE DISHES & SALADS

SOUTHWESTERN CHILE BEAN SALAD

- 1 can (about 15 ounces) pinto beans, rinsed and drained
- 2 medium tomatoes, diced
- 1 jalapeño pepper, seeded and minced
- ½ cup chopped green onions
- 1 large stalk celery, thinly sliced
- 2 tablespoons tomato juice
- 4 teaspoons red wine vinegar
- 1 teaspoon vegetable oil
- ½ teaspoon paprika
- ¼ teaspoon ground cumin
- ¼ teaspoon salt
- ¼ teaspoon black pepper
- ½ cup (2 ounces) shredded sharp Cheddar cheese

1. Combine beans, tomatoes, jalapeño, green onions and celery in large bowl. Toss gently.

2. Whisk tomato juice, vinegar, oil, paprika, cumin, salt and black pepper in small bowl. Pour over salad; toss gently to coat. Top with cheese.

MAKES 4 SERVINGS

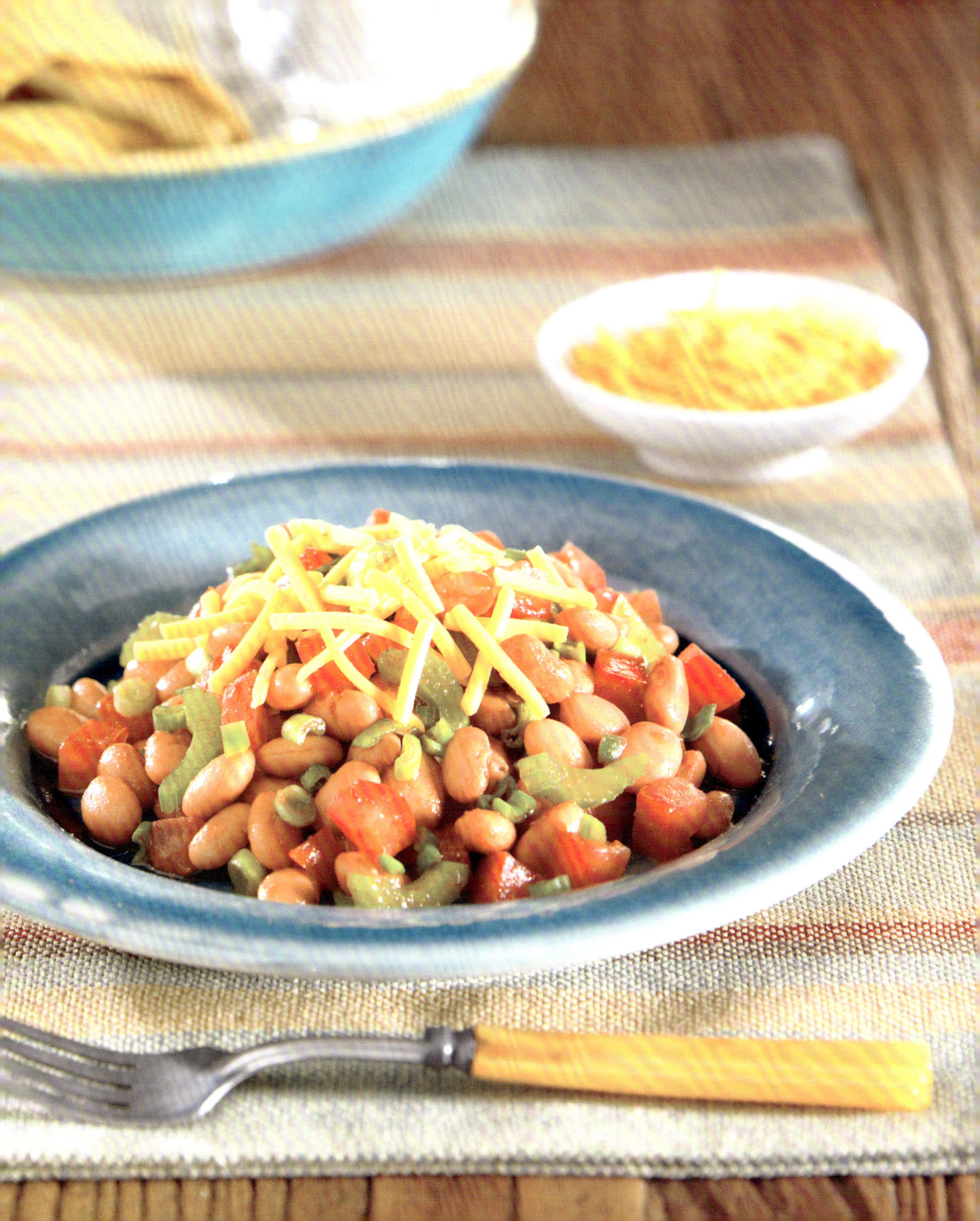

CORN AND ROASTED RED PEPPER RICE SALAD

- 2 tablespoons plus 1 teaspoon vegetable oil, divided
- 3 cloves garlic, minced
- 1 package (10 ounces) thawed frozen corn
- ½ cup roasted peppers, drained and chopped
- 2 cups cooked brown rice
- ¼ cup chopped fresh cilantro
- ¼ cup lime juice
- 1 tablespoon ground cumin
- Salt and black pepper

1. Heat 1 teaspoon oil in large skillet over medium heat. Add garlic; cook and stir 1 minute.

2. Add corn and roasted peppers; cook and stir 1 minute or until heated through. Transfer to large bowl; add rice and cilantro.

3. Whisk remaining 2 tablespoons oil, lime juice and cumin in small bowl. Add to rice mixture; toss to coat. Season with salt and black pepper. Refrigerate 1 hour before serving.

MAKES 4 SERVINGS

FIESTA BREAD

- ½ pound Mexican chorizo, casings removed
- ½ cup chopped onion
- 1¼ cups all-purpose flour
- 1 cup cornmeal
- 1½ teaspoons baking soda
- 1 teaspoon ground cumin
- ½ teaspoon salt
- 1 cup Mexican beer
- 1 cup (4 ounces) shredded Cheddar cheese
- 1 can (4 ounces) diced green chiles, drained
- 1 egg, beaten

1. Preheat oven to 375°F. Grease 8-inch square baking pan. Brown chorizo and onion in medium skillet over medium-high heat, stirring to break up meat. Drain fat.

2. Combine flour, cornmeal, baking soda, cumin and salt in large bowl. Combine beer, cheese, chiles and egg in medium bowl. Add flour mixture; stir just until moistened. Stir in chorizo mixture. Spread in prepared pan.

3. Bake 20 minutes or until toothpick inserted into center comes out clean. Cool in pan 10 minutes. Serve warm. Refrigerate leftovers.

MAKES 8 SERVINGS

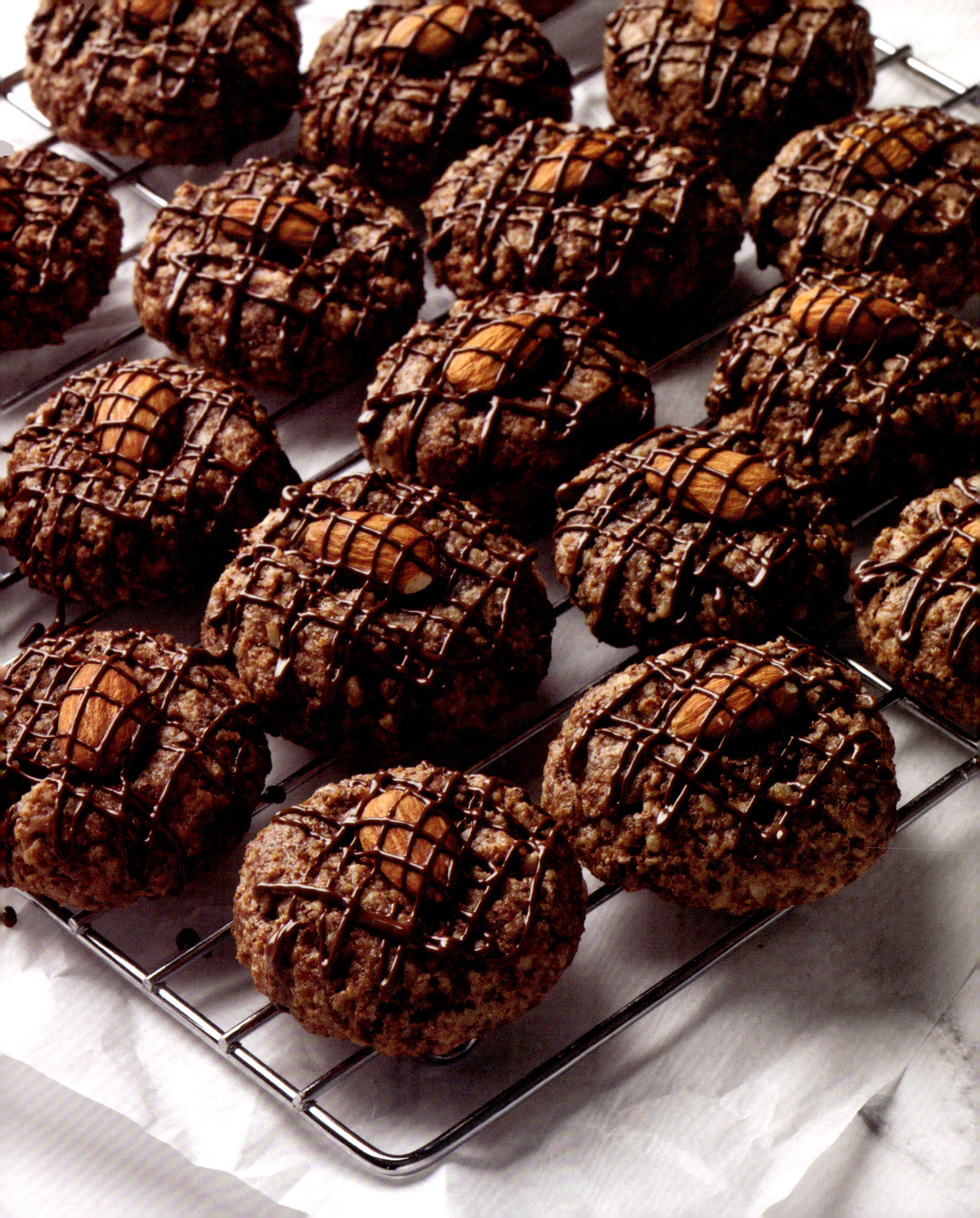

DESSERTS & DRINKS

CHOCOLATE-CINNAMON MACAROONS

- 8 ounces semisweet chocolate, divided
- 1¾ cups plus ⅓ cup whole almonds, divided
- ¾ cup sugar
- ½ teaspoon salt
- 2 egg whites
- 1 teaspoon ground cinnamon
- 1 teaspoon vanilla

1. Preheat oven to 400°F. Grease cookie sheets.
2. Place 5 ounces of chocolate in food processor; process until coarsely chopped. Add 1¾ cups almonds, sugar and salt; pulse until mixture is finely ground. Add egg whites, cinnamon and vanilla; process just until mixture forms moist dough.
3. Shape dough into 1-inch balls. (Dough will be sticky.) Place 2 inches apart on prepared cookie sheets. Press 1 whole almond into center of each dough ball.
4. Bake 8 to 10 minutes or just until set. Cool on cookie sheets 2 minutes. Remove to wire racks; cool completely.
5. Melt remaining 3 ounces of chocolate. Place in small resealable food storage bag. Cut off small corner of bag. Drizzle chocolate over cookies. Let stand until set.

MAKES ABOUT 2 DOZEN COOKIES

DESSERTS & DRINKS

MEXICAN COFFEE

- 6 cups water
- ½ cup ground dark roast coffee
- 2 cinnamon sticks
- 1 cup half-and-half
- ⅓ cup chocolate syrup
- ¼ cup packed dark brown sugar
- 1½ teaspoons vanilla, divided
- 1 cup whipping cream
- ¼ cup powdered sugar
- Ground cinnamon

1. Place water in drip coffee maker. Place coffee and cinnamon sticks in filter basket of coffee maker. Combine half-and-half, chocolate syrup, brown sugar and 1 teaspoon vanilla in coffee pot. Place coffee pot with cream mixture in coffee maker. Brew coffee; coffee will drip into chocolate cream mixture.

2. Meanwhile, beat cream in medium bowl with electric mixer at high speed until soft peaks form. Add powdered sugar and remaining ½ teaspoon vanilla; beat until stiff peaks form. Pour coffee into coffee cups; top with dollop of whipped cream. Sprinkle with ground cinnamon.

MAKES 10 TO 12 SERVINGS

CLASSIC MARGARITA

Lime wedges
Coarse salt
4 ounces tequila
2 ounces triple sec
2 ounces lime juice
Lime slices or wedges

1. Rub rims of two margarita glasses with lime wedges; dip in salt.

2. Fill cocktail shaker with ice; add tequila, triple sec and lime juice. Shake until blended; strain into glasses. Garnish with lime slices.

MAKES 2 SERVINGS

Frozen Margarita

Rub rim of two margarita glasses with lime wedges; dip in salt. Combine tequila, triple sec, lime juice and 2 cups ice in blender; blend until smooth. Pour into glasses; garnish with lime slices.

Frozen Strawberry Margarita

Rub rim of margarita glasses with lime wedges; dip in salt. Combine tequila, triple sec, lime juice, 1 cup frozen strawberries and 1 cup ice in blender; blend until smooth. Pour into prepared glasses; garnish with lime slices and strawberries.

DESSERTS & DRINKS

SUGAR COOKIES (POLVORONES)

- 1 cup (2 sticks) butter, softened
- ½ cup powdered sugar
- 2 tablespoons milk
- 1 teaspoon vanilla
- 1 teaspoon ground cinnamon, divided
- 1½ to 1¾ cups all-purpose flour
- 1 teaspoon baking powder
- 1 cup granulated sugar
- 1 ounce semisweet chocolate, finely grated

1. Preheat oven to 325°F. Grease cookie sheets.

2. Beat butter, powdered sugar, milk, vanilla and ½ teaspoon cinnamon in large bowl at medium speed of electric mixer until light and fluffy, scraping down side of bowl once. Gradually add 1½ cups flour and baking powder, beating at low speed until well blended, scraping down side of bowl once. Stir in additional flour with spoon if dough is too soft to shape.

3. Shape tablespoonfuls of dough into 1-inch balls; place 3 inches apart on prepared cookie sheets. Flatten each ball into 2-inch round with bottom of glass dipped in granulated sugar.

4. Bake 20 to 25 minutes or until edges are golden brown. Cool on cookie sheets 3 minutes.

5. Meanwhile, combine granulated sugar, grated chocolate and remaining ½ teaspoon cinnamon in small bowl. Transfer cookies, one at a time, to sugar mixture; coat both sides. Remove to wire racks; cool completely.

MAKES ABOUT 2 DOZEN COOKIES

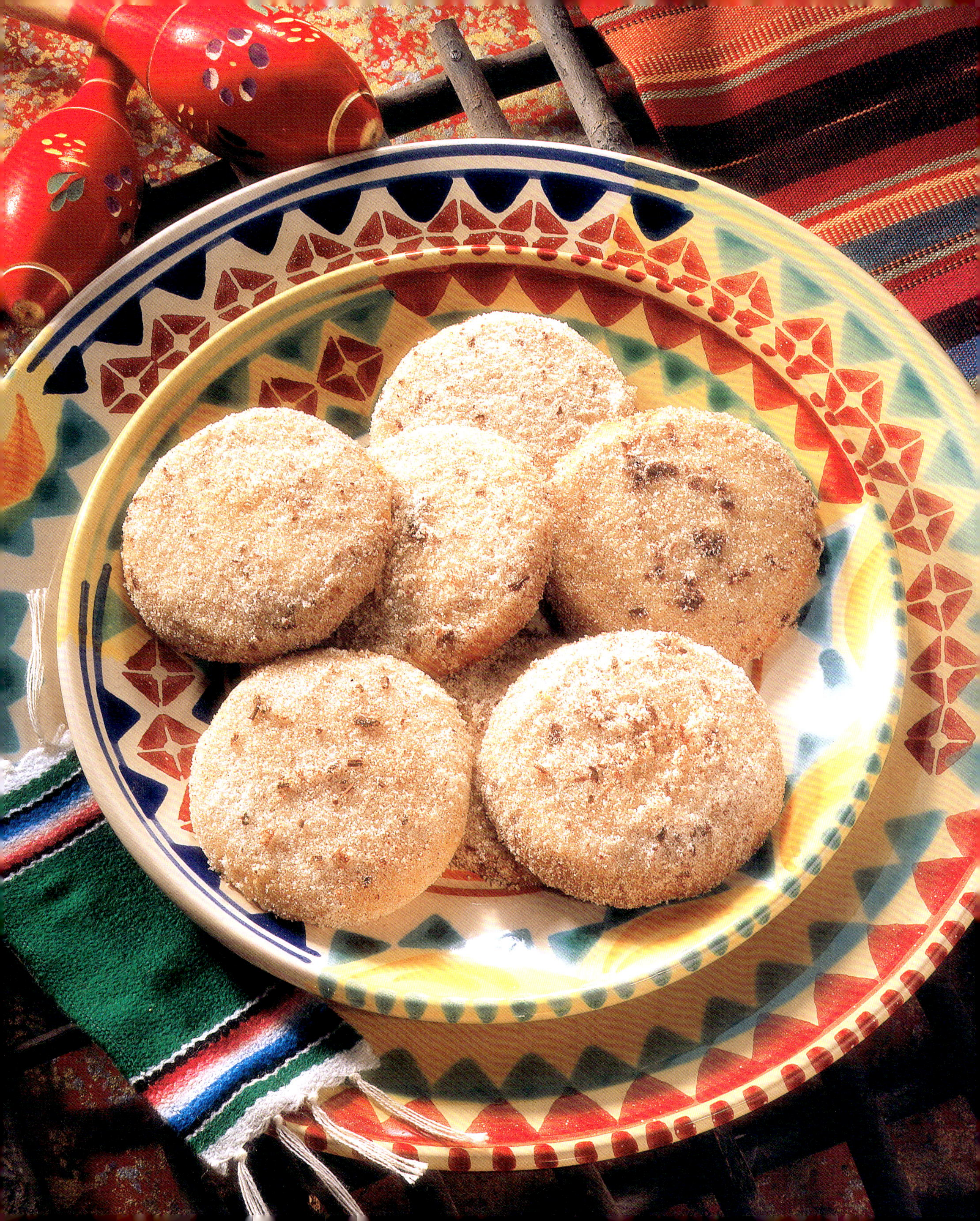

DESSERTS & DRINKS

CAJETA Y FRUTAS

1 can (14 ounces) sweetened condensed milk

3 cups sweetened whipped cream

Berries or peaches

1. Simmer milk in double boiler 1 to 2 hours or until milk is light caramel color, stirring occasionally. Pour cooked milk into large bowl. Beat with electric mixer at low speed until milk is smooth and creamy. Cool to room temperature.

2. Fold in whipped cream; stir just until smooth. Cover and refrigerate 2 hours or overnight. Divide among dessert dishes; top with fruit.

MAKES 12 SERVINGS

CANTARITO

Lime wedges
Coarse salt
1½ ounces tequila
½ ounce lime juice
½ ounce lemon juice
½ ounce orange juice
Grapefruit soda
Lime, lemon and/or orange wedges

Rub rim of Collins glass with lime wedge; dip in salt. Fill glass with ice; add tequila, lime juice, lemon juice and orange juice. Top with grapefruit soda; stir until blended. Garnish with citrus wedges.

MAKES 1 SERVING

DESSERTS & DRINKS

MEXICAN WEDDING COOKIES

- 1 cup pecan pieces or halves
- 1 cup (2 sticks) butter, softened
- 2 cups powdered sugar, divided
- 2 cups all-purpose flour
- 2 teaspoons vanilla
- ⅛ teaspoon salt

1. Place pecans in food processor; pulse until pecans are ground but not pasty.

2. Beat butter and ½ cup powdered sugar in large bowl with electric mixer at medium speed until fluffy. Gradually add 1 cup flour, vanilla and salt at low speed, beating until well blended. Stir in remaining 1 cup flour and nuts. Shape dough into a ball; wrap in plastic wrap. Refrigerate 1 hour or until firm.

3. Preheat oven to 350°F. Shape dough into 1-inch balls. Place 1 inch apart on ungreased cookie sheets.

4. Bake 12 to 15 minutes or until golden brown. Cool on cookie sheets 2 minutes.

5. Meanwhile, place 1 cup powdered sugar in 13×9-inch baking dish. Transfer hot cookies to powdered sugar. Roll cookies in powdered sugar, coating well. Let cookies cool in sugar in dish. Sift remaining ½ cup powdered sugar over cookies just before serving.

MAKES ABOUT 4 DOZEN COOKIES

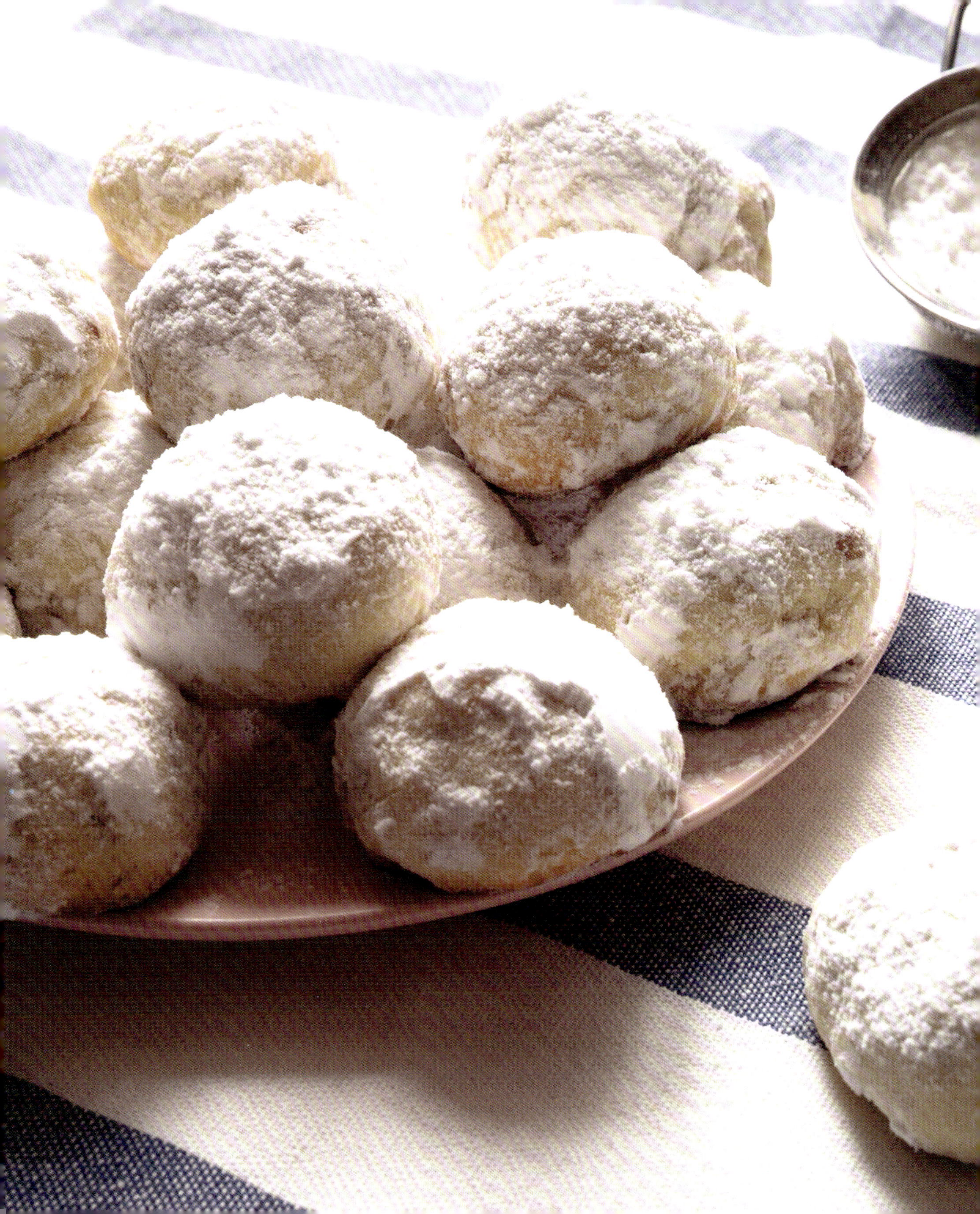

INDEX

A
Avocado Salsa, 48
Avocados
    Avocado Salsa, 48
    Guacamole, 50
    Mexican Omelet Roll-Ups with Avocado Sauce, 6
    Shrimp Tacos, 114

B
Bacon: Chicken Bacon Quesadillas, 91
Bean and Corn Nachos, 40
Beans
    Bean and Corn Nachos, 40
    Beef and Bean Enchiladas, 132
    Beef Fajita Soup, 64
    Black Bean and Mushroom Chilaquiles, 12
    Black Bean Flautas, 104
    Black Bean Soup, 56
    Breakfast Beans and Rice, 20
    Cauliflower Mushroom Tacos, 92
    Chunky Ancho Chili with Beans, 62
    Confetti Black Beans, 169
    Double Decker Tacos, 86
    Fiesta Beef Enchiladas, 128
    Grilled Chicken Tostadas, 98
    Grilled Steak and Black Bean Tacos, 102
    Huevos Rancheros Casserole, 22
    Jalapeño Beans, 155
    Mexican Breakfast Burrito, 18
    Mexican Hot Pot, 78
    Mexican Pizza, 88
    Mini Cheese Burritos, 44
    Picante Pintos and Rice, 158
    Salsa Verde Chicken Stew, 53
    Southwestern Chile Bean Salad, 174
    Southwest Gazpacho Salad, 160
    Taco Salad Supreme, 120

Beans (continued)
    Taco Stew, 74
    Turkey Taco Salad, 166
    Vegetable Fajitas, 110
Beef
    Beef and Bean Enchiladas, 132
    Beef and Cheese Nachos, 28
    Beef Fajita Soup, 64
    Beefy Tortilla Pie, 144
    Carne Asada, 119
    Chipotle Strip Steaks, 142
    Chunky Ancho Chili with Beans, 62
    Double Decker Tacos, 86
    Fiesta Beef Enchiladas, 128
    Grilled Steak and Black Bean Tacos, 102
    Guadalajara Beef, 138
    Layered Taco Salad, 172
    Mexican Pizza, 88
    Picadillo, 146
    Salsa Beef Burritos, 90
    Shredded Beef Tacos, 106
    Steak Fajitas, 122
    Super-Easy Beef Burritos, 117
    Taco Salad Supreme, 120
    Taco Stew, 74
    Tamale Beef Squares, 152
Beef and Bean Enchiladas, 132
Beef and Cheese Nachos, 28
Beef Fajita Soup, 64
Beefy Tortilla Pie, 144
Beer
    Chicken Wings in Cerveza, 32
    Chile Verde Chicken Stew, 70
    Chipotle Strip Steaks, 142
    Fiesta Bread, 177
    Guadalajara Beef, 138
    Jalapeño Beans, 155
    Mole Chicken, 136
    Puerco Sabrosas (Savory Pork), 140
Bell Peppers
    Beef Fajita Soup, 64
    Black Bean and Mushroom Chilaquiles, 12
    Black Bean Soup, 56
    Breakfast Burritos, 25

Bell Peppers (continued)
    Chicken Fajita Nachos, 34
    Chili Corn Bread, 164
    Chorizo and Cheddar Breakfast Casserole, 10
    Chorizo Hash, 5
    Confetti Black Beans, 169
    Fiesta Corn Salad, 156
    Fish Tacos with Cilantro Cream Sauce, 100
    Green Chili Vegetable Salad, 168
    Guadalajara Beef, 138
    Picante Pintos and Rice, 158
    Pozole, 60
    Red Snapper Vera Cruz, 143
    Steak Fajitas, 122
    Vegetable Fajitas, 110
Black Bean and Mushroom Chilaquiles, 12
Black Bean Flautas, 104
Black Bean Soup, 56
Breakfast Beans and Rice, 20
Breakfast Burritos, 25
Burritos
    Breakfast Burritos, 25
    Grilled Baja Burritos, 84
    Mexican Breakfast Burrito, 18
    Mini Cheese Burritos, 44
    Salsa Beef Burritos, 90
    Super-Easy Beef Burritos, 117

C
Cajeta y Frutas, 185
Cantarito, 184
Carne Asada, 119
Casseroles
    Chicken Chile Relleno Casserole, 148
    Chorizo and Cheddar Breakfast Casserole, 10
    Huevos Rancheros Casserole, 22
    Mexican Rice Olé, 170
    Tamale Beef Squares, 152
Cauliflower Mushroom Tacos, 92

INDEX

Chicken
  Chicken Bacon Quesadillas, 91
  Chicken Chile Relleno Casserole, 148
  Chicken Enchilada Soup, 58
  Chicken Fajita Nachos, 34
  Chicken Fajita Roll-Ups, 96
  Chicken Tortilla Soup, 81
  Chicken Wings in Cerveza, 32
  Chile Verde Chicken Stew, 70
  Chipotle Chicken Quesadillas, 30
  Green Enchiladas with Chicken, 124
  Grilled Chicken Tostadas, 98
  Mole Chicken, 136
  Pozole, 60
  Quesadilla Grande, 109
  Salsa Verde Chicken Stew, 53
  Tacos Dorados, 112
  Weeknight Chicken Tacos, 83
Chicken Bacon Quesadillas, 91
Chicken Chile Relleno Casserole, 148
Chicken Enchilada Soup, 58
Chicken Fajita Nachos, 34
Chicken Fajita Roll-Ups, 96
Chicken Tortilla Soup, 81
Chicken Wings in Cerveza, 32
Chile Verde Chicken Stew, 70
Chili Corn Bread, 164
Chipotle Chicken Quesadillas, 30
Chipotle Strip Steaks, 142
Chocolate
  Chocolate-Cinnamon Macaroons, 179
  Mexican Coffee, 180
  Mole Chicken, 136
Chocolate-Cinnamon Macaroons, 179
Chorizo
  Chorizo and Cheddar Breakfast Casserole, 10
  Chorizo and Eggs, 15
  Chorizo Hash, 5
  Fiesta Bread, 177

Chorizo and Cheddar Breakfast Casserole, 10
Chorizo and Eggs, 15
Chorizo Hash, 5
Chunky Ancho Chili with Beans, 62
Classic Margarita, 181
Confetti Black Beans, 169
Cookies
  Chocolate-Cinnamon Macaroons, 179
  Mexican Wedding Cookies, 185
  Sugar Cookies (Polvorones), 182
Corn
  Bean and Corn Nachos, 40
  Chili Corn Bread, 164
  Corn and Jalapeño Chowder, 80
  Corn and Roasted Red Pepper Rice Salad, 176
  Corn Salsa, 42
  Fiesta Beef Enchiladas, 128
  Fiesta Corn Salad, 156
  Grilled Fish with Chile-Corn Salsa, 150
  Lime-Poached Fish with Corn Salsa, 126
  Mexican Hot Pot, 78
  Salsa Verde Chicken Stew, 53
  Savory Corn Cakes, 162
  Southwest Gazpacho Salad, 160
  Spicy Mexican Frittata, 8
  Tamale Beef Squares, 152
  Tamales, 130
  Tortilla Pizza Wedges, 36
  Turkey Taco Salad, 166
Corn and Jalapeño Chowder, 80
Corn and Roasted Red Pepper Rice Salad, 176
Corn Bread
  Chili Corn Bread, 164
  Fiesta Bread, 177
Corn Salsa, 42
Corn Tortilla Chips, 38
Creamy Roasted Poblano Soup, 68

D
Dips
  Avocado Salsa, 48
  Corn Salsa, 42
  Guacamole, 50
  Salsa, 39
  Salsa Fresca, 51
  White Spinach Queso, 27
Double Decker Tacos, 86
Drinks
  Cantarito, 184
  Classic Margarita, 181
  Frozen Margarita, 181
  Frozen Strawberry Margarita, 181
  Mexican Coffee, 180

E
Eggs
  Breakfast Burritos, 25
  Chorizo and Cheddar Breakfast Casserole, 10
  Chorizo and Eggs, 15
  Huevos Rancheros Casserole, 22
  Mexican Breakfast Burrito, 18
  Mexican Omelet Roll-Ups with Avocado Sauce, 6
  Scrambled Eggs and Tortillas, 14
  Spicy Mexican Frittata, 8
  Spicy Scrambled Eggs and Tomatoes, 24
  Spinach and Egg Quesadillas, 16
Enchiladas
  Beef and Bean Enchiladas, 132
  Fiesta Beef Enchiladas, 128
  Green Enchiladas with Chicken, 124

F
Fajitas
  Steak Fajitas, 122
  Vegetable Fajitas, 110
Fiesta Beef Enchiladas, 128
Fiesta Bread, 177
Fiesta Corn Salad, 156

189

INDEX

Fish
    Fish Tacos with Cilantro Cream Sauce, 100
    Grilled Baja Burritos, 84
    Grilled Fish with Chile-Corn Salsa, 150
    Island Fish Tacos, 94
    Lime-Poached Fish with Corn Salsa, 126
    Red Snapper Vera Cruz, 143
Fish Tacos with Cilantro Cream Sauce, 100
Frozen Margarita, 181
Frozen Strawberry Margarita, 181

G

Green Chile Rice, 161
Green Chili Vegetable Salad, 168
Green Enchiladas with Chicken, 124
Grilled Baja Burritos, 84
Grilled Chicken Tostadas, 98
Grilled Fish with Chile-Corn Salsa, 150
Grilled Steak and Black Bean Tacos, 102
Grill Recipes
    Carne Asada, 119
    Chipotle Strip Steaks, 142
    Grilled Baja Burritos, 84
    Grilled Chicken Tostadas, 98
    Grilled Fish with Chile-Corn Salsa, 150
    Grilled Steak and Black Bean Tacos, 102
    Guadalajara Beef, 138
Guacamole, 50
Guacamole
    Beef and Cheese Nachos, 28
    Grilled Baja Burritos, 84
    Guacamole, 50
Guadalajara Beef, 138

H

Huevos Rancheros Casserole, 22

I

Island Fish Tacos, 94

J

Jalapeño Beans, 155

L

Layered Taco Salad, 172
Lime-Poached Fish with Corn Salsa, 126

M

Mexican Breakfast Burrito, 18
Mexican Coffee, 180
Mexican Hot Pot, 78
Mexican Omelet Roll-Ups with Avocado Sauce, 6
Mexican Pizza, 88
Mexican Rice Olé, 170
Mexican Shrimp with Hot Chili Butter, 134
Mexican Tortilla Soup, 66
Mexican Turkey Quesadillas, 101
Mexican Wedding Cookies, 185
Mini Cheese Burritos, 44
Mole Chicken, 136
Mushroom and Zucchini Quesadillas, 116
Mushrooms
    Black Bean and Mushroom Chilaquiles, 12
    Cauliflower Mushroom Tacos, 92
    Mushroom and Zucchini Quesadillas, 116
    Tortilla Pizza Wedges, 36

N

Nachos
    Bean and Corn Nachos, 40
    Beef and Cheese Nachos, 28
    Chicken Fajita Nachos, 34

O

Olives
    Bean and Corn Nachos, 40
    Beefy Tortilla Pie, 144
    Mexican Rice Olé, 170
    Pozole, 60

P

Picadillo, 146
Picante Pintos and Rice, 158
Pickled Red Onions, 92
Poblano Peppers
    Breakfast Beans and Rice, 20
    Corn Salsa, 42
    Creamy Roasted Poblano Soup, 68
Pork
    Chunky Ancho Chili with Beans, 62
    Pork Chili Verde, 54
    Puerco Sabrosas (Savory Pork), 140
    Shredded Green Chile Pork Tacos, 108
Pork Chili Verde, 54
Potatoes
    Chile Verde Chicken Stew, 70
    Chorizo Hash, 5
Pozole, 60
Puerco Sabrosas (Savory Pork), 140
Pumpkin: Spicy Pumpkin Soup, 76

Q

Quesadilla Grande, 109
Quesadillas
    Chicken Bacon Quesadillas, 91
    Chipotle Chicken Quesadillas, 30
    Mexican Turkey Quesadillas, 101
    Mushroom and Zucchini Quesadillas, 116
    Quesadilla Grande, 109
    Spinach and Egg Quesadillas, 16

R

Red Snapper Vera Cruz, 143
Rice
    Breakfast Beans and Rice, 20
    Corn and Roasted Red Pepper Rice Salad, 176

INDEX

Rice *(continued)*
 Green Chile Rice, 161
 Mexican Rice Olé, 170
 Picante Pintos and Rice, 158
 Turkey Albondigas Soup, 72

S

Salsa, 39
Salsa Beef Burritos, 90
Salsa Fresca, 51
Salsa Shrimp, 46
Salsa Verde Chicken Stew, 53
Savory Corn Cakes, 162
Scrambled Eggs and Tortillas, 14
Shredded Beef Tacos, 106
Shredded Green Chile Pork Tacos, 108
Shrimp
 Mexican Shrimp with Hot Chili Butter, 134
 Salsa Shrimp, 46
 Shrimp Tacos, 114
Shrimp Tacos, 114
Slow Cooker Recipes
 Beef Fajita Soup, 64
 Beefy Tortilla Pie, 144
 Picadillo, 146
 Salsa Beef Burritos, 90
 Shredded Green Chile Pork Tacos, 108
 Super-Easy Beef Burritos, 117
Southwestern Chile Bean Salad, 174
Southwest Gazpacho Salad, 160
Spicy Mexican Frittata, 8
Spicy Pumpkin Soup, 76
Spicy Scrambled Eggs and Tomatoes, 24
Spinach
 Quesadilla Grande, 109
 Spinach and Egg Quesadillas, 16
 White Spinach Queso, 27
Spinach and Egg Quesadillas, 16
Steak Fajitas, 122
Sugar Cookies (Polvorones), 182
Super-Easy Beef Burritos, 117

T

Taco Salad Supreme, 120
Taco Stew, 74
Tacos
 Cauliflower Mushroom Tacos, 92
 Double Decker Tacos, 86
 Fish Tacos with Cilantro Cream Sauce, 100
 Grilled Steak and Black Bean Tacos, 102
 Island Fish Tacos, 94
 Shredded Beef Tacos, 106
 Shredded Green Chile Pork Tacos, 108
 Shrimp Tacos, 114
 Tacos Dorados, 112
 Weeknight Chicken Tacos, 83
Tacos Dorados, 112
Tamale Beef Squares, 152
Tamales, 130
Tomatillos
 Chile Verde Chicken Stew, 70
 Pork Chili Verde, 54
Tomatoes
 Avocado Salsa, 48
 Beef and Bean Enchiladas, 132
 Beef and Cheese Nachos, 28
 Beef Fajita Soup, 64
 Black Bean and Mushroom Chilaquiles, 12
 Black Bean Flautas, 104
 Breakfast Beans and Rice, 20
 Confetti Black Beans, 169
 Double Decker Tacos, 86
 Green Chili Vegetable Salad, 168
 Grilled Fish with Chile-Corn Salsa, 150
 Layered Taco Salad, 172
 Lime-Poached Fish with Corn Salsa, 126
 Mexican Hot Pot, 78
 Mexican Omelet Roll-Ups with Avocado Sauce, 6

Tomatoes *(continued)*
 Mexican Tortilla Soup, 66
 Mole Chicken, 136
 Picadillo, 146
 Picante Pintos and Rice, 158
 Puerco Sabrosas (Savory Pork), 140
 Red Snapper Vera Cruz, 143
 Salsa, 39
 Salsa Fresca, 51
 Shrimp Tacos, 114
 Southwest Gazpacho Salad, 160
 Southwestern Chile Bean Salad, 174
 Spicy Mexican Frittata, 8
 Spicy Scrambled Eggs and Tomatoes, 24
 Spinach and Egg Quesadillas, 16
 Taco Salad Supreme, 120
 Taco Stew, 74
 Tacos Dorados, 112
 Tamale Beef Squares, 152
 Turkey Taco Salad, 166
Tortilla Pizza Wedges, 36
Turkey
 Mexican Turkey Quesadillas, 101
 Turkey Albondigas Soup, 72
 Turkey Taco Salad, 166
Turkey Albondigas Soup, 72
Turkey Taco Salad, 166

V

Vegetable Fajitas, 110

W

Weeknight Chicken Tacos, 83
White Spinach Queso, 27

Z

Zucchini
 Mushroom and Zucchini Quesadillas, 116
 Turkey Albondigas Soup, 72

METRIC CONVERSION CHART

VOLUME MEASUREMENTS (dry)

1/8 teaspoon = 0.5 mL
1/4 teaspoon = 1 mL
1/2 teaspoon = 2 mL
3/4 teaspoon = 4 mL
1 teaspoon = 5 mL
1 tablespoon = 15 mL
2 tablespoons = 30 mL
1/4 cup = 60 mL
1/3 cup = 75 mL
1/2 cup = 125 mL
2/3 cup = 150 mL
3/4 cup = 175 mL
1 cup = 250 mL
2 cups = 1 pint = 500 mL
3 cups = 750 mL
4 cups = 1 quart = 1 L

VOLUME MEASUREMENTS (fluid)

1 fluid ounce (2 tablespoons) = 30 mL
4 fluid ounces (1/2 cup) = 125 mL
8 fluid ounces (1 cup) = 250 mL
12 fluid ounces (1 1/2 cups) = 375 mL
16 fluid ounces (2 cups) = 500 mL

WEIGHTS (mass)

1/2 ounce = 15 g
1 ounce = 30 g
3 ounces = 90 g
4 ounces = 120 g
8 ounces = 225 g
10 ounces = 285 g
12 ounces = 360 g
16 ounces = 1 pound = 450 g

DIMENSIONS

1/16 inch = 2 mm
1/8 inch = 3 mm
1/4 inch = 6 mm
1/2 inch = 1.5 cm
3/4 inch = 2 cm
1 inch = 2.5 cm

OVEN TEMPERATURES

250°F = 120°C
275°F = 140°C
300°F = 150°C
325°F = 160°C
350°F = 180°C
375°F = 190°C
400°F = 200°C
425°F = 220°C
450°F = 230°C

BAKING PAN SIZES

Utensil	Size in Inches/Quarts	Metric Volume	Size in Centimeters
Baking or Cake Pan (square or rectangular)	8×8×2 9×9×2 12×8×2 13×9×2	2 L 2.5 L 3 L 3.5 L	20×20×5 23×23×5 30×20×5 33×23×5
Loaf Pan	8×4×3 9×5×3	1.5 L 2 L	20×10×7 23×13×7
Round Layer Cake Pan	8×1½ 9×1½	1.2 L 1.5 L	20×4 23×4
Pie Plate	8×1¼ 9×1¼	750 mL 1 L	20×3 23×3
Baking Dish or Casserole	1 quart 1½ quart 2 quart	1 L 1.5 L 2 L	— — —